The Intuitive Way

A GUIDE TO LIVING
FROM INNER WISDOM

PENNEY PEIRCE

FOREWORD BY CAROL ADRIENNE

BEYOND
WORDS
Publishing
I N C

Beyond Words Publishing, Inc.
20827 N.W. Cornell Road, Suite 500
Hillsboro, Oregon 97124-9808
503-531-8700
1-800-284-9673

Shamanic Healing Diagram, Yarn Painting © 1995 by Eligio
Carrillo, used by permission of Amber Lotus, San Francisco,
Calif., and The Huichol Art Center, Yelapa, Mexico.

Editor: Ann Bennett
Cover design: Principia Graphica
Typesetting: Jane Aukshunas
Proofreader: Marvin Moore
Printer: Lithocolor Press, Inc.

Printed in the United States of America
Distributed to the book trade by Publishers Group West

Library of Congress Cataloging-in-Publication Data
Peirce, Penney.
    The intuitive way : a guide to living from inner wisdom /
  Penney Peirce.
      p. cm.
    ISBN 1-885223-55-2
    1. Intuition (Psychology).   2. Intuition (Psychology)—
  Problems, exercises, etc. I. Title.
  BF315.5P45 1997
  153.4′4—dc21   97-21813
                                  CIP

The corporate mission of Beyond Words Publishing, Inc:
Inspire to Integrity

For Valerie, Julia, and Malina,
who helped me remember my innocence

Contents

Acknowledgments

Birthing a first book can feel first like a dream, then like psychic surgery. I find that I am quite transformed internally—for the better—by the process. My deep gratitude goes out to the talented "psychic surgeons" who assisted me so closely: to my editor, Lorraine Anderson, whose neutrality, keen mind, and compassionate communication style allowed me to see the good sense; to my agent, Sheryl Fullerton, who helped me achieve focus and become more visible; and to my publishers, Cindy Black and Richard Cohn and the staff at Beyond Words, who practice what they preach ("Inspire to Integrity").

Various astute and literate friends provided me with invaluable feedback about the book. Thanks so much to Carol Adrienne, whose unflagging support and enthusiasm has often kept me afloat, and to those who mindfully read early manuscripts and nudged me forward: Joan O'Hannesson, Jabarra Athas, Rod McDaniel, Colleen Cayes, Peter Howard, Wendy Young, Allen Hicks, Donna Hale, Larry Leigon, Sarka Christova, Colleen Mauro, Richard Heinberg, and Mark Bryan. Thanks to my sister Paula Peirce and to Marcus True, who listened and helped me become clear.

I wouldn't be who I am without the inspiring contributions of my colleagues Dr. William Kautz, Joan Grigsby, Kevin Ryerson, Dr. Dale Ironson, David Finch, the good people at Ananda's East-West Bookstore, and my many magical Japanese collaborators: Toshi and Yasuko Yamakawa, Lisa Yoshimi Vogt, Yoshie Usuba, Masako Watanabe, Naoyuki Sekino, and Takiko Koizumi, to name a few. Finally, I want to thank my parents, Mid and Skip Peirce, for believing in me and supporting me when I didn't do the traditional thing.

Foreword

If you have picked up *The Intuitive Way,* you can safely assume that your life is about to change radically. Your intuition, already strong and insistent, is prompting you to get ready for a new journey of discovery. Why?

A purpose deep within you is steadily unfolding. This purpose is not about to let you sleep your way through this lifetime. You may have already noticed an increasing number of synchronicities that seem to indicate you are supposed to be doing something different from what you've been doing until now. You may have noticed you yearn for more meaningful activities or associations. You may have been feeling estranged from some of the old gang or thinking of leaving your occupation and striking out for something new. But what? What to do?

These are the questions that many of us—in the millions now—are currently asking. You, along with other like-minded people, are awakening to your individual path, knowing without knowing that something more is being required of you. You are one of the people who was born to participate in this creatively explosive time of transformation. Trust that.

It is no accident that Penney Peirce's book, *The Intuitive Way,* has found its publisher at this time. This book and others like it that speak to the work of the soul are born in response to the very questions currently arising in people's hearts and minds, questions such as "What's it all about? What is the purpose of this life I've been given? How can I make the most of my time? What should I be concentrating on? Can I really make a difference?"

We live with these personal life questions and often feel that no one else understands these rather vague but persistent longings. What we wish most is that someone would tell us what to do. We cry out for clarity. In my own work the most frequent question is "I know my life is changing. I can feel something new is just about to happen—but I don't know what it is. Which step am I supposed to take first?"

Because we are creatures of our conditioning, because we are taught to do what's expected of us, we think our answer will be found by some epiphany in the external world. We are used to taking our cues from external sources—advice from parents, spouses, friends, religious leaders and mentors, professional groups or union leaders—and playing by the rules of whatever community has authority over us. We might look at labor statistics that tell us what the hottest job markets are or try to second-guess what the new retail trends will be so we may align ourselves with what we perceive to be powerful—so that we can be powerful.

This externalization of truth keeps us on a treadmill of confusion, doubt, and anxiety. We are driven by fear of not keeping up, of being left behind. In a media-driven environment we are so brainwashed by aggressive marketing tactics that we don't even notice anymore—so inundated are we by data that is meant to make us respond with our credit cards. We are awash in motivational theories and systems for self-improvement. Our days are often indiscriminately filled with broadcasts of other people's fears, brutalities, and peccadillos. It's easy to lose ourselves.

Because we are so overmarketed and trained to respond with a purchase or a pill to any of life's events, we continue to experience a queasy truce with our lives, hoping that somehow everything will turn out all right. Eventually, if we are lucky, life gets painful enough that we are forced to turn away from what we know and turn toward what we don't know. Our journey intensifies when we begin to engage the unknown and take the road less traveled. Once we become aware of our inner need for something more, something real, something that speaks to our soul, we start to ask for a different kind of nourishment. We begin to grow into our individuality.

That time of individualization must be at hand for you or this book would not have found its way to you. In reading *The Intuitive Way* you will be given the kind of nourishment that feeds your soul and asks you to trust yourself and take the unknown path.

I can think of no better teacher for this material than Penney Peirce.

Penney and I met synchronistically several years ago when we were both asked to be guests on a television show about intuition. We immediately hit it off—for one thing, we both shared a strong interest in the system of numerology. The focus of our friendship has always been on discussing the patterns we see in individual life stories as well as in discovering what works in teaching metaphysical principles. More than once we have laughingly commented on being in the same "soul group" and appreciate being able to check out our intuitive understandings with each other.

This kind of collegial relationship is precious to me. Penney and I have also co-facilitated groups on helping people develop their own application of James Redfield's *Celestine Prophecy* insights, focusing on the development of intuitive guidance as the first step in living a more fulfilling life. Penney's skill in leading both beginners and advanced students down the intuitive path is exceptional. I continue to be impressed with Penney's commitment to her work and her ability to interpret complex data with simplicity and clarity so that it makes sense to people in all walks of life.

Not only does Penney excel as a teacher and intuitive counselor, but she also has the ability to tune in to the expanded field of evolutionary trends. For example, she invited me to attend one of her lectures on future trends, and as I was listening, I couldn't help scribbling down her forecasts and interpretations of current events. I wound up including a big section of that evening lecture in one of the chapters in the book I was currently working on with James Redfield, *The Tenth Insight: An Experiential Guide*. I have recommended many clients to Penney for a life reading and have listened with fascination to her reports of working with clients all over the country and beyond, especially in Japan. We have discussed many times the unique qualities that appear in the psychic fabric of individuals from different cultures and have been able to see archetypal patterns working in both the collective and personal consciousness.

To me the most exciting frontier we can explore today is working with psyche and soul. The most empowering and practical tool we have—already within us—is the ability to receive intuitive guidance, linking it with our rational and emotional processes, and taking action based on our authentic responses to the moment. With intuition and logic working hand in hand, we can clearly see what is needed and do exactly what is required of us—rising to the occasion with inspiration and trust. Our world may be filled with questions, insecurities, and ever-changing circumstances—and it will continue to be filled with chaos until we leave this earth plane. Yet we live in a world where anything is possible. We crave to be challenged and to succeed. We want to live in the mystery.

Once we shift our perspective, we can never turn back. Using our intuition, we stand poised like a deer sniffing the wind—alive! With this new way of looking inward for direction, watching for tiny clues, we see how important our relationships are—to our souls and to each other. We realize that not only can we make a difference in the world, but this is the real reason we were born. When we grasp the paradox that nothing is fixed and ordained nor is it random and accidental, we have made the shift into truly living our mission. We begin to see that our role is to engage with life, to participate, to enjoy and have fun.

We are born to create and to use the details of our lives as our artistic medium. In the midst of this wonderful, unpredictable life, we always have our inner guidance, the inborn navigational field that God intends for us to use. We are never alone; we are always in direct contact with our inner source. This is true whether we are driving in the car, doing higher mathematics, rocking our baby, painting the kitchen, or sleeping in a subway station. All we have to do is tune in.

Let your adventure with intuition begin!

Carol Adrienne

To the Reader

The animal soul has given birth to all the fetishes.
A fetish made of wood is a little like a garter snake,
But a fetish made of energy is closer to a dragon.
To snap a wooden idol in two is extremely easy;
But to break a dragon is a task beyond our power.

Rumi

Intuition is the long-lost juice of life. It brings us fluidity and joy, instantaneous answers, and abundant knowledge just for the asking. Living by intuition is an art that when mastered produces a thrill like no other. It is into this experience of living and perceiving intuitively that *The Intuitive Way* guides you.

You may have picked up this book because you feel blocked intuitively—maybe you're overwhelmed or untrusting, or unable to see the way out of the comfortable or uncomfortable box you inhabit. It may be a chronic flatness that plagues you, or a temporary solidity of mind or emotion. Don't worry. This is part of the natural ebb and flow of intuitive knowing. The wonderful thing about intuition is that it can return at any time and become fully activated at any age. It is an innate gift of your soul; you can forget to pay attention to it, but you can never lose it entirely. The material in this book will help you dissolve self-doubts and blockages and find your intuitive way forward.

You may be interested in intuition for a variety of reasons. Perhaps you're looking for deeper answers. Or maybe you'd like greater clarity in your life direction, or more insight into your relationships with others. Maybe you want to undam your creativity, increase the vividness of your

All societies, ancient or modern, primitive or sophisticated, have guided themselves by values and goals rooted in the experience of "deep intuition."

Willis Harman

dreams, cultivate more magical synchronicity, or even improve how you find parking spaces. One of my clients wanted to improve his intuition so he could become a professional gambler in Las Vegas. Another man, a successful headhunter, wanted to increase his capacity to "read" his clients' true abilities and sense which job would be a perfect fit. Intuition can bring increased success and satisfaction in every realm—be it material, emotional, or spiritual—and can also bring many joys, both tiny and great.

Cutting through the Chaos

Intuition can make your life smoother and more fun, but it may also be the crucial skill of the future. Everywhere I travel, I speak with people whose physical and emotional lives are in turmoil, who can no longer rely on jobs, relationships, or possessions to provide meaning, who sense something intense occurring under the surface. The "normal" beliefs and forms people have identified with are shifting like sands in the Sahara. In addition, information is proliferating at such a frenzied rate that even with our personal computers and cellular phones (or perhaps because of them) we are increasingly overwhelmed and paralyzed. There are more opinions, demands for attention, and slick media experts today than ever before. We need direct access to answers that are both authentic and appropriate to our lives. Only intuition can cut through the noise, only intuition can provide calm in the face of chaos.

Our own intuition is the catalyst for self-improvement and self-realization, because when it comes to making deep and lasting changes in one's personal life, only subjective experience, not facts, registers as real. And yet, when I listen to my inner authority and receive its insights openly and quietly, and when I share my views in the same spirit, I usually find that I'm not unique. Other people have been sensing, thinking, or dreaming similar things. Intuition becomes especially strong when we share it with each other—we find then that the synthesis of our shared intuitive knowing validates truth more powerfully than does reading books by erudite scholars.

The Intuitive Way will give you the simple truths I have gleaned from my own zigzagging path toward becoming a clear lens. It will empower you to know what you need to know, just when you need to know it. It will help you become one of the voices of love and truth in the world and give you the advantage of extended perception, heightened clarity, and a renewed sense of magic about life. With intuition, as you will see, miracles are not only possible, they're *probable*.

Myths about Intuition

A number of myths surround intuition. One is that you have to be born with "the gift." I am living proof that you don't have to be born special or psychic to become a skilled intuitive; my intuition opened later in life. I had absolutely no surprising intuitive experiences as a child—never saw angels, had no imaginary friends, didn't conk my head and see visions, didn't have a near-death experience. My destiny never showed up in a dramatically convincing way. Part of me wishes I had weird and colorful stories to tell about the origin of my intuition, but I was phenomenon-free. Over the years I've come to see real value in being the girl-next-door from the Midwest with a fairly normal developmental process. I learned firsthand that the intuitive process, or what I call "direct knowing," is a natural human ability and not the realm of a special few. If I could learn to be intuitive, you can, too.

As you contemplate opening your intuition, you're sure to encounter another myth about intuition. Many people associate being intuitive with being psychic. Do you think that if you open your intuition you just might pick those winning lottery numbers or know when and where the next big earthquake is going to hit? Intuitive ability is much more than predicting the highs and lows of the stock market or communing with spiritual entities. Psychic phenomena, as it turns out, are often just the first signs of a much greater and all-encompassing wisdom. We notice these paranormal ways of perceiving first because they're dramatic. If you persist in the search for a more elegant, more efficient, more loving, more uplifting way of knowing, you'll follow the intuitive way deeper and deeper into life. Eventually you'll discover what I have discovered: intuition is not just about knowing who's calling you on the phone—it's about attaining crystal-clear perception.

You'll also realize that intuition is not the opposite of logic—it is a cyclical process, a comprehensive way of knowing life that includes both left-brain analytical thinking and right-brain communion states. This marvelous process has been called many things: the process of creativity, self-recovery, evolution, transformation—even enlightenment. In the end, the intuitive way is truly a spiritual path. Follow your intuition and eventually you'll experience your soul, in your body, as your personality. Intuition is a powerful tool that can heal the painful split we all feel between our earthly, mundane selves and our divine, eternal selves. When we realize that our spiritual knowledge is in us right now and always has been, we become filled with light—light-hearted and enlightened.

How My Intuition Evolved

The pursuit of intuition became a passion for me in my twenties, building gradually from an interest in art, photography, animals, and nature, and from an insatiable curiosity about the mysteries of life. The path first led me to become a graphic designer and corporate art director, using intuition to create advertising, brochures, and logos—sensing what symbolic image might capture the essence of a product or company. Then, for the past twenty years, I plunged into the art of knowing and perceiving, teaching workshops on intuition development and using my expanded intuitive ability to sense the fundamental patterns and purposes in people's lives, offering guidance and healing perspective in private counseling sessions.

I see now how important it is to trust the pull of your interests. I flowed quite unsuspectingly from sketching trees and birds to photography, to design, to a fascination with oracle systems like handwriting analysis, to reading books on psychism, to studying meditation, to doing life readings, to teaching workshops, to writing a book. Trusting the current to carry you to your destiny, or destination, is a big part of intuition. By doing this I learned that the process itself is the teacher.

To me, there have always been too many questions and not enough satisfying answers. My training as a designer taught me to think originally and be a problem-solver; I wanted answers that were essential, not surgical or superficial. Eventually, to get answers that felt really right, I had to enter the intangible world of metaphysics. I wanted to know how consciousness, and the world, worked—from the inside out.

I looked into the inner dynamics of events and people's lives and discovered that when I paid close attention, if I could relax into a softer, less defined identity, I could "become" a whole new field of knowledge that included more data than I'd been aware of as my earthbound "Penney" personality. I practiced entering this expanded field over and over again, translating the information I found there into words of insight for thousands of clients from many countries and walks of life.

I couldn't get enough about the invisible mechanics of how human beings come to be, know, create, and grow. I was a spiritual detective, rediscovering through intuitive observation what priests and sages from every culture in the world have always known. Our lives are based on natural laws. Everything we know occurs within those laws, and evolution moves in accordance with innately harmonious mathematical patterns. I began to think in geometry. I could feel *patterns* of knowledge. Sacred geometry, it turned out, was not so far from graphic design.

I began to travel internationally, and a long-term involvement with the Japanese turned me inside out. They gave me a profound understanding of an ingenious way of ordering reality that was diametrically opposed to our Western way of thinking in almost every detail. As I allowed myself to be absorbed into their cultural reality, my thoughts and body were repatterned, and I was stretched into a new kind of intuitive perception.

My intuitive growth has come from a blend of diverse insights from many disciplines and cultures. Each insight has always made sense—eventually—and never contradicted anything else. I simply added it to the stew.

Meeting the Luck Dragon

The intuitive way of perceiving has always put me in touch with the effortless, truly joyful nature of life and showed me how, when we approach our experience with childlike innocence and awe, miracles abound. As I was contemplating writing this book, for example, I had a bigger-than-life experience that was marked by the kind of flow that always signifies to me that a greater reality, or an important teaching, is trying to emerge from my deeper mind. Intuition was talking to me in its strange language of omens, dreams, and synchronicity.

A couple years ago I responded to an inner call that said, "Get in your car and drive to Santa Fe, New Mexico." I was only halfway through an experimental study group I'd been participating in with my friend, author Carol Adrienne. She was developing exercises for the experiential guide for *The Celestine Prophecy*, which she was co-authoring with James Redfield, and I was serving as a guinea pig, giving her feedback from an intuitive's point of view. In particular we had been discussing the concept of synchronicity and coincidence, and the meaning of the themes that popped into our heads. This trip, with its nonrational, other-dimensional origins, seemed like a perfect chance to practice what we'd been studying.

On the first night in Santa Fe I had a simple but powerful dream. I was riding on the back of a giant sea serpent, far out in the ocean. Along with me, other people were straddling the massive coils that looped up from the waves, and we were having the ride of our lives. Every so often the huge serpent would turn its head slowly around and look back at us with a kindly expression, as if to say, "Is everyone doing OK back there?" When I woke, my first impression was, "This must be a symbol for my trip!" But what did it mean?

Two days later I went hiking with friends in a canyon. As I trailed along at the end of the line, an exquisitely marked snake suddenly crossed my path. Its energetic impact was phenomenal, as it stopped and actually stared at me. The creature reminded me of something ancient, mythological, and eternal, something just at the edge of my consciousness. Later I wondered, "Why was I the only one who saw it? And was it trying to say something to me?"

The next day I had a highly synchronous meeting with a writer who was instrumental in helping me launch this book. I also saw the movie *Sirens*, which features a snake meandering from scene to scene. Then my marching orders came again: "Drive to Denver and see your sister." I spent the next week in suburbia communing with my sister and two nieces.

One day I rented a video for the girls—one of my all-time favorites, *The NeverEnding Story*. It's a magical piece of work, a mythological hero's journey for children as well as for adults. In the story the hero rides around the kingdom of Fantasia on the back of a lovable luck dragon named Falkor, facing down frightening monsters and passing innumerable life-or-death character tests. As I watched it for the second time with my three-year-old niece Julia, she announced, "This is gonna be a scary part"—mostly just to let her body get prepared for an upcoming shock. Moments later she said, "But Falkor's gonna be here pretty soon. Falkor's a *luck dragon*." I could feel her getting comfortable again. She could get through the scary parts as long as she knew she had a friend.

Driving home across the desert, I thought about my book, about the trip, about synchronicity and what I would tell Carol. Then, with a jolt, I noticed the toy rubber snake curving up to greet me from its place amidst the rock collection I carry on my dashboard. I realized that the snake image had twined its way through my entire journey. And Falkor was the sea serpent in my dream! I didn't know what it meant but was fascinated at the repetition of the theme.

"Well, Penney, don't you see?" exclaimed Carol on the phone. "The luck dragon is just like the process of synchronicity and intuition! It's magical and fun, full of wisdom, and it has the same energy of everything we've been talking about. Penney, this must be the spirit of your book. It's your personal 'intuition mascot.'"

As Carol raved on enthusiastically, I felt that profound shiver which for me always indicates truth. This luck dragon image was something that was close to my heart of hearts, and it carried an energy of childlike simplicity. Just look how Julia had identified with Falkor and overcome her fear. Hey, I'll admit it—*I wanted to ride on Falkor, too.* So, in my imagination the luck dragon and I became partners. I practiced embodying the qualities he represented. If I forgot to feel his wise and happy energy, the world would remind me in some unique way.

Since those first dreams and omens, the dragon image has followed me relentlessly. Everywhere I look, I see dragon movies, dragon coffee mugs, dragon children's books, dragon puppets, dragon statues. A friend sent me an illustration of the Chinese goddess Kwan Yin standing on a sky dragon, and in a Tokyo museum I saw a happy little Buddha perched on a dragon's back. I even saw a rope dragon from Tibet in a catalogue with this caption: "Within my mind I was riding atop my powerful friend. Do you have a dragon in your heart?" And just this morning, as I drove to breakfast, I noticed I was following a car with the license plate I M DRACO.

OK, OK—I'm listening! For some reason the voice of my intuition has been speaking loudly on this subject. For centuries, especially in the East, the dragon has been the archetypal symbol of transformative power, immortality, wisdom, and good luck. It binds all the phenomena of nature: dwelling in the earth or water, flying through the air, and breathing fire. It represents the basic, spiraling, sine-wave movement of our life-force energy, or *kundalini,* rising from the depths of the earth, up through our spine, and out the top of our head, bringing wisdom as it wings its way heavenward. In Asia, the dragon is represented holding the pearl of fertility and enlightenment in its claws. With its rippling, undulating movement, the dragon seems to represent the need to equally embrace both the highs and lows of life.

Since our intuition blossoms when we play with images, I had to agree with Carol—what better symbol for the intuitive way? And once I merged with the luck dragon in my imagination, I found that the fluidity of my own intuition improved, and this book found its way out of my mind and heart and through the circuitous channels of the publishing world. I share this story with you because the image that came to me may speak to you as well. If it does, embody it and let it guide you. If not, as you work with the material in *The Intuitive Way,* keep your eyes and ears open for your own vibrant symbol for this amazing process of living and knowing. Although intuition is a practical tool that can be applied to daily tasks, let's not forget that it also keeps us pure and direct and feeds our childlike sense of delight. In the end it may be the quality of our deep inner experience that counts the most to our souls, not just what we accomplish in the world.

Bastian flushed with pleasure. "Is that true, Falkor?" he asked. "You wouldn't mind carrying me?"

"Of course not, all-powerful sultan," said the dragon with a wink. "Hop on and hold tight."

. . . Bastian vaulted directly from mule to dragon back and clutched the silvery white mane as Falkor took off. . . . Riding a white luck dragon was something else again. If sweeping over the ground on the back of a fiery lion had been like a cry of ecstasy, this gentle rising and falling as the dragon

adjusted his movements to the air currents was like a song, now soft and sweet, now triumphant with power. Especially when Falkor was looping the loop, when his mane, his fangs, and the long fringes on his limbs flashed through the air like white flames, it seemed to Bastian that the winds were singing in chorus.

Michael Ende, *The NeverEnding Story*

Getting the Most from This Book

There is only one journey. Going inside yourself.

Rainer Maria Rilke

The Benefits of Active Intuition

Marcus has had a fascinating life. And he credits this to his "little voice," which he says has piped up in an unavoidable way at key times, telling him first as a teenager during World War II to leave his family, ride his bicycle across the German border at night, and flee to Canada. He worked as a scenic carpenter in Canada until his little voice told him to start carving sculptures from wood and showed him just what shapes to make. Then it told him to open an art gallery, which became quite successful. Next his inner voice told him to study psychology. And as he completed his university studies and developed a thriving practice, his voice commanded him: "Go to California!" Today he uses his intuition actively in his work as a therapist and can't imagine what his life would have been like without it.

Though it didn't always make sense to his logical mind, Marcus could hear the voice of his own intuition and was willing to take the risks involved in trusting it. So many people I speak with tell a different story: how they *didn't* listen to their inner voice, follow their hunch, or try to manifest the vision they got in a dream—and how they almost immediately became snagged, took a turn for the worse, became depressed or sick, or even lost a valuable situation or possession. This seems to be such a common experience that people joke about overriding or second-guessing their intuitions. "When will I ever learn!" they say, rolling their eyes toward heaven.

Lee, one of my students, tells me, almost incredulously, that she has just realized, "When I sense something strange is going on, it usually is. And if I keep feeling funny about a situation, if it keeps coming up again and again, I'm starting to believe it does need to be attended to." Lee has learned the hard way to trust her bodily-felt intuitions. She grew up in a family where she learned to override her gut instinct and "do what was expected," even if she didn't want to, even if it went against her best interests. In fact, she never knew what her best interests were. Now, after years of unconsciously sacrificing much potential joy, she is learning to recognize the subtle sensation in her body that tells her, "I don't want to do this"—and actually have it be OK to go against her "shoulds." Her intuition is waking up, and she admits it's both exciting and scary to dare to become more of her true self.

Whether you're tuned in to your intuition as Marcus was or learning to listen to it in new ways, like Lee, the intuitive way of life offers you many benefits:

- You'll learn to slow down, be present, and pay attention to the amazingly wise process of your experience.
- You'll develop a positive, life-enhancing attitude.
- Your natural talents will be revealed.
- You'll become more alert and aware of detail and nuance.
- You won't waste time and energy on inappropriate thoughts and actions.
- You'll find and stay in touch with your life purpose and lessons.
- You'll be better able to understand your spiritual path.
- Your creativity and imagination will increase.
- You'll experience more grace, synchronicity, good luck—and even miracles.
- You'll manifest your dreams in less time than ever before.
- You'll have more confidence and personal power.

As You Prepare to Begin

To receive the greatest benefits from this book, it helps to start the journey with the best "intuitive attitude." Truly successful students possess a natural "beginner's mind" and can temporarily suspend what they know to listen, act, receive, and process new data with childlike innocence and directness. With a beginner's mind you will not be threatened by not knowing or by having personal experiences that vary from the norm. You'll feel fresh and sincere. You'll trust yourself, trust the process of learning, and trust that whatever you need next will be revealed in a way you can understand. Like children, students with a beginner's mind are truly "full of themselves" in the best way and don't question the appropriateness of their observations and creations. They stay open to learning and expressing themselves because it feels good.

As you begin, look at the basic attitudes you bring to this experience. Are you optimistic or pessimistic? An optimist, when turned down for a job or rejected by a lover, naturally finds a way to interpret the experience as a benefit. Pessimists, on the other hand, use the setback as an excuse to revalidate their negative views about life. When working with the intuitive process, a pessimistic attitude can kill the flow of information and energy. Beware of unnecessary negativity. On the other hand, *needing* things to be positive can lead to gullibility, which allows intuition to flow but can prevent you from discriminating what's practical from what's titillating. We need a little skepticism to temper our openness. Without common sense, intuition can turn to delusion. Yet without optimism, it's difficult for intuition to occur at all.

No pessimist ever discovered the secrets of the stars, or sailed to an uncharted land, or opened a new heaven to the human spirit.

Helen Keller

Attitude Assessment

Imagine a thermometer with markings from one to ten. Ten indicates the highest response; one the lowest. Ask your inner mind to give you a reading on the following questions. Take the first answer you get and write it in your journal.

1. When presented with new information, how readily do you accept the ideas as presented?

2. Do you first check with your own inner sense of things when judging the validity of new information?

3. How much do you need answers to be positive?
4. How skeptical are you about new information?

Are you willing to suspend your preconceived ideas about intuition and slip into a beginner's mind? Are you willing to become a child again, fascinated with perception and learning, engrossed with the magic of creating something new and original? Are you willing to receive the experiences your soul wants to facilitate in you as a result of following the material in this book—without demeaning them or yourself in any way? The more open you are to surprises, the more fun you'll have with the intuitive process. At the same time the more honest you are with yourself, the higher your accuracy level will be. Are you willing to know what might block the clear-running waters of your intuitive insight? Are you willing to examine both the highs and lows of your experience, looking for the hidden "gifts in the garbage"?

A Natural Progression of Steps

Intuition is spontaneous and free-form. But there is an orderliness to the development of intuitive skill, a natural progression of insights that allows an easy, fluid integration of nonlinear, "holographic" perception with our more familiar linear, logical, hierarchical way of perceiving.

This book is organized to guide you through that sequence. The text is divided into three parts:

1. **Creating a Clear Lens**
    Recognizing the Intuitive Process
    Choosing the Intuitive World View
    Living in Alignment with the Creation Cycle
    Unlocking the Secrets of Your Subconscious Mind

2. **Accessing Subtle Information**
    Becoming Aware of the Invisible
    Hearing Your Body Talk

3. **Making Intuition Useful**
    Harnessing Dreams and Imagination
    Receiving Superconscious Guidance
    Applying Intuition in Everyday Life
    Staying in the Natural Flow

The first phase of the intuition development process focuses on creating a clear lens. If your binoculars are dirty or covered by a cap, no matter how fantastic the view, you won't enjoy it or benefit from it. Where intuition is concerned, a clear lens means a clear mind.

To aid you in becoming lucid, Chapter 1 helps you recognize the ways you've been using intuition and how you may have resisted expanding your intuition. It also identifies intuitive abilities you might develop. Chapter 2 takes you further, helping you understand how your attitudes and world view influence the flow of your perception—and what you will allow to become real in your life. You'll begin to learn about the intuitive number three and about the three parts of your mind and how to shift your viewpoint, and therefore your reality, from one part of your mind to another at will.

Chapter 3 models for you the ideal, frictionless, optimally creative use of your awareness. It shows you how to flow intuitively with the current of your own cycle of creation and how to recognize the intuitive signals that indicate a backward flow. Chapter 4 takes you on the hero's journey, helping you deal with the inevitable bumps and distortions you'll encounter along the intuitive way; it provides you with a simple procedure for transforming negativity into intuitive insight.

Once you're able to create and maintain mental clarity, the second phase of intuition development prepares you to access intuitive information. Chapter 5 teaches you techniques for becoming receptive and neutral and for maximizing your sensitivity to subtle information. Chapter 6 takes you into your body, where intuitive information first makes itself known, and helps you increase your ability to access and interpret nonverbal, sensory information.

In the third phase of the intuitive development process, we'll practice using intuition in a variety of ways. Chapter 7 helps you trust and build your imagination and use it to generate and interpret symbols and imagery—one of the main "languages" of intuition. You'll learn techniques for expanding your dreams. Chapter 8 teaches you to use your intuition to acquire clear guidance for yourself and others. Chapter 9 helps you apply your intuition in improving communication, making decisions, enhancing creativity, healing yourself, and manifesting what you need. Finally,

Chapter 10 gives you tips on avoiding common pitfalls along the intuitive way and maintaining your newfound clarity.

What Often Happens on the Journey

Beginning the process of intuition development is like putting a canoe in a river with some exciting white water downstream. You intend to shoot the rapids and come out into a broad, gently flowing section of water you've heard exists somewhere ahead. First you check that your equipment is in tip-top shape. You launch your craft and put your paddle in the water. You practice your strokes in an easy section of the river, then gradually proceed downstream toward the unknown. The current carries you, and if you pay attention, it guides you around the rocks. You learn to read the ripples. As you enter the rapids, you must surrender your fears and draw upon the wisdom in your body, becoming one with the flow of the river. You are so involved with the endeavor that time seems to stop. As you emerge from the first set of rapids, you've learned something about yourself. But there's an even bigger challenge up ahead! Get ready, get centered, here you go again . . .

The Intuitive Way will launch you on a journey through new territory. As you complete the work in each chapter, you'll synchronize yourself with a universal process. Just as each adventurer goes through the same sequence of rapids and bends in the river, so you'll naturally enter the next phase of the intuitive process, and the next, and the lessons will feel timely and uncannily relevant to what's happening in your life. Each chapter discusses a specific theme, and as you proceed through the material, your life will come to epitomize these themes. Each person making a river run carves his or her unique groove down the channel, through the sequences of rough and smooth waters. Similarly you will find your passage through the intuitive development process to be purely your own. Please don't measure yourself against anyone else.

Coincidence and Synchronicity

As your life falls into alignment with the stages of growth outlined in this book, you may notice an increase in coincidences and synchronicity in

The highest way asks nothing hard.

Seng Ts'an

your life. You'll see odd repetitions of phrases, symbols, events, and motifs, just as I was continually reminded of the luck dragon. One week everyone you know will be experiencing fatigue and sleeplessness; the next week they'll be talking about people they know who've suddenly married. Maybe you'll see someone with a bouquet of balloons—twice in one week—*and* you'll see an image of balloons in a magazine. What does it mean? Maybe a friend will ask you why you think she has developed heel spurs. You intuitively respond, "Because you've been digging your heels in." The next day a man you've never met, describing his job situation, says, "I dug my heels in and refused to be transferred overseas." You hadn't heard the phrase for years, and now you hear it twice in two days. Why? The Mystery is starting to talk to you. Take note!

Your Wish Is Our Command

You may also notice it takes less time for your insights and wishes to manifest as reality. No sooner had you said you'd like to take French lessons than a French woman phones, a friend of a friend who is in town, and wonders if you have time for lunch. Or you have vague misgivings about a business partner, and the next week you find he's been secretly organizing a hostile takeover of your company. Maybe you're a counselor who's been so busy seeing clients that you silently wish for more quiet time to work on projects at home. The next week the phone hardly rings, and you wonder where all the people went. Your negative beliefs and behaviors may reveal themselves to you as well. You gossip about a friend and are found out instantly. You lose patience with a slow checkout clerk and that afternoon are reprimanded by your boss for not being productive enough.

The more you ask for guidance from your soul and act on your intuition, the more your outer life will show itself to be a direct result of your inner thoughts, beliefs, and commands.

Pandora's Box Opens Wide

Though you might hope that opening your intuition will bring only sweetness and light, you'll probably dip briefly into the mud before winging your way to the heights. As you progress through the chapters and ask

There are only two ways to live your life. One is as though nothing is a miracle. The other is as though everything is a miracle.

Albert Einstein

for more truth, more love, more "reality," everything that is not true for you anymore, everything that has outgrown its usefulness, everything that is illusory will rise from your deep subconscious to the surface of your conscious mind. These old ideas will appear in two ways: they will be obsessive, anxiety-producing thoughts that cycle around and around in your brain, or they will occur as actual situations or events that symbolize the beliefs you're coming to grips with. These are the "rapids" that you must navigate with full presence and attention—and it's absolutely normal. The material in chapters 2 through 4 will help you deal with this part of the process and travel through any turbulence you encounter.

Perhaps you've been frustrated by feeling relatively invisible. As you open your intuition and the quality of your insights becomes clearer, you will gain the power that comes from being authentic. This energy of truth and loyalty to yourself always attracts attention. People start to notice you—both those who appreciate and praise you and those who are envious or even afraid of you. You may find you're dealing with people who want unreasonable things from you or who betray you out of jealousy. Can you keep going without collapsing into the sinkhole of ego, disappointment, or anger? A ballerina once told me that if she falls at a critical moment in her performance, though humiliated and shocked, she has no time for self-indulgent behavior. The only relevant question to ask is "What's next?"

The Monkey Mind Scurries, Chatters, and Leaps

As you enter the intuitive process, if your beginner's mind is not in place, you'll be tempted to bargain with your soul. You might say, "If I trust you, you'd better give me some important stuff . . . or else I'll return to my old way of thinking where I never recognize you." Or "If I open up, don't you dare give me scary information or anything ugly. I'll only accept information from ascended masters and angels." Of course, this approach is bound to attract what you resist. Trust can't be conditional.

As you receive insights and guidance, you may be tempted to look the gift horse in the mouth. You may find your inner Skeptic emerging from the shadows. You may be besieged by a barrage of "yes, buts": "Yes, I did get a sense that I should tell Peter about my dream, but my intuition should have shown me that it was a precognitive dream. How was I supposed to know?" Or "OK, I asked a question and received an answer, but it's not a very good answer." Or "Yes, I want to do the exercises in my diary, but I don't have time." Or "Yes, I did gain insight about how to solve my problem, but it's probably just a projection from my mind." Or "Yes, I asked—but I didn't get anything. See, it doesn't work for me." Watch out for too much internal dialogue and static-producing self-talk. Carlos Castaneda's Don Juan says, "A warrior is aware that the world will change as soon as he stops talking to himself."

Navigating the River

The material in the early chapters will orient you, give you maps to use on the journey ahead, and teach you how to handle whatever you'll face downstream. Take it slowly. You may want to leap ahead. Please don't. Just as successful athletes take time to fully visualize their intended performance, you will have better results if you slow down now and do the groundwork. The early chapters should trigger memories, put you in touch with unconscious resistance, and begin clearing you of fear. Remember, the first phase of any process involves *conviction* and *commitment*.

As you progress through the material, you will learn to let go of control, to be neutral, to receive. Here's where you'll encounter the cleverness of your "monkey mind." You may feel vulnerable, irritable, and anxious. You may experience doubt, panic, delusion, inflation and deflation, adrenalin rushes, and boredom. Hold steady and keep going. The second phase of the process is about *courage* and *effort*.

Finally, as you come through the rough waters, you'll find glimmerings of new authority, new skills, new knowledge about life. You'll want to use your capabilities in larger arenas, take on greater challenges, apply them to practical situations. You may want to share your knowledge with others. At this point, it's important to practice, practice, practice. Be careful about getting caught up in a premature, false sense of grandeur. The third phase of the process is about *honesty, humility,* and *rededication.*

Once you finish the process, you may find you'd like another go. Each river run has its own unique twist because the currents are never the same. Every time you go through the process of expanding your intuition, you'll navigate it differently. Your skill and facility will increase, your attentiveness and involvement will be more complete. And remember, life is not static—there is always a flow, and you can enter it whenever you choose and stay in it as long as you want.

How to Proceed: The Guidelines and Tools

Mindfulness is the path to immortality.
Negligence is the path to death.
The vigilant never die,
Whereas the negligent are the living dead.
With this understanding,
The wise, having developed a high degree of mindfulness,
Rejoice in mindfulness,
Paying heed to each step on the path.

The Buddha

Make Time and Space

You'll need to give about an hour each day of attention to *The Intuitive Way*. You may cover a chapter a week, or you may want to take longer. Decide when and where you'll reserve private time, then be consistent. Your body will appreciate following a regimen.

Complete Three Main Activities

Read the Chapter Through

First, each week read the chapter. As you read, involve your body. Mark up the pages, underline passages in bright colors, write comments and questions in the margins, and check exercises you've completed. Give it your imprint. For the next few months this book will be your buddy.

Take it with you in the car, into restaurants, to work, on business trips. It's fine to read a little, do an exercise, read some more, write a bit, read more.

Spiritual Aerobics: Do the Exercises

You'll find exercises scattered throughout each chapter. Many involve using a notebook; others are experiential and are meant to be done out in the world or in a meditative state. After you complete the experiential exercises, document what happened in your journal. What were your insights? What data did you receive? What difficulties or surprises did you encounter?

Doing the meditations, visualizations, and exercises daily is like spiritual aerobics. You stretch your capacity and tone yourself, just as you do with physical aerobics. Intuitive exercises that engage the full imagination and the "reality sense" of the body can stimulate you physically. You are running energy of a higher frequency through your brain and nerves, and until you become used to it, you may feel "wired" with energy, then sleepy. Rushes of energy come as you open new circuits in your body and mind. The sleepiness comes when your conscious mind has absorbed as much as it can and needs time to digest the material. With practice, you'll become intuitively "fit."

Keep a Journal: Your Intuition Diary

Writing daily observations in your journal and doing written exercises is the colored thread that weaves through the fabric of your intuitive development, revealing your unique pattern. The daily journal is a powerful tool. It documents the contents of your inner mind, recording your rhythms and subtle patterns. It measures your growth and proves the reality of your intuitive prowess to your inner Skeptic. Because the intuitive process is a function of the mind becoming one with the body, you must include your body in the learning process. Your body is like a simple animal; it loves physical, sensual, repetitive, and ritualistic acts. It loves the splash of color, swooping bold lines, swirling water, pungent odors, movement of any kind. If your body is to trust you and willingly give you the wealth of knowledge it possesses, you must spend companionable time with it, much as you would play with a three-year-old.

TROUBLESHOOTING TIP
Guiding Yourself in Meditation Exercises

Find a quiet place where you won't be disturbed. Read the exercise several times and feel the natural order of the steps. Study the instructions until you know the sequence by heart.

Close your eyes and run through all the steps. Practice in a cursory way several times, then do it for real.

Develop an authoritative Soul Voice inside your mind. When it instructs you, agree to follow and see what you get. Let this voice lead you in the meditations.

As an alternate technique, record your meditations on a cassette tape, leaving enough blank space to allow unpressured responses from your intuitive self. Then follow your taped voice.

Ask a friend to read the instructions to you, pausing occasionally to give you time to get the results you need.

Keep your journal nearby so you can record immediately what you received during the exercise.

To open your intuition and keep it flowing, establish a ritual. You need stimulation your body can count on, something you do consistently every day. Just as your dog or cat orients itself to the exact time you feed it and pesters you unrelentingly for food if you forget, so will your body quickly acclimate itself to relaying information to you from your soul. Ask and you will receive—*if* you create a reliable, consistent method for receiving. Give your body a notebook and a colorful pen, fun things to do with that pen, and watch out. Create a new habit: write, doodle, sketch, make lists. Use your favorite pens, ones that make broad, bold strokes, ones that roll slickly across the surface, pens of different colors for different days, fountain pens with character, fine-line drafting pens. See what ideas flow with different nibs.

Buy a thick notebook with plenty of pages so your entire process will fit into a single journal. Nothing too fancy, neat, or precious—unless you are truly compelled by your inner voice. Too much emphasis on the perfect form can interfere with spontaneity of content. With the intuitive process, freedom is like gold. Feel free to be messy, make mistakes, draw sketches, write poems, and scratch out whole lines. As writing teacher Brenda Ueland says, "Keep a slovenly, headlong, impulsive, honest diary." [1]

Write to Prime Your Intuition Pump

The Exercises

The exercises in each chapter should stimulate your imagination, bring themes into your conscious mind, and jump-start the process that will evolve as you work with the material. You may begin your writing each day by doing one or two of these exercises. If you miss a few in any given week, return whenever it occurs to you and do them. The timing will always be appropriate. If you want more practice, try the additional exercises listed in the appendix, "Delving Deeper."

Direct Writing

Direct writing is a method of writing directly from your innermost self, letting a stream of words emerge without censorship, without rereading them, as a spontaneous flow of commentary. At the end of each chapter you'll find a list of seven questions. These are suggested "magnets" for triggering a response from the deeper part of your mind. After working with the exercises in each chapter, flip to the end and see which direct writing suggestions feel "juicy." As you use this method, you'll be surprised with what you're writing, because it will be fresh, direct, and quirky but right on target. You'll feel it in your gut.

Here's how direct writing works: Get quiet and centered. In the beginning you might pretend that your writing partner is your inner child or your soul itself. Your mind's job is purely secretarial. Write a magnet question in your notebook: "Why is my work not being recognized?"

Tune in to honest, wise, simple You and encourage the answer to come. Let the inner voice address you directly, then allow words to emerge, one by one. Don't think ahead, don't analyze what's being said. If a strange word comes into your head, write it down. Whatever word is supposed to follow that one will simply occur. Don't stop and reread what you've written. You are taking dictation. Wise You begins:

> When you put yourself out into the world and don't receive the results you think you deserve, it's not necessarily because your work is substandard or because you're doing something wrong. You must keep going, keep walking, taking the steps that come from the deepest impulses. What makes people notice you and your work is power, and you have not built up enough of it. Power accumulates by consistently using the talents you were given, from doing what you love repeatedly in the world. Be creative every day. *Be* the artist and *do* the artwork. Don't siphon energy into other activities and people. Be convincing. You must saturate your energy field with who and what you are.

Direct writing is "soul writing." Whether you are using this device in a conversational fashion or writing in the first person without hashing over or belaboring your thoughts, you'll receive the clearest insight if you write straight from your body. Brenda Ueland says, "And so, in your diary, if you write fast, as though you vomited your thoughts on paper, you will touch only those things that interest you."[2] My normally neat and tidy client,

Sandra, found that her direct writing helped loosen and clear a creative block. Her journal contains the following passage that looks like it was written by a manic alien from another planet. The handwriting scratches, marches, stomps, and billows beyond margins, at some points almost off the page:

> My handwriting is getting so many glitches in it! I hate that! I'm trying to be legible like my grade school teachers wanted, but something in me is rebelling! But who cares? Right now, right NOW, it can be whatever way it wants! Using the computer, I've lost touch with my body, the unique form it gives my thoughts, as hand-written words, coming loaded with nerve force. See? I can write with more pressure, like I'm doing now, Wow! but it takes too long and I feel like Frankenstein. I can write really soft like this, hardly pressing at all, but I can't feel the paper. It's like I'm skating over water, but I notice the ease of the flow. This is neat—I can see how lightening up the pressure can free my writer's block! and change my brain! and my inner rhythms! See how the shape of my handwriting is changing already? It's getting big and more and more illegible but prettier. Ooooool!

Document Your Process and Insights

You can also use direct writing to describe the entertaining or surprising openings of your intuition, the blocks you encounter in your perception, the breakthroughs. It lends itself well to a fluid, free-form description of your process. Spend some time each day documenting your insights in the order they come—we're aiming for a spontaneous, stream of consciousness style. Some odd little experience or perception may have caught your attention, but until you write about it in this manner, you may not understand its significance. Start by writing an interesting anecdote, then continue with direct writing:

> The strangest thing happened when I shared my dream with Pamela, whom I had just met at a party. . . . Pamela had had the exact same imagery in a dream last week! That got us to talking about how it was possible for this to happen, and then we both realized that we

With the wild nature as ally and teacher we see not through two eyes but through the many eyes of intuition. With intuition we are like the starry night, we gaze at the world through a thousand eyes. The wild woman is fluent in the language of dreams, images, passion and poetry.

Clarissa Pinkola Estes

might be tapping into some global theme. And maybe there were other people who were dreaming the same thing! Now I'm thinking about how interconnected I am to everyone. . . .

Write about small miracles, and then see, through direct writing, why these things might occur:

I was thinking yesterday that I needed an exercise bike and at work today Steve mentioned he had one to sell at a reasonable price! Why did this happen to me? This happened to show you that you can have what you ask for! To show you there is no limit on how life can provide for you and how quickly your ideas can become real.

Write about energy: "I haven't been able to sleep for a week. I feel some kind of electricity running through me as soon as I lie down." Write about what you see in your dreams and meditations, about odd things people say to you—out of the blue. The waitress asks what you're writing and you say you're opening your intuition. She says, "Oh, I meditate every morning! Three breaths, in through my nose and out through my mouth for ten long counts. Works like a charm." Everything that happens to you can trigger a deeper insight.

Your Agreement with Yourself: Pay Attention

I invite you to treat yourself to a purely private endeavor, something you need not share with anyone. The material in this book is for you. I invite you to make an agreement with your soul and your body to pay absolute attention to them. During the next several months, vow solemnly to give to yourself and others—and even to the inanimate objects of the world—what you're always complaining *you* don't get: loving, unbiased interest and attentiveness.

REMEMBER
▼
*What you find
fascinating holds the
ultimate authority.*

Vow: a solemn pledge, esp. one made to God or a god, dedicating oneself to an act, service, or way of life
Solemn: from *sollennis*, yearly, hence religious (from annual religious festivals); done according to ritual; sacred in character; deeply earnest; arousing feelings of awe

To make a successful agreement to complete the process outlined in *The Intuitive Way,* you must realize there is no outside authority to resist. The book is not out to get you; neither am I, the author, going to punish you if you don't follow each guideline. You are your own master teacher, and it is the authority of your perception that makes life meaningful to you. Where would you like to invest authority? If you can see it within yourself, as well as in all others, you will have no problem making a commitment. There will be no one and nothing to resist!

God is in the details.

Ludwig Mies van der Rohe

"I, _____, *commit to trust and pay attention to the subtle insights, feelings, and hunches I have for the next few months. I agree to participate fully in the process of considering the deeper meaning in everything I notice and to find the wisdom in my own life process.*"

Part I
Creating a Clear Lens

The first phase of the intuition development process

focuses on creating a clear lens.

If your binoculars are dirty or covered by a cap,

no matter how fantastic the view,

you won't enjoy it or benefit from it.

Where intuition is concerned, a clear lens

means a clear mind.

I

Recognizing the Intuitive Process

Intuition isn't separate from life. To find it, you must fully enter life and learn to move as life moves. You've been using intuition every day, but you probably aren't aware just how and when. Chapter 1 helps you assess your current level of active intuition and gives you ideas about what's possible. The first phase of any process is like a seed sprouting, pushing up through the soil but still in the dark. The ideas in this chapter are like seeds; let them prompt you to notice new ways of knowing. Stay loose and open.

It seems that we have made a dreadful mistake by identifying ourselves exclusively with our consciousness, by imagining that we are only what we know about ourselves. There is much more to us, parts that speak in tongues that take some getting used to. To learn their language, we need to lend a very attentive ear to the strange myths of the mind, and take a careful look at whatever happens, regardless of whether or not it accords with orthodox explanations. For, as Jung says, "It is important and salutary to speak also of incomprehensible things."

Lyall Watson

Beyond Information Overload

When you awoke this morning, did you immediately start making lists and worrying about how much you'd accomplish today? Do you feel pressured to be smarter or faster so you can digest all the data you should to do a good job? Is your mind a petty tyrant who needs to organize and control the people and environment around you to establish serenity? We're so used to living by the wiles of our logical left brain that we've come to accept these stress-filled conditions as normal. "Help!" I want to yell some days, "I'm being held hostage by my linear mind."

Maybe you're like Cynthia, who co-founded a successful Silicon Valley software company and relies heavily on her intuition to make decisions. Cynthia receives more than a hundred e-mail messages, faxes, and phone calls daily and barely has time to delegate them, let alone sort through them personally. She says she's losing herself and her intuitive edge in a clutter of information.

Cultivating the kind of knowing that doesn't depend on following paper trails and keeping up with proliferating piles of information seems essential as our world speeds up and problems become more complex. Imagine if we surrendered our compulsion to devour information and instead trusted intuition, if we listened to first impressions and acted from a deep sense of harmony. Operating this way, what we needed to know would simply occur to us, and whoever was supposed to do the task would be the first to do it.

Colleen, a systems analyst for a high-technology company, says that when she stays in that open state of mind, each person who drops by her cubicle to chat seems to be purposeful. John serendipitously has the report she needs to complete her spreadsheets, Sarah provides a key insight, and Howard knows the person she should call about a new industry sector.

We're about to discover a way to have things work faster, more harmoniously, and more efficiently—without the tyranny of the left brain. *Could it be that just beyond the Information Age is the Intuition Age?*

No matter how many facts we gather, if we cling to logic alone, we're using only a small percentage of our capacity to know (some scientists say only 10 percent)—and knowing a relatively small world, at that. Our left brain perception is flat and rather boring when compared with direct intuitive knowing, revelation, and wisdom. These are experiential and bloom through seemingly magical intervention from a greater force. Intuition, I'm convinced, is where the other 90 percent of our brainpower lies. Through intuition we get the big picture, the simultaneous understanding that puts us and all the facts in our proper relationship to something beyond us. A friend of my mother, who in her sixties had started opening to her intuitive nature, summarized it when she exclaimed, "Going backward now and living that old way—well, it'd be like turning into a *worm!*"

Intuition used to be associated primarily with women, artists, mystics, poets, oracles, or even lunatics and other fringe elements of society. Though intuitive knowing is still pooh-poohed by intellectuals as soft and self-indulgent, we see many signs that the public's understanding is changing. Authors such as John Bradshaw, Marianne Williamson, and Carolyn Myss are popularizing an inner-directed philosophy, encouraging us to examine the way we create our reality through the use of our minds.

When reason rules, then dreams and prophecies, psychic insights and unconscious forces, go underground and fester. Rationalism's success in cutting off access to our deep psychic and spiritual dimensions suppresses half our life.

Jean Houston

Advocates for extrasensory perception and other-dimensional experience, such as astronaut Edgar Mitchell, physician Deepak Chopra, and near-death expert Raymond Moody, encourage us to explore the transpersonal realms of consciousness to improve the quality of our lives. In addition, physicists like Fritjof Capra tell us that to understand our "holographic" universe and solve today's complex problems we must go beyond mechanistic thinking. Intuition, it seems, is finally becoming useful.

Noticing Intuition

Information, as well as openings to greater knowledge, can come in strange, illogical ways. We're not as practiced in recognizing and validating intuitive truth as we are concrete, scientific proof. For example, have you ever had butterflies of recognition about a place or person you've never seen before? Have you ever pursued meeting certain people just because you saw a special quality in their photo or because the sound of their name rang a strong inner bell? Sometimes all we need to do is come near a person, hold an object, or stand on a certain spot of land, and a pattern of knowledge is activated (or reactivated) within. Suddenly pictures appear in our mind, or our bodies telegraph a sense of safety or danger.

Intuitive insight often comes in a form that doesn't relate to our usual concepts of time, space, and personal identity. At first we may not understand. When I first studied historical cultures and spiritual societies like ancient Egypt and the Essenes, I felt displaced in time and had a distinct sense that I already knew everything I read. I was a young art director then with no place to apply my mystical insights, yet those glimpses of possible expertise made me wonder, "What might I really become if I could reintegrate everything I've ever been?" The strange intuitive sense of recognition eventually gave me the confidence to leave my corporate job and risk becoming a spiritual teacher and intuitive counselor.

If we're patient and wait for the larger context to reveal itself, eventually the pieces fit together and make sense in an awe-inspiring way.

REMEMBER
▼
There's no right or wrong way to be intuitive!

How Has Intuition Appeared in Your Life?
In your journal, tell two or three stories of your most intriguing experiences with intuitive knowing: "I had a dream that came true.

I narrowly avoided an accident by _____. I was thinking about George, and I ran into him at the movies." What questions did each experience trigger in your mind? What was your emotional response to each experience?

Intuition can as easily bring us highly specific, mundane answers, for example, whom to trust or what not to eat, or an instant understanding of complex intellectual patterns. The fields of mathematics and chemistry are full of stories about breakthroughs derived from a revealing dream or a serendipitous insight. Mathematician Jacques Hadamard, for example, reports, "On being awakened by an external noise, a solution long searched for appeared to me at once without the slightest instant of reflection on my part." Even Pythagoras was said to have made an intuitive leap—discovering that the relative pitch of vibrating chords is determined by the ratio of their lengths—as he noticed the sound changing when the blacksmith hammered different rods.

Even if you haven't had unusual intuitive experiences, rest assured intuition *has* been active in your ordinary life, right under your nose. Intuition is a normal way of perceiving the world. Why did you prefer to wear yellow this morning and then find the person you met for lunch was wearing the same color? Why did you take the scenic route home and miss a ten-car pileup on the freeway? Was it chance? Or was it intuition?

Perhaps the experiences we discount as "mere coincidence" come from a normal human perception we've not yet become accustomed to. Imagine if it were normal to know that you could meet or communicate with anyone, anywhere, on any level, any time you wanted. What if it were *normal* to know anything you wanted to know—immediately?

Intuition becomes active whenever you're so engrossed in concentration that you lose track of time. As a child maybe you drew animals or planes, caught up in the magic of the lines, shapes, and colors appearing out of your hand. What activities captivate you the same way today? Do you get lost working among the flowers in your garden? Forget to eat lunch when you're in your woodshop or at your drafting table or computer? Whenever you merge so totally with your self-expression, intuition sky-

The intellect has little to do on the road to discovery. There comes a leap in consciousness, call it intuition or what you will, and the solution comes to you, and you don't know how or why.

Albert Einstein

rockets. You don't question your next move, your choices and insights, or how the process will end. You're in the natural flow. When you can recognize the subtle sensations of intuition, wherever it's currently manifesting for you, it's much easier to extend those qualities of experience into other areas of your life.

It is the soul's duty to be loyal to its own desires. It must abandon itself to its master passion.

Rebecca West

Identify and Transfer the Intuitive Sensation

1. Take a moment to reimagine, in every sensory detail, an activity that captivates you. As you imagine it, you'll re-create the good feelings in your body and emotions. Take your time, and go through the stages of the activity you love. For example, if it's gardening, smell the dirt and fertilizer, see and feel the shiny trowel and the leaves of the plants, notice the rich colors and textures, feel the sun on your face and back, put on your gardening gloves, and imagine yourself digging and turning soil, planting seeds, watering, and weeding.

2. Now imagine an activity you don't like. Let's say it's public speaking. Imagine the same sensory details coupled with your anxiety.

3. Finally, while thinking about giving a speech, re-create the rich sensations of gardening and overlay those sensations on the new activity. Notice how relaxed you become, how you open to the sensory information from the audience and the lecture hall. Imagine each step in the process of public speaking to be as satisfying and interesting as gardening. Do you feel more timeless? Less pressured? As you're talking, notice how spontaneously a new idea comes. Or how effortless it is to answer questions or even be funny.

4. Write about the attitudes and conditions you have created in yourself that allow you to feel at ease, fluid, and intuitive.

In observing the way intuition works and feels, we're brought face-to-face with the following principles:

With intuition, we know what we need to know, right when we need to know it. The universe, it seems, doesn't waste time or energy. Intuition presents information to us when we need it, not a moment too soon or too late, and uses any means available to reach us.

One of my students, Molly, told me that she'd been looking for a job for over a month, going through all the normal channels. She mapped a detailed plan of action for each week and was following it, without much success. "This week I'll market myself to the human resources departments of large corporations, take out three ads, make twelve cold calls, go to five networking meetings. . . ." She was steeped in worry. Yet in the midst of her search she impulsively decided to attend a poetry-writing class. Once there she followed her next impulse to share a poem she'd written with the woman sitting next to her. They began talking and discovered they had common interests and had reached similar transition points in their lives. Synchronously the woman knew of a job that had *just become available* at her well-known company. And Molly could have first crack at it.

If Molly had realized that she could trust her intuition to bring her the opportunity she needed, she could have saved herself needless stress. And yet she was open enough to follow her intuitive urge to write poetry and not discount it as off-purpose. When you trust your intuition implicitly, solutions may not fit your expectations, and experiences are no longer right or wrong—they're just right.

When you look at the world intuitively, the question and the answer always exist together and arise in the same instant. You're driving down the road and for no reason you think, "I wonder how my friend Nancy is doing? I haven't talked to her for ages." When you get home, you discover she's left a message on your answering machine. Did the thought occur to you because she called? Or did she call because you thought of her? The designer is focused on a tricky floor plan. His mind wanders, and suddenly the symbol of a wave flashes before his mind's eye. It represents the perfect solution: he needs curved walls, not straight ones. Did his higher mind have the *answer* first, and to manifest it physically, did it plant the *question* in his logical mind? The logical mind thinks there must be a cause in time and space. But using intuition, we glimpse a higher characteristic of consciousness—simultaneity and omnipresence.

Intuition cuts through the normal limitations of time and space. Our consciousness can know the past and future as if they were *now.* Or we can

REMEMBER
▼
Anything is possible.

be in other locations as if they were *here*. All knowledge is available to us. Intuitive knowing is direct knowing—knowing without time-consuming, linear reasoning; knowing without external proof. With intuition, your here-and-now bubble of experience expands and contracts, encompassing more or less time and space, like a camera's zoom lens. You do this all the time, probably without realizing. One moment you're focused intently on a writing report, and your world is tight and task-oriented. The next moment you lean back and look out the window. Your mind drifts, absorbing the view, moving through time. In a few minutes, you envision an ingenious way to illustrate your next point.

Using intuition, if you focus on a broader view or an up-close-and-personal one, your reality and the knowledge you can access will change accordingly.

If I Could Increase My Intuition . . .

List ten ways you'd use your intuition positively if it were open, active, and at your beck and call: "I'd know who was calling before I picked up the phone. I'd use my hands to help heal people. I'd remember my dreams and be able to control them more. I'd do more artwork." Fire up your imagination and shoot for the stars.

Intuition Is More Than a Magic Show

Intuition is more than a lightning bolt striking you, being possessed by the Muse, or having direct access to unlimited realms of knowledge. At its best the intuitive process brings clarity and accuracy to your ordinary awareness and transports you into an experience of awe about your own divine nature. But intuition is often reduced to the level of a magic show.

If you use intuition to play "Twenty Questions" or to read the past and future, you become what I call a *psychic*. Sometimes psychics are accurate, but their orientation is usually toward what, not how and why; toward form, not process. When we worship form alone, we easily miss experiencing the process that preexisted and created the form and the even deeper experience of the state of being, or spirit, that underlies the process of life. With this bias, we quickly find detailed answers that seem credible but miss the organizing context that gives the answers their deeper

In one of the Pali scriptures there is an anecdote recording Buddha's own characteristically dry comment on a prodigious feat of levitation performed by one of his disciples. "This," he said, "will not conduce to the conversion of the unconverted, nor to the advantage of the converted." Then he went back to talking about deliverance.

Aldous Huxley

meaning. When we're fascinated by form alone, psychic (or parapsychological) phenomena can easily captivate us, and we risk bypassing the whole process of learning to live more artfully.

Psychic abilities—like psychokinesis, astral projection, or mediumship—are part of the intuitive process, but not the greater part, and they are not necessarily the goal. Perhaps you've experienced an unusual psychic phenomenon. If you have, you're not crazy. As your intuitive and spiritual awareness opens and you enter a more mystical communion state, you'll feel comfortable with how intimately connected you are with all knowledge, all dimensions of existence and stages of the manifestation/creation process. You'll know that these phenomena are not supernatural but natural. In fact, psychic abilities often stabilize and become integrated life skills as a by-product of work on a spiritual path.

The process, not necessarily the answers, is the sacred thing. The intuitive process is a way of living, a way of aligning yourself with what is truly real. The great spiritual teacher Yogananda, who drew his inspiration from both Eastern and Western religious traditions, said, "It is very difficult to define intuition, for it is too near to every one of us. . . . It is through intuition that humanity reaches Divinity. . . . This intuition is what all the great savants and prophets of the world possessed. Thus it is by intuition that God can be realized in all His aspects." [1]

To become expert in the intuitive process, your mind should be calm and trained to align with universal truths. Fears that contract your body's natural sensitivity must be encouraged to surface and must then be dissolved through the kindness and understanding of your heart. If we can clear ourselves of interference, we won't inadvertently distort the truth with a filmy lens, and we won't be tempted to stop at merely being psychic. Accurate intuition is a function of what Buddhists call "skillful perception," and skillful perception takes effort and patience to cultivate. Brain/mind researcher and author Robert Ornstein says, "Developing instant comprehension, paradoxically, takes time and is a process too subtle for those who demand everything immediately." [2]

When you continue beyond psychism to developing intuition and practicing honesty and awareness of yourself, others, and the unknown, miraculous results occur. Life takes on new dimension, and you may

TROUBLESHOOTING TIP
When a New Phenomenon Overwhelms You

If you are suddenly opened into an unfamiliar way of perceiving, or if you receive information that frightens you, try these techniques:

1. Assume you cannot know something without being ready for it. Relax and be with the experience. Give yourself an extra moment to "pause and consider." Take your time. You don't have to know what to do right away.

2. Assume that some part of you knows what to do and that this part will soon enter your conscious mind if you allow it.

3. Consider that the experience or insight you have received may be true at a literal or symbolic level. Maybe the experience is simply to free up energy in your body and emotions. Consider three or four possible interpretations.

4. In a meditation, or with your journal, ask your soul to help you understand what to do. Listen for instructions as they come through your body. Record them.

become psychologically mature and physically healthy. Life flows naturally with grace and precision, without struggle.

With intuition, trust increases, both in yourself and others. You can see the good reasons for why things happen. You experience less anxiety-producing hopelessness and hopefulness about the past and the future and a more acute awareness of your surroundings. There's more synchronicity. Inspiration increases. Enthusiasm expands, because when things flow, you feel happy. When you're happy, creativity and productivity soar and satisfaction becomes profound. For instance, you rush frantically to the grocery store to do the weekly shopping, squeezing in the errand between work, time with your children, and repairs on the house. You could make the experience entertaining and magical if you pay attention to the smells, shapes, and colors of the foods and packages and the emotional tones of the people you meet in the aisles. You might enjoy the smooth motion of your grocery cart or notice exactly which piece of fruit your body wants to select.

Does this mean you should float through life, living for the moment and giving up goals? Or not balance your checkbook or save money? Of course not. We're here to participate fully and take care of the details. This is a world of action and accomplishment; doing and having, as well as being, are a natural part of the creative process.

There will always be a place for logic, compartmentalization, and management by objectives. But the intuitive process expands the extent of your understanding, gives you more clarity in every phase of the creative process, streamlines logistics, and brings a unifying world view and new enjoyment to each task and accomplishment.

Each moment fully perceived contains eternity.

There is one common flow, one common breathing. All things are in sympathy.

Hippocrates

Make a "My Successes" List

Reserve several pages in your journal for a "My Successes" list. It's important to remind yourself of what you're doing that meets your inner standards of excellence and makes you happy. Look at the glass half full. How did you trust your intuition this week? How often did you follow up on a hunch? Did you remember a particularly colorful, symbolic dream after you said you wanted to? Did you get a sudden insight about a situation immediately after you asked for guidance from your inner self? As you work more consciously with your intuition over the next few months, continue adding items to this list. They can be significant or absolutely mundane.

How Intuition Comes: The Three V's

In the early stages of the process, intuitive information, like all other information, comes to us through our five senses. Intuitive insights most commonly show up via three modes: vision, voice, and vibration. At first one of these orientations will likely dominate your perceptions.

Vision

Have you had visions, either in a dream, fantasy, or meditation, where you received information about your own life, the future of others, or the future of the planet? Have you ever flashed on the image of a friend before you unexpectedly met? Have you had a déjà vu experience, where suddenly you realize you've seen it all before?

James, a counseling student doing his internship, often makes decisions about what to work on in his therapeutic process by examining the imagery in his dreams from the night before. He also has had profound insights about colleagues by looking at the collages, masks, and sculptures they make in his art therapy group.

Voice

Has a "little voice" ever told you that you shouldn't leave the house, but you did anyway and later discovered you forgot your wallet? Or the little voice said, "Don't get involved with this person," but you did anyway and he stole your heart, money, and car? Have you been awakened by a ringing telephone or a knock at your door, only to find that no one was there? Can you hear tension in the tone of a person's voice? Have you ever caught yourself humming a tune and realized that the lyrics were the answer to a problem that had been plaguing you all day? Do you hear music too high for the human ear?

Allen, an art director, regularly uses an auditory sense of intuition to slow the process of producing advertising and graphics, to sense when a mistake is in the works. He says he taps into the flow, and a voice whispers, "Allen—something's wrong with this print run; did they use

Man, surrounded by facts, permitting himself no surprise, no intuitive flash, no great hypothesis, no risk, is in a locked cell. Ignorance cannot seal the mind and imagination more securely.

Albert Einstein

matte varnish instead of gloss?" or "This client is going to require lots of special handling."

Vibration

Have you ever felt cold and clammy when entering a strange house? Do certain people make you angry or highly nervous before they even say a word? Can you tell when your pet is upset? Do you absent-mindedly squeeze a friend's shoulder and she says, "Oh, you just hit the perfect spot!" Have you felt that someone touched you, but when you turned around, no one was there?

Diane uses her tactile sense of intuition when she's working with a massage client; her fingers somehow know the exact spot where the person is experiencing pain. In addition, Diane uses her "scanner" to scope out public situations where she might encounter danger. She describes getting an all-over "body sense" about whether to give money to a panhandler who approached her at the post office. Was he truly homeless or a drug addict?

Your Pathway through the Senses

Intuitive information can also come to you through your senses of smell and taste. Have you smelled a friend's distinctive cologne only moments before he telephoned? Do you ever say, "Something smells fishy!" or "I smell trouble here"? What about "How sweet it is!" or "I want that so much, I can taste it!" or "I just can't swallow *that*!"? One of my friends loves to eat and passionately refers to certain people and new ideas as "yummy" and "delicious."

You probably have a preferred mode of perceiving, and as you begin to use your intuition, your information will be colored by that sense. As you progress it's normal to evolve through the rest of your senses until your ability to receive is fully rounded. Later, as you develop more sophistication, you may find that your senses blend together into a less definable, more direct experience of what many of my students call a simple "knowingness."

My intuitive development began with a strong visual orientation. When I first did life readings, I saw images and odd symbols superimposed over parts of the client's body—a ballerina, an olive, a flashlight, a sofa.

REMEMBER
▼
Drama doesn't make it better.

Sometimes I'd see answers spelled in different typefaces: bold, italic, or caps if the message was important, lowercase if it was familiar or personal. The problem with this symbolic visual method was that it took time to interpret each image.

Gradually I started to hear a whisper in my ear. It would begin, "Tell them they are learning the lesson of courage by standing up for _____" or "Tell them their mother dominated them when they were growing up, but now they are taking back their own space by _____." I would relate the message, and somewhere in the midst of it, the voice would drop off and my words would keep pouring out.

After a while, even that seemed too slow, and I would just get the gist of the message. I then began to feel textures of energy in the person's body and around them: sandpapery, pockmarked textures for people who had abused drugs; ashen gray, dishwater energy for people who were emotionally exhausted; prickly, electrical energy in people who were anxious or self-critical.

In time that kinesthetic mode gave way to a more subtle discernment of the higher vibratory patterns in a person's life. Today an insight most often appears without an identifying carrier, right in the center of my mind. And yet, as it occurs, I feel my mind is spread evenly through my entire body and that varying patterns are impressing my whole field. I can't identify which sense I'm using.

You will have your own developmental pathway through the five senses. Begin by noticing your own sense preferences and when your dominant sense is active. Listen for the sense-oriented adjectives and verbs you use. Do you say, "I see," "I hear you," "I feel," "It sounds like," or "That's touching"? Then start using all your senses more consciously and see what you know about someone's house, or a store you walk into, by smelling it instead of seeing it, for instance.

Your Sense Preferences

In your journal, describe how the world makes an impression on you. Are you primarily visual, auditory, or kinesthetic? How often are you aware of the subtle smells and tastes around you? What senses predominantly fill your conversation? List your common sense-oriented phrases.

Next, think about memorable intuitive experiences you may have had. Have they come via vision, voice, or vibration? Or perhaps smell or taste? Describe the sensory details connected with your intuition.

Now, notice the developmental pathway of your intuitive sensitivity. Have you already explored more than two different sense preferences? What was first? What came next? What sense are you interested in exploring next? Write about your process: "As a child, I _____" or "When I stop trying to figure things out and relax my mind, my intuition pops in via _____" or "The last time I noticed sound in my dreams, I was _____," and so forth.

With easy access to so many avenues of intuitive information, I often wonder why we doubt ourselves so much. We have the innate tools to know anything, anytime, anywhere. Our inherent capacities always will be more sophisticated than our computers, satellite dishes, and cellular phones—especially if the attention we put on refining ourselves matches to any degree the effort we put into high technology. By now you should have some ideas about what might be in that unused 90 percent of your brain and what kinds of abilities are possible to develop. We've planted seeds. Now we water, till the soil, and patiently prepare conditions for the survival of our seedling intuitive abilities.

BE INTUITIVE TODAY!

Seek guidance from vision, voice, and vibration.

Be on the alert today for intuitive information coming to you through your senses of sight, hearing, and touch.

1. Make a decision based on how something looks to you. Does the situation have a lot of light on it? Does it have the right color? Does it have a pleasing design?

2. Make a decision based on the way something "sounds" to you. Does the situation sound screechy, shrill, melodious, quiet, hollow, or harmonious?

3. Make a decision based on the way something "feels" to you. Does the situation feel smooth, rough, sharp, soft, cold, hot, slippery, or sticky?

Most of your experiences are unconscious. The conscious ones are very few. You are unaware of the fact because to you only the conscious ones count. Become aware of the unconscious.

Sri Nisargadatta

Direct Writing Questions

Sit down with your journal and get quiet. Empty your mind. Pick one of the following questions and be with it for a few moments. Ask that you be able to receive creative insights from your deepest level of truth. Let the question serve as a magnet. Allow the first word to pop into your mind. Write it down. Let another word pop in. Write it down. Let words proceed forth, without judging them, without second-guessing where the answer is going. Don't jump ahead. Don't stop and read back over what you've written until the writing stops of its own accord. Helpful techniques: write as your own soul, innocent child, or future self; address your personality in the second person, by name; don't try to be too significant! Let your handwriting change shape. Change your speed and your rhythm, or write with your opposite hand.

- "What areas of life (work, romance, spiritual practice, physical exercise, pleasure, etc.) would I, the soul, like you, the personality, to pay the most attention to right now? Why?"

- "If I had all the time in the world, with no deadlines or responsibilities, what would I do first? Then what would I do? How would I feel as I was doing each thing? How would the activity change my present state of mind? What would I learn from each activity?"

- "What do I need to know to understand the 'good reasons' behind my problem with _____?"

- "What are the main questions I am unconsciously asking about my life right now?" (For example: "I want to know why I can't find a good relationship. I want to know why my family keeps rejecting me. I want to know why so many people are dying from AIDS.") Take each question and continue asking, "What do I need to know about _____?"

- "What do I, the innocent child (little _____), love to do? Why do I like to do each thing?" Write as a three-year-old, in the present tense, and describe your experience in rich detail as you imagine doing your favorite things.

- "If I could have accurate answers to ten questions, what would they be?"

- "What ideas do I need to let go of to be more intuitive? How does each idea interfere with my direct knowing?"

2

Choosing the Intuitive World View

*When the higher flows into the lower,
it transforms the nature of the lower
into that of the higher.*

Meister Eckhart

The Power of Your Personal Attitude

One simple thing can immediately help your intuition become a steady, consistent part of your life—an attitude of positive expectancy and trust. Keep reminding yourself that the intuitive state is the natural state of your soul. Mental and emotional confusion and turmoil are not your birthright. *Expect* intuition to return in the next breath whenever you lose it. Doing nothing more than consciously choosing the best world view, one that enhances your experience of interconnectedness, trust, and love, will always, without fail, activate your intuition.

Each of us adheres to a particular way of viewing the world, influenced by a combination of love and fear beliefs, that helps determine how our life unfolds. To develop clear, conscious intuition, we must become familiar with this unconscious mental structure that can both expand and limit our life experience. Like a faucet that turns to release the flow of water through a hose, your deep attitudes can turn intuition on or off, or allow intuition to arise only in the areas you pay attention to or authorize to be real.

Ellen had an attitude of open experimentation with the process of manifesting what she needed in her life. She was playing with the idea that somehow life would always support her. When her car died and she

Unlike a car, which you can drive without knowing how the gas relates to the pistons or axle, your mind is a vehicle you must know intimately if you want to develop consistently clear intuition. Chapter 2 teaches you about the power of your fundamental world view, the blocks that can distort intuition, the three kinds of personal consciousness, and your two important choices.

couldn't afford a new one, she didn't panic. Her intuition stayed open and, following a hunch, she mentioned her situation to a wealthy massage client. Lo and behold, he had a red sports car sitting in his driveway that he didn't use and his wife didn't like—so he gave it to Ellen for as long as she needed. Ellen's world view was based largely on love and faith; therefore it allowed the possibility of synchronicity and miracles. This sort of self-empowering world view actually invites intuition to occur.

If, on the other hand, your world view has been shaped by early fear-based, negative experiences, your intuition may only bring you information that warns of further danger and negativity. It will be difficult for you to trust your own insight, let alone that of anyone else.

Darlene booked an appointment with me for a life reading, and by hearing her on the phone, I knew she was afraid she wouldn't get her money's worth. Then, the evening before her appointment, my tape recorder froze. I didn't have another but was sure there was an extra at the bookstore where I was to meet her in the morning. I arrived early only to find none available. When she arrived, I apologized and offered other options—and her immediate response was, "The story of my life . . ." While she stood sighing disgustedly, arms crossed tightly over her chest, one of the bookstore staff came to the rescue with a recorder he'd found hidden in the stockroom.

As I talked to Darlene about the patterns in her life, she kept glancing at her watch. "Am I going to get the full amount of time?" she wanted to know. After every sentence she said, "Well, that doesn't fit; I can't relate to any of this." And as I was about to describe the current transition in her life, she interrupted to say, "Well, what's happening to me now?" Darlene's husband had left her a few years earlier and had remarried. Since then, she'd been severely depressed. Her main concern was "When will I get married again and stop having to be alone?" Yet she was prickly and critical of the men she had met. She told stories of how hard she'd tried to date, be social, even do volunteer work—but every attempt had degenerated into something she didn't want. The world seemed to be against her. She had quit her lucrative job with the city and was now a waitress. She complained she didn't have enough money or time to do the things she really enjoyed.

REMEMBER

▼

Your intuitive ability increases when your world view supports growth, connectedness, and trust.

Darlene was caught in a no-win situation of her own making: she believed deep down that she never got what she wanted. She talked to herself constantly about what wasn't working; what she didn't like about other people; what she didn't have; what her horrendous, destitute, isolated, probable future would look like. Under it all, she was just the opposite: warm, generous, funny, nurturing; but she couldn't see that part of herself. When I tried to point it out to her, she changed the subject: "Yes, but when am I going to find a husband?"

Talking to her was like wrestling an octopus whose every arm was intent on validating her negative world view from which she was deriving emotional juice. She left upset that I hadn't given her the name of her next boyfriend and the date of their marriage. Darlene's subconscious mind had a stranglehold on her; she was caught in a self-defeating web of beliefs that prevented her from enjoying the richness of her daily life, receiving the love that ordinary people gave her constantly, and valuing the time she had created to discover her inner nature. Her intuition was so blocked she had deliberately quit a good job and was repeatedly choosing men with poor character. I had to wonder, as I took my tape recorder into the repair shop, if her intense belief system might even have had a negative psychokinetic effect on my machine.

How you perceive the world may be somewhere between Ellen's and Darlene's, but like most of us, you're probably influenced by "old programming," or fear-based decisions that were made in the past that lie buried in your subconscious mind. To open your intuition, you must realize how much unconscious negativity shapes your view of life, how attached you are to the false security your limitations seem to give you, and how much joy and ease you'll allow yourself. One of the most useful skills you can develop is the ability to catch yourself when you're coming from your negative world view so you can turn it around quickly.

Basic Ideas That Influence Your Perception

1. Write about your self-defeating world view. What behaviors in others upset you? Why? What do you constantly tell yourself you never get? Are there areas of your life where you feel

you're sacrificing? What can't you allow yourself to do? What are your worst possible scenarios? What beliefs do you hold that trigger anger, criticism, panic, or avoidance? What adages epitomize your negative world view?

2. Write about your self-empowering world view. What kinds of things do you *know* are possible? What behaviors in others please and amuse you? What do you constantly tell yourself that you *are* getting? What are your beliefs about giving and receiving? What are your best possible scenarios? What adages epitomize your positive world view?

REMEMBER
▼
You can't see the gift in what you resist.

You're in charge of your moods and attitudes. In the exercise above you identified some beliefs connected with your two world views. From now on, listen to your internal self-talk when your negative thought system takes over. Can you catch yourself midstream when you're running negative thoughts and suspend them? Next, to develop even greater intuitive sensitivity, become aware of the actual state your body goes into—your "inner posture"—when each world view is activated. How does your voice sound when you're speaking from each world view? How do you stand, hold your head and face, breathe, contract your muscles, or walk when you're in the positive and the negative "stances"? Once you identify your fear-based inner posture and the bodily sensations that go with it, you can choose to shift out of it and into a world view that turns on the intuition faucet. With conscious bodily awareness, it's easier to return to the more comfortable feelings of natural flow associated with the positive world view.

How Does Contraction versus Flow Feel to Your Body?

1. Recall a time when you were intensely afraid of, resisting, or frustrated by something. Visualize and feel it in your imagination. Let your body go into the "inner posture" that corresponds to each condition.

2. Write about the sensations in your body using as many adjectives as you can. Are you tense? Cold? Are you aware of your lower body? Upper body? What parts of your body are affected? Which muscles? What's happening to your breath-

ing? How do your face, eyes, jaw, and neck feel? At this moment do you trust your intuition?

3. Clear your mind and body, and rest a moment. Recall a time when you experienced synchronicity and everything seemed to work effortlessly. Let your body go into the "inner posture" that corresponds to the condition of flow.

4. Write about the sensations in your body using as many adjectives as you can. Do you feel relaxed? Excited? Warm? Are you aware of your lower body? Upper body? What parts of your body are affected? Which muscles? What's happening to your breathing? How do your face, eyes, jaw, and neck feel? Do you trust your intuition right now?

5. Return to the inner posture that results from feeling contracted. Make a conscious choice, and shift to the inner posture that results from feeling things flowing. Track the subtle internal changes in detail. Review the stages of the shift several times until you can do it quickly.

To help you learn to shift your intuition-blocking world view to an intuition-enhancing one, let's enter the hidden dynamics of your mind and learn to identify the different kinds of awareness you flow from and into all day long. By understanding the three parts of your mind, you'll gain greater control over the incredibly vast, seemingly unwieldy mechanism of your perception. Then you'll know how to set yourself up for clarity every time.

The Three Kinds of Mind

Psychology breaks consciousness into three components: the subconscious mind, the conscious mind, and the superconscious mind. These correlate loosely with the metaphysical terms for the same aspects—the body, mind, and spirit. The superconscious and subconscious minds are actually experiences, or environments from which to perceive the world. They are also storehouses for different types of memory. The conscious mind, on the other hand, is a roving point of awareness and choice. It contains no memory.

The degree to which one understands Three is a fair indication of the degree to which he or she is civilized.

John Anthony West

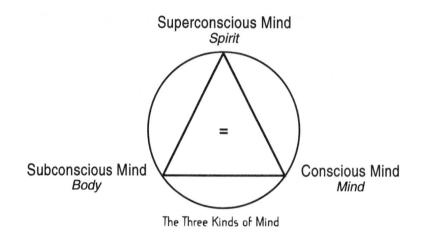

Superconscious Mind
Spirit

Subconscious Mind
Body

Conscious Mind
Mind

The Three Kinds of Mind

The Superconscious Mind

Have you ever had a transcendent experience where your normally petty mind suddenly broadened and revealed the hidden benefits of a difficult situation? Perhaps you saw how essential divorce was to the growth of both you and your ex-partner and were able to release all rancor. Or maybe you glimpsed a global view of the importance of forests or oceans to the planet's future, or a vision of how your career might evolve. If so, you were perceiving from your superconscious mind.

The superconscious realm is known in many spiritual traditions as Heaven, the Upper Kingdom, or the Pure Land. It is the clear, collective consciousness of all life forms characterized by spontaneous flow, perfect coordination, and appropriateness. The superconscious mind knows no fear, no blocks, no ignorance. It's the part of you that contains higher purpose, the God's Eye View, where all experiences are simultaneous and omnipresent. We might equate the superconscious mind with the soul's awareness. (I define *soul* as the function of consciousness that interconnects individuality and universality.) Its specific focus in the body is the heart, the neocortex of the brain, and the top four chakras, or energy centers.

This higher mind sees the interconnection and mutual inclusiveness of everything that exists in time and space and how we continually emerge from and return to spirit. It contains the memory of all events, throughout all time, in which you acted in full awareness of your true nature as a divine being. These are memories of actions taken in love, in alignment with universal principles characterized by grace, luck, flow, and joy. Your natural talents originate here.

When intuition is sourced from your superconscious mind, you often feel a light turning on in your head. What you sense may be predominantly visual, frequently an abstract geometrical pattern. It's also common for superconscious intuition to reveal itself as a blending of all your senses, an all-over "direct knowing," often accompanied by a feeling of openheartedness.

The Subconscious Mind

As native peoples and mystics have always known, everything is conscious: mammals, birds, reptiles, insects, plants, bacteria, individual cells—even crystals, metals, plastic, and wood. The subconscious mind contains all this physical, biological planetary knowledge as well as impressions of every organism, personality, and period in history we have passed through in our evolutionary ascent. It knows the raw energies of birth and death, transformation and war. Because its essence is primal, the subconscious mind contains information relating to survival and the mythological human rites of passage.

The subconscious contains memories of all experiences in which you were *reacting* from a survival instinct and made decisions in partial awareness of your true self, not understanding the whole situation, not seeing the superconscious God's Eye View. Fear, panic, confoundment, self-protection, and lack of trust characterize these memories—and in effect, they condense and become "hot potatoes" that you don't want to touch. Every subconscious memory is actually an incomplete experience that the soul has not fully understood and digested. If we could see them, these paralyzed chunks of unavailable knowledge might look like black spots in our energy field. If we have lots, we may seem energetically thick, ash-colored, and opaque. In the Western therapeutic tradition they're called *subconscious blocks*; in the Eastern religious tradition they're known as *karma*. In the body the subconscious mind is focused in the brain stem and reptile brain as well as in the three lower chakras, or energy centers.

The subconscious mind contains an untapped wealth of knowledge about our physiological origins, but it is also harbors a darker side since it

Neither by suppression of the material streaming out of the consciousness, nor by permanent surrender to the unshaped infinity of the unconscious, but rather through affectionate attention to these hidden sources— thus have all the great artists worked.

Herman Hesse

is the home of negative emotions. We often call it the Lower Kingdom, the Underworld, the Shadow, or the Dark Cloud. Mythology represents it as chock full of monsters, dangerous obstacles, and tests of character. To reach heaven (the superconscious) you must first complete the process of understanding these experiences or make "the hero's journey": quest for treasure in the depths of the cave, battle the serpent or fire-breathing dragon, or endure what the Vedic rishis called "the great passage."

When intuition is sourced from your subconscious mind, it comes through one of the five senses, often with a slight edge of tension or confusion such as a tangible feeling of anxiety, a dark image, or a choking odor. Since not all information in the subconscious mind is negative, you may also receive intuitions about your physical body or the archetypal meanings of animals or plants, for example. This information comes from an all-over physical "felt sense."

⚡

I can't do anything about the thoughts that come into my head, but I *can* do something about the ones that stay there!

The Conscious Mind

The conscious mind, in contrast to the other two kinds of consciousness, contains no memory and knows nothing. It is a point of awareness, your sense of "I am," the viewing point, or the eye of the soul. The conscious mind is also the agent of your free will, a moving point of choice and personal identity—it gives you the experience of being an individual. By choosing different views and identifying with what it sees, the conscious mind determines your experiences. Perhaps this is why Edgar Cayce called it "the architect of our existence."

The conscious mind is relational. As soon as it perceives something outside itself—be it a person, object, situation, or place, it creates a relationship or an association: "I notice Tokyo." Next it forms a meaning: "I live in Japan." Finally it defines an identity: "I am Japanese." Then, as it roves around and notices other things, it separates from the first set of ideas, and as the meanings and identities dissolve, it then reassociates with something new: "I'm a student. Now I'm a husband. Now I'm a Little League coach. Now I'm a serious businessman." Thus the conscious mind creates a flickering film of on-again, off-again images, meanings, and movements. The conscious mind views the spherical bubble of the movie we call life and asks, "Who am I?" Then, as it sees something and connects

The Three Kinds of Mind

The Superconscious Mind	The Subconscious Mind	The Conscious Mind
Love	Fear	Point of choice, or will
Unity, grace	Separation, defense/attack	Point of view, or focus
Wisdom, truth	Ignorance	Point of identity
Complete, whole perception	Partial perception	"Who am I? I am that."
Collective consciousness	Isolation consciousness	Allowance of existence of individual
Trust, supply	Doubt, attachment	Window into this world
Creativity	Survival, frozen beliefs	Source of duality and movement
Freedom	Polarization and conflict	Architect of our earthly existence
Memory of loving experiences	Memory of fearful experiences	No memory
Godhead	Material world	Personal self

with it, it registers a meaning and answers itself: "I am this" or "I am that."

In the body the conscious mind is focused in the center of the brain. In fact, neurologists have found that destroying the midbrain's limbic cortex causes complete loss of the sense of self. They can remove any other part of the brain or body with little effect on the experience of individuality.

How Many Identities Do You Have?

Notice the activity of your conscious mind and the many associations it makes. Start a "My Many Faces" list. Describe the inner characters who express themselves through your personality. On your list might be such notables as the critic, the slave driver, the cheerleader, the ancient wise one, the maniac driver, the bag lady, the business leader, the brilliant scientist, the inspired artist, the wet blanket, the crusader, the expounder, the wallflower, and so on. What does each character say to the world? What is each trying to receive? To give? How do other people respond when you're playing each role? Add to this list over the next few months. List some roles you'd like to play.

Two Choices: Two Sources of Intuitive Guidance

As the vehicle of free will and the point of choice, your conscious mind shapes your daily life. The attitudes and ideas you identify with determine

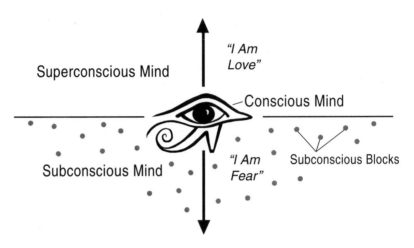

"Who Am I?" The Conscious Mind Uses Free Will to Choose
Identity Based on Love or Fear

the kind of people and situations that will manifest for you. Luckily, only two choices, two views, two sources of guidance exist. You can look toward the superconscious mind or toward the subconscious mind—and your intuition will flow from the source you identify with.

As the conscious mind looks out into its world, it asks, "Who am I?" When it looks toward the superconscious realm, it answers, "I am whole and complete, purposeful, wise, loving, and full of truth, beauty, and harmony. I love myself and the world." When you choose the superconscious world view, your intuition brings you superconscious guidance. You'll feel lucky and self-empowered.

If instead it looks toward the subconscious, your conscious mind might answer, "I am afraid, unworthy, and ugly. I don't like myself or the world." When you choose the subconscious world view, your intuition will bring you guidance based on a fear-related understanding of life. You'll feel you have "gaps" in your understanding. Eventually you'll become a victim.

It's simple, really—two life choices. One facilitates the experience of flow, love, and truth; the other perpetuates immobility, fear, and ignorance.

The study in Christian mysticism called *A Course in Miracles* emphasizes this same choice and identifies only two basic emotions: love and fear. If you have love, you cannot experience fear. If you have fear, you cannot

⚡
I can be bothered, irritated, and aggravated, *or* I can choose to be amused.

The Feelings Identified with the Conscious Mind	
The Subconscious Mind = FEAR	**The Superconscious Mind = LOVE**
Reactive	Responsive
Protective	Explorative
Confrontive, avoiding	Communicative
Willful	Willing
In denial	Receptive
Worried, doubtful	Lucky, optimistic
Stressed, depressed	Excited, peaceful
Restless, bored	Interested
Limited, hoarding	Abundant, generous
Separate	Connected
Partial, incomplete	Whole, complete
Unconscious, wandering	Alert, attentive
Attached	Detached
Can't stop or start	Fluid
Blaming, punishing	Understanding, forgiving
Martyr, tyrant	Able to serve and be served
In the past and future	In the present
"It *should* be this way"	"It's OK the way it is; it's OK if it changes"
"I can't have, can't do _____"	"I'm entitled"
No time, no space	All the time and space needed

experience love. They are mutually exclusive. We can look out on a world characterized by separation, fear, and ignorance, or we can turn 180 degrees and observe wholeness, connectedness, and love.

In the table above, which column attracts your attention?

Shifting from Fear to Love

1. Scan the left-hand column of the table. For each word, jot down the situations in your life that provoke those responses: "I become protective of myself (or another) when _____. I feel rooted in the past when _____. I feel like I can't do _____ because _____."

2. For each situation, look at the corresponding words in the right-hand column. How could you apply the opposite trait or attitude to the situation? For example, "I blame my boss for being

insensitive and never acknowledging me" might change into "I understand my boss is under pressure from her boss—and I can forgive her for being too frantic to notice that I'm doing a good job."

3. If you were to apply a superconscious perspective to the problems in your life, what would your next actions be? What might be the outcome? If you forgive your boss for being scared, maybe you'd send her a thank-you note telling *her* what a good job *she's* doing! Maybe she'd pick you for the next challenging assignment.

Shifting to a Superconscious World View

⚡

Harmony exists
in everything,
if you notice it.

If you developed a negative world view in your youth—if you feel mired in limitations and only now realize it—don't despair. You can learn to suspend your involvement with negativity, even if it's just for a moment. This will give you the fraction of a second you need to realize you do have another choice. And if you've practiced remembering the bodily sensations that accompany the superconscious world view, you can practice consciously leaving the state you don't want and entering the state you desire. You may need to practice this shift many times a day until it becomes a new habit. Shifting is not hard—but remembering to pay attention can seem difficult. You'll need to slow down and drop into a deeper sense of what's real and how you want to feel.

Practicing the God's Eye View*

Sit quietly, eyes closed. Focus into the center of your head and pull your energy inside your skin. Breathe regularly. Be aware that you are in the here and now. Imagine a being of shiny diamond light standing behind you. Invite it in, and as you do, feel it gently penetrate you, melting into your energy. As it fills you, tension dissolves; you feel fresh and new. Imagine that this being is your Divine Self, the Self of Infinite Wisdom. You now share your reality with it.

Scan your body and personality, dedicating each part to the Divine Being. Feel it fully as you say, "My feet are God's feet. Let

---

* If you resist the term *God*, please substitute any concept, term, or feeling that gives you a real sense of a higher, more loving consciousness.

God show me how to take a stand in this world, how to make contact with the earth. May I transmit divine energy into the planet. My legs are God's legs. Let the Creator show me how to move forward in my life and where to go. May I carry forward the divine intent into this world. My emotions are God's emotions. May God show me how to feel; may I be the vehicle to share God's feeling with others. My stomach is God's stomach. May I eat and be nurtured by whatever God brings to me. May I honor the food I am given.

"My vitality and power is divine power. May God show me how to express it and where to apply it so that I influence others as God would have it. My heart is God's heart. May I know compassion as the Creator knows it; may I extend divine balance and understanding to others. My hands and arms are God's hands and arms. Let the Creator show me how to reach out and when to help; let me use these hands creatively. My voice is God's voice. May I be shown how to speak with truth and beauty, how to communicate what God wants me to say.

"My ears are God's ears. May I hear the world the way God would hear it. May I understand the real messages coming to me from others. My eyes are God's eyes. Let God show me what to see and help me see fully. Let the Creator see the world through me. My mind is God's mind. May I be shown the way to perceive, the way to make choices, the way to release thoughts. Let God perceive the world through me and teach me how to know."

Life assists us in becoming clear. As the days pass, pieces of the puzzle constantly appear to us. We have many opportunities to grow and become sophisticated, graduating from petty jealousies and simplistic answers to greater tolerance and respect for diversity. We begin to understand that events occur so we can learn. We realize the way people treat us relates to how we treat ourselves.

Sometimes, if we have strongly identified with a particular world view, it takes a personal crisis to prompt us to look for a better way. The insights that come when we face our human vulnerability often lead us to review and revise the unconscious fear beliefs we made early in life with our immature mind.

Intuition reproduces, on our scale, the original mystery of a great Gaze: a mighty glance that has seen all, known all, and that delights at seeing bit by bit, slowly, successively, temporally, from myriad points of view, what It had once wholly embraced in a fraction of Eternity.

Satprem

Matt, a client, was a competitive athlete and energetic entrepreneur. He had been a lobbyist in Washington, D.C., and was comfortably wealthy by age thirty. His world view was "Look out for number one and win at any cost—and show my father I'm better than he is." He was self-absorbed, charming, and hard-edged. Though he had a strong intuition, he used it only for survival and self-aggrandizement. I saw him over an eight-year period during which a crisis forced him to lose most of his money. Eventually he exited the rat race and developed an understanding that there's more to life than getting attention and material rewards. He rebuilt his business and practiced empowering his employees, expressing appreciation, and creating opportunities for others. His world view had evolved from one based on ego and lack of self-worth to an expression of universal love. His world view became "The first will be last and the last will be first."

By continuing to be honest about how you want your body to feel, how much trust you want to practice, and how loving you want to be, you can accelerate the natural evolution of your positive world view until it becomes permanent. You can also improve your ability to maintain a superconscious world view by learning to attend to what's at hand for longer periods of time without judging. Being addicted to defining things, jumping to conclusions, or settling for pat answers result in a partial understanding of life's dynamics and a subconscious world view. If you stop your explanation early, your world view will be small.

REMEMBER

▼

When you have nothing else, you always have choice.

If you remain open to the unknown, you'll find your understanding increases and you actually prefer world views modeled on love and natural order. You'll also find that the more loving and superconscious your world view, the more accurate your intuition. As you increase your attention span in your observation of life, your insights will be broader and more accurate spiritually.

If you ask three people with different attention spans the same question, you'll get answers supporting three different world views. If you ask, "What is love?" Jennifer, who believes life is basically about survival, answers, "When you get married and have kids." Michael, who believes the goal of life is to overcome suffering, says, "When you actively care about others and serve your community." Terry, who believes everyone is

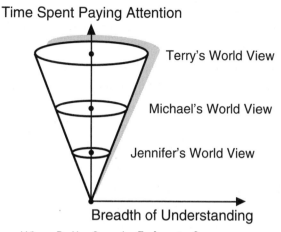

Where Do You Stop the Explanation?

worthy and perfect as they are and life is a celebration of creativity, says, "Love is the experience of everything in life fitting together perfectly."

Terry's broad-minded world view naturally and compassionately includes the views of Michael and Jennifer. They, on the other hand, may think Terry is living in a fantasy world. You may recall the story of Magellan, who, approaching the shores of the Yucatan for the first time, could see the natives, but because the Mayans had never known great sailing ships, they could not see him.

Extending Your View

Notice something you glossed over or handled too quickly in the past day or two. Did you do a cursory job cleaning the bathroom or thinking through the content for a report? Did your child try to tell you something as you were dashing out the door?

Go back and pay attention. Take it further. Put your full awareness on the task and sink into it. Notice what benefits and insights you missed the first time. Write about what your attention revealed.

BE INTUITIVE TODAY!

Change your perception by changing your view.

Consciously shift into your superconscious, intuitive world view today on three occasions. Document what happens in your journal.

1. The first time, do it while you're with another person or a group. Notice your observations and insights immediately after shifting. Communicate aloud the appropriate parts of those insights.

2. The second time, make the shift when you're bored. Notice what your superconscious mind suggests as your next action immediately after shifting. Do it.

3. The third time, make the shift when you're feeling pressured. Notice what message your superconscious mind may be trying to give you immediately after shifting. Speak it aloud to yourself; then act on it if you can.

Direct Writing Questions

Sit down with your journal and get quiet. Empty your mind. Pick one of the following questions and be with it for a few moments. Ask that you be able to receive creative insights from your deepest level of truth. Let the question serve as a magnet. Allow the first word to pop into your mind. Write it down. Let another word pop in. Write it down. Let words proceed forth, without judging them, without second-guessing where the answer is going. Don't jump ahead. Don't stop and read back over what you've written until the writing stops of its own accord. Helpful techniques: write as your own soul, innocent child, or future self; address your personality in the second person, by name; don't try to be too significant! Let your handwriting change shape. Change your speed and your rhythm, or write with your opposite hand.

- "What is the superconscious vision for my life's work?"
- "What positive lessons did I learn from the 'negative' events of my youth?" Pick one or two experiences and write about the "gifts in the garbage."
- "What does my subconscious mind tell me about (1) money, (2) my current relationship situation, and (3) my body? What does my superconscious mind tell me about (1) money, (2) my current relationship situation, and (3) my body?"
- "If I could reverse three situations or chronic habits in my life, what would they be? And how would I do it? What would my life look like then?"
- "What does my superconscious mind know about (1) my destiny, (2) the secret of having good relationships, (3) where I should live, and (4) how to enjoy my life more fully?"
- "What's the worst event that could happen in my life? Why would it be so bad?" Imagine it has happened and write how your soul guides you to act.
- "What are three things that (1) I have a morbid curiosity about, (2) I can't stand seeing, and (3) make me blindly enraged?" Write about what's underneath these feelings, what your subconscious would like to do, noticing any related images or odd connections to other subjects.

3

Living in Alignment with the Creation Cycle

You issue from God's attributes first;
Return again back to those attributes with all speed! . . .
You begin as part of the sun, clouds and stars,
You rise to be breath, act, word and thought!

Rumi

Riding the Current of Consciousness

Intuition occurs naturally when you're living in a fluid way, detached from worries, "shoulds," and strong opinions. If you can shift direction easily, adjust your speed to meet the moment's needs, initiate movement, and abandon outworn behaviors, your intuition can become a permanent part of your life. Your soul—your fundamental consciousness—and the creative force of life itself are so intertwined that at the deepest levels, it's hard to find a difference. Both you and the flow of life follow a simple, inherent pattern of movement, repeating certain basic rhythms consistently. Like your heartbeat or your breath, or the rising and setting of the sun, or the cycle of the seasons, your innate consciousness progresses through the phases of a wondrous cycle, creating and then dissolving the myriad forms of your life, again and again. When you learn to identify this cycle and its phases, feel it as it moves you, and know when it's shifting and where it's likely to go next, your intuition will never be blocked. When you forget to align yourself with this current of consciousness, you may try to

Chapter 3 helps you learn to ride the current of consciousness, to merge with the flow of your soul's journey as it descends into matter and ascends into essence. If you can learn to be conscious of where you are in the creation cycle and where the flow naturally wants to go next, your intuition will have an effortless quality. This chapter also gives you guidelines for recognizing when you have turned the creative flow backwards on itself, resulting in immobilization—and how to get it going again.

move across the flow or even backwards, forcing your way upstream. Every time you do, you'll lose your intuitive connection.

One of my clients, Ken, was a successful entrepreneur who had started a small company, which over the years was fraught with crises that Ken felt compelled to handle personally. The more competent he became at extinguishing fires, the more crises ignited. His constant involvement with his business turned him into a workaholic.

Finally, he made plans to take his girlfriend on his boat for a rare weekend of fun. He envisioned sun, swimming, laughter, and good food. But when he checked the boat that morning, the battery was dead. He had to drive to his father's to borrow a charger. When they arrived at the lake to launch the boat, his girlfriend noticed he'd left the food and drink coolers at home. Muttering under his breath, they drove to the nearest grocery, where he bought a new supply of food. When they came out of the market, Ken discovered he'd locked his keys inside his truck. Now he had to call a locksmith while his frustrated girlfriend waited and the potato salad got warm.

Ken's soul had been trying to send a message to him for a long time. His deepest self was telling him to slow down, let go of handling emergencies all the time, stop forcing things to work, and use his intuition instead to see what the flow of life would naturally create. But Ken's mind was deriving a strange identity from being a rescuer and problem-solver. He didn't want to admit that the way he'd set up his business just wasn't working. He was due to make big changes, but he didn't want to face the prospect and wouldn't pause to hear his inner voice of guidance. As a consequence, Ken's day of fun turned into another series of blocked movements and problems to be solved.

We all flow through many cycles of creation; some take a minute, some an hour, some a day or a month or a year. Yet it's common to become confused halfway through each cycle and revert to our subconscious world view. Learning to identify when the flow hits the dam and how you can release it to continue its natural direction is an important skill in intuition development. In this chapter you'll learn to become conscious of the dynamics of this process. First, we'll talk about the basic oscillating movement of your soul; second, we'll break that movement into the three phases in any cycle of creation.

Your Soul's Shifting Focus

If you pay attention, you'll notice that you oscillate constantly between two worlds or two points of view. One minute you'll be aware of solid objects, the next, of empty space. Your attention will be absorbed entirely with a physical task, then by a period of distraction. You'll feel loving and superconscious one moment, and the next you'll be preoccupied with anxiety and the "yes, buts" of the subconscious mind. We constantly descend into the physical world, then ascend again into the heavens. We materialize and dematerialize, manifest and dissolve, involve and evolve.

When your soul's consciousness approaches and "lands," you'll suddenly become aware of your body and individuality. When it lets go and moves up and out again, you'll remember how interconnected you are with life and the universe. We travel into the higher reaches of our soul's superconscious awareness when we go to sleep. We "materialize" each morning. We may "space out" while we drive on the freeway, then suddenly "come to" just as our exit appears.

Your soul descends or drops in vibration constantly, giving you the experience of being "down to earth" or "grounding an idea." Have you ever had the experience of "showing up" in the midst of a situation that felt like a surrealistic dream and then thought, "How did I get here?" Or perhaps you've been seized with an idea on which you had to take

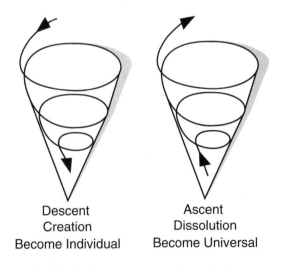

Descent	Ascent
Creation	Dissolution
Become Individual	Become Universal

The Soul's Path into and out of the World

Between the conscious and the unconscious, the mind has put up a swing; all earth creatures, even the supernovas, sway between these two trees, and it never winds down. Angels, animals, humans, insects by the million, also the wheeling sun and moon; ages go by, and it goes on. Everything is swinging; heaven, earth, water, fire, and the secret one slowly growing a body. Kabir saw that for fifteen seconds, and it made him a servant for life.

Kabir (translated by Robert Bly)

immediate action, or maybe you had an *aha!* where an abstract idea suddenly made sense. If so, you've experienced a mini-cycle of your soul's descent.

On the other hand, you don't have to wait for the day of your death or enlightenment to ascend to the heavens. Your soul also ascends or moves upward in vibration constantly. Every time you relax or lose concentration, every time you're bored with an activity or have a daydream, your soul is expanding into the superconscious realms to get new energy and new information. Every time you stretch your attention to sense the possibilities or to feel the future or the past, your awareness increases its scope. Pausing before you speak, taking catnaps, meditating: each pause is a mini-ascension.

Your basic awareness is continually moving. In and out, up and down, appearing and disappearing—your soul rocks itself the same way we rock our babies. We rock into clarity, then confusion; into motivation, then apathy; into specific goal-orientation, then expansive overviews. We wake, we sleep; we inhale and exhale. Through this ongoing rhythm, we're remembering the two extremes of our nature. And through this cyclical oscillation, eventually, we integrate our spirit with our personality.

Your consciousness rocks into the superconscious realm to obtain higher perspective and a vision for your next period of self-expression. Then it rocks back into the physical and subconscious realm to take action and manifest the vision, one task at a time. At the end of each task, it rocks back to check the collective consciousness and see if any minor revisions to the plan are necessary.

To enhance your intuitive ability, learn to recognize these subtle movements of your awareness and be conscious of which phase you're in: are you coming down from the superconscious place of wisdom, ready to make things concrete? Or are you lifting up and outward from the physical world of form, ready to be inspired? Once you know, go with the movement until it changes naturally to its opposite flow.

Rocking In and Out
Catch yourself when you've popped back after being spaced out. How long were you gone? What was your first thought on

returning to your personal reality? What were you doing or thinking about right before you became unconscious?

Practice stopping your internal dialogue. Go blank. Imagine you're being drawn into superconsciousness. In a moment, a thought will occur to you, and it will be more superconscious than the one before. Notice what it is. Then blank out again and imagine that the collective wisdom in the superconscious realm is repatterning you. Notice the next thought that comes naturally. Repeat this process of rocking in and out for five minutes. As you allow your thoughts to arise from the superconscious and not from previous thoughts, they will become increasingly insightful.

Do you ever feel stressed and overwhelmed, or have you suffered panic attacks, manic/depression, or chronic fatigue syndrome? Do you sometimes feel pressed to accomplish the amount of work before you? Your subconscious mind is probably in survival mode, trying to please others, to not fail, to hold its ground.

One of my clients, Rita, was a stockbroker specializing in the high-stress world of options trading. She came to me at a point of physical and mental breakdown, needing desperately to know how to keep up. Rita's awareness was so focused on succeeding in the complex physical world she had created that she had unconsciously become a talented psychic.

She had all her feelers out, constantly scanning for pertinent information and checking for what potentially could go wrong, while her body was going ninety miles an hour achieving goals. Unwittingly she was using her intuition to get a bird's-eye view of her environment and the near future so she could answer questions like "What will I encounter on this path of action? Where will I hit log jams? How many balls must I keep in the air while I juggle the ten million things I 'have to' do?"

Rita constantly received intuitive input about the big picture, but because of her internalized sense of urgency, her poor body sensed it was somehow supposed to manifest the entire vision *immediately*! Her body was in a panic because it could not accomplish that many things in so short a time. Its circuits were jammed. Your soul can know everything at once, but your body does one task at a time. The debilitating stress Rita was living with was caused by her not understanding how to flow gracefully back and forth between the tight focus of the physical world—action and results—and the expansive focus of the spiritual world—purpose and visions. She was unconsciously trying to cram her entire superconscious vision into one moment in her physical life.

Here's how she could remake her situation. Rita realizes she has many general goals and specific deadlines to meet. She becomes motivated to do the work. Instead of scattering herself in pursuit of ten simultaneous tasks, she seeks quietude, opens her awareness, and senses the greater picture. She reminds herself that at a higher level everything is coordinated perfectly and that there's a way it can happen harmoniously. She chooses the super-conscious world view. While she meditates on these thoughts, she keeps her body relaxed and receptive, knowing that when she must act, a higher part of her own self will tell her what to do. She sits mindfully until she feels full and happy. Then she becomes aware of her body. It's definitely ready to do something now. She asks that the overview filter gradually into her present, into her real-time personality, so she can take the right action. She knows her intuition will tell her the sequence of tasks to be attended to today.

Suddenly she has a strong sense that she should start the day by copy-writing a promotional brochure, then do an errand—not the other way around as she had planned. While she's writing, the phone rings and the caller is an important contact she needs to make, someone who's hard to reach. If she'd been at the bank, she'd have missed him. Later, while driving to the printer and daydreaming a bit, she has an incisive idea on how to solve a complex problem. She can even accomplish the first step on the way back to the office!

After each action, Rita stops and regroups. What should happen now? Once again she chooses the superconscious view, checking her intuitive sense of the overall picture while letting her body rest. Then, when she feels happy and full, a new urge percolates into her conscious mind, and intu-itively she knows what she wants to do. By having fun performing each physical task—even if it's just sending a buy order or locking her car door—and then letting her body rest while she checks the overview, Rita maximizes her day. Through synchronicity and natural efficiency she accomplishes more than she ever could through will power and worry.

⚡

I feel anything and everything my body wants me to know.

She also finds serendipitously that the people she deals with are more cooperative and that new colleagues are volunteering to assume more of her work.

Balancing Your Two Worlds

Become aware of the times during the day when you start a new action. At these times, identify fully with your physical body and let it have a grand time. Be engrossed in whatever you're doing. Physical bodies are like three-year-olds or puppy dogs. They enjoy anything with sensory stimulation. While you're in action you'll probably forget your superconscious self. Yet as the task comes to completion, you may space out.

Let yourself have that moment's pause. Expand your conscious mind to feel and enjoy the spaciousness, the rest, the opening of your imagination. You're now realigning yourself with the blueprint for your next action. While you're in this state, you may not be aware of your body. In a moment, however, you'll receive an impulse or picture of something you'd like to do, and you'll focus physically again.

To increase your intuition even more, learn to make smooth transitions between the two phases of your awareness. At the end of the descent phase, embrace silence and the pause. At the end of the ascent phase, embrace curiosity and courage. Flow in and out without getting stuck in attachment, fascination, fear, or resistance.

REMEMBER

▼

Trust endings and beginnings; it's your soul changing direction.

The Creation Cycle: *Be-Do-Have-Be*

By looking at the movement of your awareness in terms of the metaphysical trinity of body, mind, and spirit, you will understand more how your perception creates your reality. The creative process is an identical twin to the intuitive process. Being well-acquainted with and able to move smoothly through the three phases of any cycle of creation will also keep your intuition flowing.

To create anything, your consciousness must pass through three phases: (1) moving down from spirit as inspiration, and occurring in your mind as concepts and plans, (2) moving from your mind as motivation, and occur-

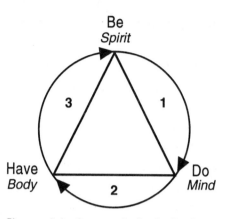

The Three Phases of the Creation Cycle: *Be-Do; Do-Have; Have-Be*

ring in your body as results and form, and (3) moving up from your body as completion, and being experienced again at spirit as renewal. This movement through spirit, mind, body, and spirit again correlates with three simple actions: *be, do, have,* and back to *be.* The three arcs in the illustration above depict the three phases in a cycle of creation. The first two arcs represent your soul's descent from *be* through *do* to *have,* while the third arc shows the ascent from *have* back to *be.*

Creation begins with the spirit, or *being.* Here, in the superconscious realm, purpose resides, here we are in tune with the collective wisdom of humanity and the planet, here we know the most about love and are aware of the big picture. This is the part of us that funds our physical existence.

The mind, or conscious mind, correlates with action, or *doing.* It's the function of awareness that focuses, compartmentalizes, chooses, registers impressions, makes associations, determines meaning, implements, catalyzes. Mind is the personal will, combining thought with desire to create action.

The body correlates with the experience of manifested form, or *having.* It's at this stage that action precipitates results and there's an outcome to ideas. Until this point, nothing is concrete, tangible, or stable. The body is part of the subconscious realm.

Be-do-have. For anything to manifest, consciousness must follow these three simple steps, in order.

The Descending Phase of Creation: *Be-Do-Have*

Let's trace the process of how we create our personal reality.

The first phase in the process, the downward swoop of *spirit-be* into *mind-do*, is the *aha!*, the spontaneous, impulsive influx of inspiration. Natalie Goldberg, who teaches writing as a spiritual practice, advocates writing from "first thoughts" as opposed to second and third thoughts, which the inner censor has rehashed many times. She says, "First thoughts have tremendous energy. It is the way the mind first flashes on something. . . . First thoughts are also unencumbered by ego . . . [and] if you express something egoless, it is also full of energy because it is expressing the truth of the way things are." [1]

Activating Phase One of the Creation Cycle
1. List five new ideas that excite you.
2. List five first impressions you felt about people or situations.
3. List five sense-oriented experiences you crave.
4. List five hunches you followed today.

As the first phase of the cycle occurs we're full of superconscious guidance, enthusiasm, purpose, and the desire to expand. We're motivated, curious, and imbued with a childlike innocence that knows no doubt. For example, an artist sipping coffee in a café may notice a reclining woman in a romantic dress and be inspired to pick up a pen and sketch her. Your

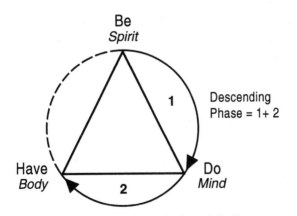

Descent: Manifesting Form through *Be-Do* and *Do-Have*

mind at this point clarifies and defines its ideas, and then it uses will power to initiate action.

In the second phase in the process, the swing from *mind-do* to *body-have,* your goal is clear. You're coming from superconscious guidance as you launch into action and become industrious. You hardly know if it's work or play. You're in the groove and applying yourself in a cause-and-effect process. The artist asks his friend for a pen and grabs a napkin to make his sketch. He scribbles furiously and loses all sense of time until he realizes the drawing is complete. We experience an increase in intensity and focus during this phase, a threshold point is reached, and physical results manifest.

So the mind receives an inspiration, registers that energy as an idea, and drops it in frequency by imaging it with the senses. The mind drops the energy further by defining it verbally and focusing it through will power. The energy then flows toward your goal. Action slows the original flow more by using some of the energy. Finally, when the energy becomes slow enough, it coalesces into a physical form, and you have results. The entire process from *be* through *do* to *have* represents the descending movement of your soul, the manifesting part of the creation cycle. It represents the dynamic and expressive power we all exercise daily.

Activating Phase Two of the Creation Cycle
1. List five activities in your life where you took action without hesitating.
2. List five times you lost yourself in what you were doing.
3. List five results that surprised you.
4. List five things you want to accomplish very much.

Getting Stuck: *Do-Have, Do-Have, Do-Have*

Be-do-have. So far our intuition has been alive and well. If only we would follow the current in the direction it's going and finish the cycle. But we complicate matters. This is how: We've followed the inspiration and motivation of spirit, decided, acted from our mind, and now have results for our body.

One of my clients, Chuck, exemplifies this process. He had an inspira-

There is no such thing as a logical method of having new ideas, or a logical reconstruction of this process. Every great discovery contains an irrational element of creative intuition.

Karl Popper

tion for a software application and later developed, manufactured, and sold it. He made a good profit and bought a car and a house. He was highly satisfied. But he needed to maintain his good feeling, his material possessions, and his ongoing venture that now supported his employees.

Chuck's awareness was focused on methods, results, and security in the task-oriented world. He had forgotten what it felt like to do anything but manufacture software: "Being? What's that? How could *being* be important? Sitting on my duff sure won't pay the bills." At this stage Chuck recognized only what was tangible. Completing the creation cycle by returning to *being* was out of the question, because he associated leaving the world of doing and having with loss, even annihilation. His mind looked out at the realm of being and saw only . . . the Void: "Choose emptiness and lose the security of my job, marriage, house, savings? Give up the attachment I have to the identity I'm getting from my successful business? Open myself to the possibility of becoming a playwright or a race car driver next? No way!"

⚡

Don't get in the way of life with thoughts that don't move.

Captured by the Subconscious World View

Although Chuck was feeling bored by doing the same thing, the idea of giving it up or changing it looked insane. Yet he was starting to have doubts, and his intuition was less reliable. As pressure built, he experienced reactionary behaviors in himself based on "a-voidance," anxiety, distrust, frustration, and hoarding. Chuck was bogged down in his fear-based subconscious world view.

Like most people confronted with this kind of discomfort, Chuck took the least objectionable route—he turned around and went back to what had worked before. He moved backward, against the natural flow: back to the mind; to doing and thinking; to familiar beliefs, thought patterns, and habitual behaviors: "Manufacturing software got me a new house and a feeling of success. Doing more of it should solve my problem." He expanded his production facility and increased hiring. Chuck was stuck now, going back and forth between *do-have, do-have, do-have.* He was no longer expressing his soul's true desires.

To continue with more doing and having at the end of the descending phase of the creation cycle is unnatural and takes its toll. Since we're using

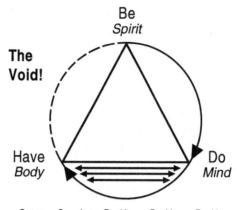

Getting Stuck in *Do-Have, Do-Have, Do-Have*

more will and less energy to manifest the results we're accustomed to, the results decrease proportionately. Chuck continued to resist the pressure to complete the cycle and return to his being for reorientation and renewal. He depleted his energy, motivation, and conviction. Repeating his original action was a tremendous effort.

What to do? Go backward *again*! But this time, to reach the same results, he had to alter his original plan by doing things *better* and *differently*: "The business isn't doing well, and I'm not motivated. But my success has been in software, so I'll improve manufacturing techniques or redesign the packaging." He cranked up his will power, applied more effort, and disregarded his body's growing unease.

As Chuck's success rate continued to drop, his panic built. He denied his desperation and became depressed; he was still afraid to face the unknown. He started having a few drinks after work and became embedded in the addictive process. *Do-have, do-have, do-have.* Going against the flow eventually resulted in an absence of vitality and loss of connection to his true self. He had blocked his intuition.

Running on Empty

What we see is what we are. As we begin the descending phase of the creation cycle, we *are* spirit; we *are* whole. The world therefore looks ripe with possibilities; we are confident and wise. We like ourselves. But as we manifest results, most of our intention and fuel has been translated into form and consumed.

At this point, at *body-have*, looking to the third phase of the process, we see through the filter of emptiness, because we *are* empty. Our reserves are gone, and we're not aware again of the universal supply. Nothingness looms. More than at any time, we tend to think in terms of emptiness, to talk about what isn't, to tell ourselves we are nobody, and to project negative thoughts into the future. We seem to have no self-esteem.

In this part of the creation cycle we can actually rest in peace and recharge. Yet after so much *do-have, do-have, do-have,* life has become so concrete that few of us remember how to recognize the intangible, let alone how pleasurable emptiness, or spaciousness, is. Buddhists view emptiness as divine. But our Western culture places a negative value on emptiness, equating it with deficiency. Some ultraconservative groups go so far as to associate the unknown with evil. We need a new life skill: how to recognize, welcome, and use the third phase of the creation cycle.

The Ascending Phase of Creation: *Have-Be*

When results have manifested and the telltale signs of dissolution begin to stir—such as loss of direction, motivation, and interest; sleepiness; anxiety attacks; boredom; the desire for your addiction of choice; and the desire to turn and backtrack into what's familiar but energetically dead—what should you do? It's quite simple: *Stop!*

It's Time to Let Go Now

Are you thinking, "I don't know if I'll be able to create anything ever again!" or "I don't know why I'm still doing this"? Are you trying too

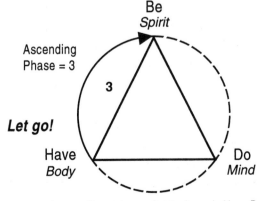

Ascent: Returning to Spirit through *Have-Be*

Inside myself is a place where I live all alone and that's where you renew your springs that never dry up.

Pearl Buck

⚡

I enter the pause that refreshes.

TROUBLESHOOTING TIP
When You Can't Remember How to Let Go

1. Catch yourself in the middle of a fear response or addictive behavior. When you notice yourself wanting to fight or going into avoidance, stay with the process. Say aloud, "Whoops, there I go again!" and "I don't have to know or do anything about this right now. It's OK to feel what I feel." Don't punish yourself. Take a deep breath. Relax.

2. Stay in the present moment and *be with what is.* Let life do what it's doing. (Hint: When you can be with what is, you're instantly back to the top of the triangle!)

3. Let yourself feel complete and receive the benefit of your current involvements. Draw conclusions, create a completion ceremony, or let yourself become bored in the old form.

4. Let your body release pent-up energy through emotional catharsis, sports, dance, spontaneous movement, or sound.

5. Cultivate an appreciation of "the pause that refreshes." Learn to enjoy suspending your mind until the new creative urge emerges spontaneously. Fill the space of waiting with a small Buddha smile. (Note: If you're having thoughts like "That's OK— I can do without; I don't need anything; I can get used to living alone," you still haven't let go. You're experiencing self-sacrifice and are still resisting the forward flow. Suspend even those thoughts.)

hard? Pushing or pulling something or someone? Ahead of yourself or chronically late? Compulsive or procrastinating? Things aren't connecting? Life full of snags and bad timing? It's time to change your tactics. Try something besides thinking and doing.

If you're using will, you've already returned to doing. If you're depressed, you're not letting go of old thoughts or concepts but are forcing them to fit a reality that's outgrown them. Cultivate this thought: "It's OK to not know or not do right now." Let go of the "shoulds" and "shouldn'ts." Pull your thoughts out of the past and future and enter the present. Let things be as they are.

I'm reminded of a cartoon showing a desperate man hanging on a flimsy bush growing from a sheer cliff. He's yelling, "Somebody up there—help me!" A deep, booming voice answers, "Let go!" The man looks up. He looks down at the vastness. He looks around. He looks up again. Finally, he squeaks, "Is anybody else up there?"

Your Being Is a Hair's Breadth Away

As soon as you allow yourself to not-know, not-think, and not-do, you're on your way to entering the third, ascending phase of the creation cycle. This takes you back to the superconscious mind, to purpose, love, and wisdom. Your intuition faucet turns on again.

Activating Phase Three of the Creation Cycle

1. List five times you've been bored and let go of something.
2. List five ways you could pause or open up more each day.
3. List five ways you could waste time positively.
4. List five things that feel like they're more trouble than they're worth. Could you let go of each one or let it turn into something slightly different? What might happen?

Being is the stuff of which thought, action, and form are made. *Whenever we cease thinking, doing, and forming, being is immediately present.* We take no time, we do not journey to get there. The trip to spirit at the top of the trinity is instantaneous and can happen wherever you are, whenever you think of it. Just stop. Let an opening occur. Suspend your

The Signs That It's Time to Let Go

You feel you have to do it all yourself	You feel desperate
You're confused	Nothing seems interesting
You're depressed	You want to sleep when you're not tired
You have no sense of direction	Your mind is fuzzy
You've run out of motivation	You have the heebie-jeebies
You indulge in your favorite addictions	You have no confidence
You don't like yourself	Things aren't fun anymore
Nothing works; even machines break down	You're pushing or pulling
You feel a sense of urgency all the time	You expect results too soon
You're ahead of yourself and others	You're chronically late
You're overwhelmed and overcrowded	You're experiencing lack and limitation
You're procrastinating	You're compulsive
Life is full of snags and bad timing	People seem to be cheating you
You're spending time in the past	You're living in a fantasy world
You're trying too hard	You're being stubborn or vindictive
You feel close to having an accident	You feel like you're in two places at the same time
No one seems to see or hear you	People interpret you the wrong way
You walk into a sliding glass door, have a flat tire, run out of gas, twist your ankle	You're sure the answer lies in thinking or doing more, better or differently

thoughts. Don't try to replace what you released. Pray or ask for help. Laugh. Shrug your shoulders. Notice the little things. Take small, non-goal-oriented actions coming from your body's instinct. Be insignificant and simple.

When you've finally entered the unknown, you'll hardly notice, because it's really not there. The panic you were feeling was the resistance to the idea of the Void. Once you enter being, by opening to what is, you'll immediately feel your soul. The unknown transforms into the known. You'll feel lit up with fresh, burning insights and motivations. You'll be un-self-conscious, brilliant, and appropriately aligned with others and your environment. Soon you'll find yourself drawn to an idea that's perfect; you'll want to move in a new and fluid direction. Your intuition will be in high gear. Without realizing it, you've emerged from being and are once again in the first phase, starting life anew.

In contrast to the emptiness you feel at the end of the descending phase

If I had only two loaves of bread, I would barter one for hyacinths to nourish my Soul.

Muhammad

⚡

I am here and it's OK to do nothing.
I am here and it's OK to do anything.

of the creation cycle, when you're at the end of the ascending phase, you're 100 percent full of energy and ideas. You naturally know everything, all at once, and you identify yourself and life through this perceptual filter. All you want to do is give birth to creations and be dynamic. Life looks full, active, and positive.

When Chuck stopped and asked himself, "Do I still like manufacturing software?" and permitted the answer to be no, he realized he wasn't using his creativity. At a summer barbeque he met a man who needed someone to head the production end of his growing multimedia company. The event marked an important point in the evolution of Chuck's career, yet he had been too immersed in his company to have thought of it.

Greasing the Wheels of Intuition

If you can achieve a state of awareness where you become the motion you're in, where you become the question, the medium, and the answer simultaneously, you'll be highly intuitive. It's just a new habit of awareness.

You can learn that going backward and living via willfulness and denial is downright uncomfortable. You can learn to add to your life the pleasure of release, of waiting as you gestate a new creation. It's your right to take time and space, to take your mind off things and be aimless, to pay homage to the greater wisdom that guides your course.

To open yourself to the flow of life and experience the fullness of your identity as a physical and spiritual being, you must complete three phases of activity: (1) inspiration to choice, (2) action to manifestation, and (3) dissolution to resourcing. *Be-do-have-be.* Each phase of the cycle is an opportunity to use your intuition and connect to higher awareness.

In the first phase, inspiration to choice, practice innocence and humility. Be receptive and fertile. Let the next urge or idea rise spontaneously from inside your body, percolate to the surface, and register on your beginner's mind. Trust the seed that has been planted there. The revelatory function of awareness is connecting you to your optimal path of thought and action.

Next, let this idea take on increased reality by using your senses. Smell it, feel it, see it happening in your imagination. Get clear about what you want. Let yourself continue receiving energy from spirit, filling up and

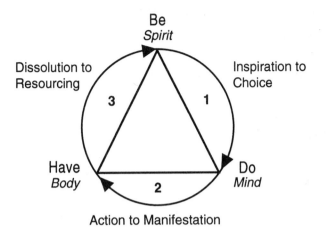

The Full Creation Cycle: *Be-Do-Have-Be*

growing fat and juicy like a ripe fruit. Don't act prematurely. Wait for the moment when the fruit naturally drops off the tree.

In the second phase of the process, action to manifestation, practice staying present and alert in your body. Be aware of the flow, step into the action stream, and become one with the motion like a kayaker going down a whitewater river. Start your motion when it starts *you*. No force or "shoulds" are necessary. Your instinct will tell you where to steer and when to go slowly. Don't jump into the future. The immediate process contains all the information you need about what results to expect; the formula for the outcome is encoded in the flow. When the payoff comes, notice what it is. It's simply the crystallization of a pattern you've been living. Love it, appreciate it, use it.

In the third phase of the process, dissolution to resourcing, practice humility once more. Notice your tension. Don't run away from how you feel. Is something ending? Should you keep this action path going? Should you hold tightly to what you manifested? Can you figure out what to do through cleverness? Probably not. At the moment your mind alone is too small to grasp the bigger plan.

Remember that the process holds the wisdom. The revelatory function of awareness is close now, comforting and guiding you. Feel relieved to know you have help and are not alone. Cooperate with the unseen. Soften your edges. Surrender to the spaciousness. Feel your heart. Notice what's real. Amuse yourself.

The Phases of Creativity

1. What seeds of ideas are percolating inside you? In your imagination, test each idea by seeing yourself involved and acting on the concept. How does it feel? Which hold your interest and make you forget time? Which excite your body? If it feels good, take one step in the physical world toward one of your ideas.

2. List the activities or projects you've started and are still doing. Which are free of pressure, originating in pure enthusiasm? Pursue these. Which involve too much will and effort, or irritate, exhaust, or frighten you? If each of these activities were to end tomorrow, what have you learned from each?

3. Ask yourself if you should end your involvement with each activity, if it's time to wait for further instructions. Complete the situations as indicated. Let yourself be limp, aimless, unfocused, happy for no reason.

And if the earthly has forgotten you, say to the still earth: I flow. To the rushing water speak: I am.

Rainer Maria Rilke

BE INTUITIVE TODAY!
Use intuition to rank ideas.

Visualize a large thermometer with ten markings along the side. Ask your inner wisdom to give you a reading about the suitability of each idea—the higher the better. Watch the liquid rise to the appropriate marking and note it. After recording each answer, clear the image from the space before you and continue the other options.

1. Of all the new ideas and projects you're excited about, which are best for you? Bring each idea to mind, visualize yourself doing it, and overlay the image of the thermometer. Get a reading on each option. Which will fulfill you the most? Which should you start first?

2. Which current ideas and involvements does your inner wisdom want you to abandon now? Bring each option to mind, visualize yourself involved with it, and overlay the image of the thermometer. Which block your intuition the most? Which should you abandon first?

Direct Writing Questions

Sit down with your journal and get quiet. Empty your mind. Pick one of the following questions and be with it for a few moments. Ask that you be able to receive creative insights from your deepest level of truth. Let the question serve as a magnet. Allow the first word to pop into your mind. Write it down. Let another word pop in. Write it down. Let words proceed forth, without judging them, without second-guessing where the answer is going. Don't jump ahead. Don't stop and read back over what you've written until the writing stops of its own accord. Helpful techniques: write as your own soul, innocent child, or future self; address your personality in the second person, by name; don't try to be too significant! Let your handwriting change shape. Change your speed and your rhythm, or write with your opposite hand.

- "I'm having trouble starting (new project) because _____."
- "I'm having trouble completing (old situation) because _____."
- "When I daydream, I go to (place) and become involved with (person/persons) doing (activities). I'm aware of (surroundings), and I'm integrating (specific lessons or qualities)." Place this daydream in the present tense, as if it's happening now. What insights do you receive about your present cycle of creativity?
- "What are the factors that influence my ability to achieve my goals? How do these factors affect me? How can I change things?"
- "How might a currently blocked situation flow if I were following the phases of the creation cycle in their natural sequence? What are my barriers?"
- "What have I gained through the significant losses in my life?"
- "If I could live for a hundred years and still be healthy and attractive, what might I do in each ten-year period to come?"
- Let your soul talk to you about the Void. What does it really feel like? What is its gift to you right now? What's a good method for you to use to enter it and receive its messages?

4

Unlocking the Secrets of Your Subconscious Mind

Search, find out, remove and reject every assumption til you reach the living waters and the rock of truth. . . . Resist your old habits of feeling and thinking; keep on telling yourself: "No, not so, it cannot be so; I am not like this, I do not need it, I do not want it," and a day will surely come when the entire structure of error and despair will collapse and the ground will be free for a new life.

Sri Nisargadatta

The Hero's Journey

You are someone who knows there's more to life than what you see on the surface. You've asked to glimpse the unseen realms for help in knowing the underlying reality. You seek clarity. Just from this deep desire, just by asking in your heart of hearts, a process has been set in motion. Now you must trust that the unseen world and your unrecognized soul are answering your call.

Everything that occurs in your life from this point on is an answer to that request. All your new experiences, positive or negative, are meant to further your progress and understanding. From now on, the intuitive process asks that you accept what comes and look into each event to unlock the secrets hidden in your most trying experiences as well as in the entertaining synchronicities and serendipitous flashes of insight. Your life is taking on a magical quality of meaningfulness.

As you get in synch with yourself, flow creatively, and have intuitive

Creating a consistently clear lens for accurate intuition results from dissolving subconscious blocks and integrating their hidden messages. Chapter 4 outlines the hero's journey toward enlightenment and shows you how to deal with your shadow and transmute fear, pain, and suffering into love so your intuition can flow freely. This chapter shows you that some of the most valuable intuitive guidance can be derived from the parts of yourself that you deny.

insights regularly, you'll realize how effortless your life can be. Then you'll crave the superconscious state and will be unable to tolerate living with interference. Before you can consistently have the greater wisdom for which you ask, any memories or beliefs stored in your subconscious that might block your ability to live superconsciously will rise to the surface of your mind to be cleared. The more intense your desire for clarity, the faster the subconscious will surrender its contents.

Practicing the intuitive way, you may at first encounter increased confusion, misunderstandings, and reactionary behavior in yourself and others. You may not understand how something as innocuous as intuition development can create such a stir. But remember, the intuitive process is really a path to spiritual enlightenment and will constantly challenge you to overcome ignorance and to re-create love and clarity.

The process of opening this Pandora's box is normal—in fact, it parallels the hero's journey that myths and religions describe. Before you can live in consistent clarity, you must deal with the shadow, the underworld, or the dark cloud. Poet Robert Bly calls it the "black bag" into which we stash all the feelings society does not authorize us to feel. In the hero's journey you face these incompletely perceived experiences, see and feel them again, and finally reach heartfelt understanding and true freedom. In this chapter, we'll delve into the process of becoming friends with the subconscious mind, of learning how to create reliable and accurate intuition.

You can begin the hero's journey by being open to use all information that comes to you, whatever the source. What are colleagues saying to you in ordinary conversations that are really messages from your depths? If your wife is "harping" at you again, what legitimate insight does she voice that you resist? What did it mean that two ravens flew into your backyard and remained for ten minutes? Why did you break your right arm? What lesson did you learn in losing your wallet? What superconscious message lies behind your mate's debilitating illness? As the saying goes, even the darkest cloud has a silver lining. It's your job now to find it.

You can use your intuition to free more intuition. Subconscious blocks represent partially understood information, and if you use your intuition to look beyond the apparent form of what's happening and listen with an open mind, they will teach you. Each subconscious block, when decoded, can be a "gift in the garbage." In fact, the easiest way to keep your intu-

REMEMBER

▼

If something negative happens, it doesn't mean you're off-purpose.

ition open is to regard your subconscious blocks as containing interesting and useful information.

One of the fastest ways to notice the tip of the iceberg of a subconscious issue is to catch yourself when you use the term "yes, but—." A friend, Allison, was considering buying a house. She said she could easily talk herself into liking almost any house, but she noticed when she described the places to her daughter she said things like "Once you get inside, it really feels good . . ." and "The bedroom does have a great view . . ."

At the end of every sentence was a blank space where the word *but* was implied. When she added the rest of the message she got ". . . *but* there are high tension lines really close to the yard" and ". . . *but* there's hardly any closet space." She realized something in her subconscious mind was attracting her to a living space that didn't fully support her health and self-expression. Seeing underneath her "yes, buts" allowed her to clarify what kind of nurturing and creativity she wanted in the next part of her life.

Intuition allows us to make karmically correct choices.

Deepak Chopra

Seeing Underneath Your "Yes, Buts"

1. List three things you've had a conditionally positive response to in the last day or two. Did you partly agree with someone in a discussion? Did you partly like a new restaurant, movie, or co-worker? Are you allowing yourself to partly commit to an action? Are you letting yourself be partly pleased with something you accomplished?

2. Use your intuition to guess why you're being agreeable when you really don't feel 100 percent that way. Write about what comes after the "but." Is there a clue to a subconscious issue lurking in what you're taking exception to? What do you really want and need?

As subconscious blocks rise into your conscious mind and become recognizable, they may often seem chaotic or significant beyond all normal proportions. One of my students, Sera, had a frightening, repetitive dream. In it, her dead grandmother stood at the foot of her bed moaning, "Feed me! Feed me!" Through meditation, we discovered that her grandmother was a symbol of the wisdom of Sera's homeland, which Sera had left as a teenager and wasn't paying much attention to now. By imagining dialogues between her and her grandmother, Sera began to remember pieces of her heritage and to heal the loneliness she felt living in a foreign country.

Christine is an executive in a large San Francisco company that was laying off thousands in a major "reengineering" move. She had devised a clever proposal for shifting her job description and job sharing with another woman in hopes that their department might survive the worst cuts. On the day she was to make the presentation to the male-dominated upper management, she experienced severe panic attacks. Her mind conjured up scenarios where she was criticized, fired, and cheated of her retirement package. She descended into such a state that she couldn't eat or sleep.

As she quieted down and used her intuition to probe the real reason she was distraught, she realized that she really needed to speak to her father and her husband about what she wanted emotionally from them and that her problem lay at home, not in her work arena. After doing that, her meeting with her bosses went smoothly.

Todd, another client, was dealing—not very well—with difficult emotions about his father's approaching death due to an incurable cancer. He suffered great pain about the prospect of losing his father yet was unable to get in touch with it consciously, to voice his feelings or cry. He just felt depressed. Trying to escape by taking a long bicycle ride in the country, Todd was hit by a car. His bike was totalled and he was cut and bruised badly but was otherwise OK. He was incensed about the loss of his expensive bicycle and vented his anger to his friends, obsessed with details of "the other guy's" insurance and possible financial resources.

When I saw him for a counseling session, the combined effect of the physical pain from his injuries and the unconscious amplification of his upset about the bicycle finally triggered a catalytic release of grief about his father. By fixating his emotional upset on a relatively inconsequential bicycle, Todd was able to break through a powerful subconscious block about his unwillingness to feel pain.

Dialoguing with a Subconscious Block

1. Scan your recent experience, listing any issues that have triggered upsets or discomfort. Define the cause of the discomfort in simple terms: "I'm uncomfortable about having to talk to my

sister; about the driver who honked at me; about losing my pay-check."

2. Imagine that the upsetting issue is the skin around a sub-conscious block. Imagine facing the issue. Converse with it: "You are making me feel _____." It responds, "I'm really your friend. I'm trying to show you _____." You say, "Show me the lie I've been buying into. What am I really afraid might happen? Show me how I can see the whole picture." Remember: Subconscious blocks want to be understood and set free. They always cooperate and give you the information you need—if you ask.

3. Make notes in your journal.

Each individual in the previous examples was able to use open-mindedness to transform a negative experience into something that helped them feel more loving. Some subconscious issues that surface for us, how-ever, are connected to lifelong themes that are not easily understood. These deep-seated constellations of beliefs can repeatedly trip us up. To live an intuitive life, to become a consistently clear lens, you must unravel these core patterns of negativity.

Brian, a client, is an example of how the soul can bring clarity and intuitive knowing through a stubbornly rooted subconscious world view. Brian came from a wealthy family and was the eldest son of a top execu-tive at a Fortune 500 corporation. His father assumed he would follow in his footsteps.

But Brian was a free spirit and studied theater arts, leaving home at an early age to write plays and act in New York. He enjoyed some success, but instead of making it his life work, Brian unexpectedly decided to start a business. He veered from his bohemian life and using his innate financial acumen built his innovative business into a several million-dollar-plus ven-ture. Then, without warning, a hostile takeover threw Brian into a chaotic maelstrom. An older partner demeaned and cheated him; he was sued unfairly and lost almost everything.

Despite a debilitating depression, Brian tried to pull himself together and reapply his considerable business skills. Yet every time he tried to repeat his old patterns, he became deathly ill. He consulted doctors and went into therapy. After several torturous years of resisting his inner urges,

⚡

There is no such thing
as a bad vibration.

Brian resumed writing. First it was poetry, finally a book drawn from his experience in applying creativity and spirituality to business.

Brian had lived through a period of clearing a large constellation of subconscious blocks. After he emerged from his long, dark tunnel, he saw that his subconscious mind had believed that if he did what he loved he would be abandoned by his father. He understood, too, the role his business partner had played in helping these deep fears surface. Once the fears cleared, Brian was free to be his creative, intuitive, and expressive self without having to rebel to do it.

Perhaps you've had a similar period where living out experiences from your subconscious world view has dulled your clarity. A time like this is often marked by drama in which you may feel either a victim or a dominator. Events may force you to take care of someone or let someone take care of you. Someone may betray or abandon you, or you may lose control in some wild way. You may feel drained, depressed, and out of touch with your true self. And during this time, your intuition is on vacation. Then, without warning, you emerge from your tunnel. The light shines again, you shake yourself off, and you exclaim: "What *happened* to me?!" What happened was that you unwittingly became obsessed by your subconscious blocks as a way to recognize and dissolve them.

Let's examine how you can maximize your hero's journey through your subconscious mind. You can transform negativity into intuitive insight, and whether you're stuck in an uncomfortable dream or a fairly long period of difficulty, the procedure is the same. As with many other things relating to intuition, this process of enlightenment, or illumination, has three phases. In this process you will journey from unconsciousness (being unconsciously superconscious), through confusion (being consciously subconscious), to clarity and direct knowing (being consciously superconscious). By knowing how the three phases work, you'll be able to reduce wasted time and increase self-expression.

Phase One: Being Unconsciously Superconscious

At the beginning of life, you're still merged with the superconscious state—close to your soul yet unaware of it. As you grow, you individuate and project your mind into external things, identifying with your body,

If you bring forth what is within you, what is within you will save you.

Jesus (Gospel of Thomas)

possessions, image, relationships, jobs, accomplishments, failures, race, or nationality. You're still not aware that your superconscious self is sourcing you.

Maybe you're emotionally involved, like Brian, in the formation of new subconscious blocks as a result of unhealthy interactions with your parents. In Brian's case his father was critical and pressured him to stabilize and be more logical. Brian soon developed a negative self-image and lack of self-worth. This is dramatic and attention-capturing stuff, and it kept his mind from the superconscious state. He covered his feelings of inadequacy with a rebellious attitude and a sarcastic, self-deprecating humor. Yet unconsciously he was echoing what his father had been telling him: "I'm a dilettante, and I'll never amount to anything unless I'm a serious businessman." To avoid that pain, he added: "But I don't care; I'm going to do what I want. I'm getting away from my old man." Though he was unaware of it, Brian's conscious mind was now identifying with his subconscious blocks.

Brian flung himself into the life of an artist in the big city. He had crazy relationships, was accepted and rejected by directors, finally wrote and had plays produced, but in the end received only modest reviews. His lukewarm success only reinforced his beliefs about his lack of self-worth. To avoid his deep emotional pain, Brian's subconscious mind decided to deny everything that made him uncomfortable. He started to think, "I'm not successful doing what I want; maybe my father was right. I'm not an artist after all." He had an idea for a business, pursued it, and became wealthy. He was still reinforcing subconscious beliefs: "I'm only good if I toe the line." Without his recognizing it, Brian's life was building to a crescendo. He was a success. He was just like his dad—but wait a *minute*!

At this point Brian's superconscious mind, or soul awareness, woke up. He was *not* just like his father—he had his own destiny. His superconscious mind always had been present but was having tremendous difficulty getting through his various resistances. When the final "lie" was reached, Brian's deep truth was drawn in to meet and match the lie. The power of his soul's truth magnetized his subconscious blocks toward the surface.

Now Brian's fixated mind had to relinquish control. He could not keep

My perception makes my world.

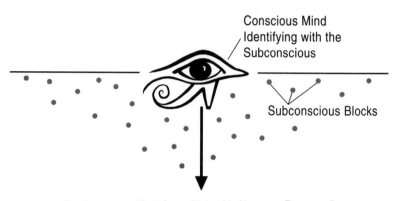

The Conscious Mind Says, "I Am My Negative Emotions"

going backwards and repeating old cycles of *do-have, do-have, do-have.* He had bouts of absent-mindedness. His ulcer acted up. He started to have a sneaking suspicion that spreadsheets weren't his real forte, that his heart wasn't in another round of motivating his sales force. His inner dialogue went like this—Soul: "I want out!" Mind: "I have to keep doing things the way my father would." Soul: "I'm coming out." Mind: "I can't *hear* you." Soul: "You will!"

Discovering What You Resist

1. Write about the conditions and "yes, buts" in your subconscious that underlie the following issues:
    a. Your incomplete projects.
    b. Your undelivered communications, secrets, or with-holds.
    c. The agreements you have not kept.
    d. Your unfulfilled expectations of yourself.
    e. The ways you want others to change before you'll be happy with them.
2. Use your intuition to project ahead and see how you would complete each item and how you'd feel afterward. What's the "gift in the garbage" hidden in each situation?

Phase Two: Being Consciously Subconscious

Brian's superconscious mind popped loose a series of "yes, buts" and worst possible scenarios; they flooded into his conscious mind. As the blocks surfaced, they clouded his vision and caused circumstances to align with his worst expectations. His life went into upheaval. Nothing meant anything anymore, and he went through a process of disillusionment. At last he became consciously aware of his subconscious mind and how powerful a grip it had had on his life. As his business crumbled and he was ejected from that reality, Brian had to reexamine his values. He had to let go.

The Wedge Experience

It almost always takes a dramatic or shocking situation to open you to the reality of the superconscious realm after you've spent so many years being subconscious. A "wedge" is driven through the fixed portion of your mind, and there is a sudden dawning of light.

This wedge might be a crisis resulting in loss such as Brian had. Maybe it's an automobile accident, a near-death experience, betrayal by a friend, or the loss of a beloved pet. Maybe an angel or being of light appears to you in a dream and gives you a powerful message. Whatever its form, the wedge experience will leave you with the impression that there's more to life than you thought. You glimpse superconsciousness, and it causes you to yearn for answers of a different kind. At this point you may pray for help and understanding. You may buy books on meditation, unsolved mysteries, past-life recall, metaphysics, psychology, and philosophy. You now have a spiritual hunger that never seems satisfied. Your intuition is opening of its own accord.

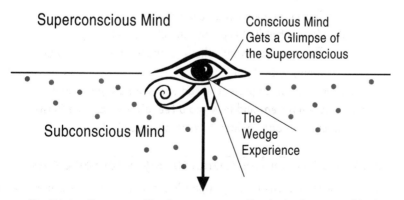

The Wedge Experience: The Superconscious Floods the Conscious Mind

You may start on a spiritual path or, like Brian, begin an intensive process of psychotherapy. The more you read, pray, or meditate, the more superconsciousness you'll magnetize into your conscious mind. Remember: Superconsciousness makes you wiser, more loving, and more intuitive. It's easier now to choose to *not* be fearful: "Who am I? I *might* be super-conscious. I *want* to be superconscious." With each victory, you become more of a magnet for your soul's wisdom. You draw in more insight. Ironically each success creates more havoc because now you're more aware of what's in your way and less satisfied to live blindly. The first time through the wake-up process, you're likely to be on automatic pilot, feeling like life is happening to you. But as the process continues, you'll find it easier to stay conscious and intuitive, and you'll be more aware of your partnership with life.

Your Wedge Experiences

Describe the times in your life when you've had a breakthrough, or a wedge experience. Think back to your childhood. Did you experience something shocking or overwhelming? Did you pray or ask for help? What answers did you receive? What conclusions did you draw? How did the experience make you feel closer to the divine or to your inner self? How did your behavior change?

The Magnet

You now enter an uncomfortable period. Your clarity becomes a magnet for your blockages. You know that something better is possible and that "monsters" lurk under the surface—and you're ready to face them: "I don't want to be a coward anymore! I'm not going to keep feeling sorry for myself." You're taking the first intentional steps on the hero's journey into the underworld. Before long the magnet draws another layer of subconscious beliefs to the surface of your awareness. More crazy events occur in your life. You total your car. The landlord sells your house, and you have to move. Brian's wife suddenly decided to divorce him when he reached this stage.

This is a crucial point in the process. You must choose each time you face fear-producing events: "I am fear" or "I am love." You can react to the upsets by backtracking: "See, another bad thing is happening to me.

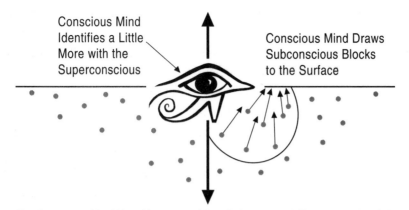

Conscious Mind Identifies a Little More with the Superconscious

Conscious Mind Draws Subconscious Blocks to the Surface

The Conscious Mind Now Magnetizes More Subconscious Blocks into Your Life

I have the worst luck. I'll never get out of this mess. How did I stop it when this happened before?" Or you can choose the God's Eye View: "I don't know why this is happening right now, but there must be a good reason. What can I learn about myself from this? If I pay attention a little longer, what does my soul tell me about the inner meaning of the events?"

If you react from the subconscious world view now, you'll stall your intuition and create more blocks. If you respond from the superconscious world view, the event will untwist, open up, and share its deep meaning with you. Energy and intuition will flow. You'll have an *aha!* Brian had an *aha!* when he realized, "My business partner was acting out a role exactly parallel to that of my father. Now I'm aware that I don't have to surrender my power to domineering authority figures." The result was that he became more loving, tolerant, and understanding.

Changing Your Habitual Reactions

1. Write about three problematic situations in your past or present. Describe your initial reactions. Describe your self-talk. What happens when your mate is distant and unavailable? When you lose your car keys? When you let someone down? When someone pressures you? Do you tend to react from a subconscious world view?

2. Use your intuition to imagine responding to each of the three situations from the God's Eye View. How might each situation change?

REMEMBER
▼
*It's never the event that
determines the response.*

Now you're feeling pretty good and fairly intuitive. You jumped some big hurdles, healed some old pain, and then suddenly you can't believe it: your soul is removing *more* roadblocks. At this point Brian had to sell his house to pay his ex-wife and couldn't find a job. Once again, you're faced with two choices, two attitudes. The subconscious world view will say, "I thought I *handled* that already! What's wrong with me? Life is pure misery." The superconscious world view will say, "Wow! This must be another layer of the puzzle I hadn't seen! What's this one all about? I'll just be with what's happening, love it, and see how it turns around." You're learning slowly how the power of your choices can shorten your periods of distress.

Transforming a Problem with Love

List something you don't like about yourself, something you'd like to get rid of. Close your eyes, get centered, and imagine the thing you don't like. Maybe it's your fat stomach or a pushy boss. Visualize the person or object surrounded with the diamond light of your soul; the light is loving and understanding, fresh and invigorating. Let the energy build and slowly enter into the object of your dislike. As the energy is absorbed, the person or thing you don't like will change, perhaps getting more exaggerated, transforming eventually into its ideal self. Watch the process. Perhaps something else is hiding inside. As energy begins to move, what does the person or object really want to become? What is its real gift to you? Why is it in your life, drawing your attention? Receive the benefit it has to offer you.

No one said the hero's journey is easy, but you only have to attend to one thing at a time and take one step at a time. As subconscious blocks arise from the netherworld, to fully clear them you must only reexperience them and see them freshly. Listen to their hidden message, perceive them completely, and you will, in effect, "digest" them. In "re-viewing" them, adopt an attitude of neutrality and look from your heart through the eyes of the divine Knower.

How to Transform Negativity into Insight

Let's say your mate just broke an agreement and stood you up at a social function that was crucial for your career success. You are furious; many upsetting emotions churn within you. Intuition? Inspired guidance? What's that? How can you release this debilitating negativity and return to the center so you can see clearly?

1. Abandon the victim/attack mode. Your mind is probably caught in a whirlwind of accusations and desire for punishment: "He let me down. Wait till I get home. I'm going to tear him to shreds. How could he do this to me?" Or it's turning the hurt and anger inward onto you: "Well, I'm never important enough, never visible enough. I won't get the promotion, and I'll probably lose my marriage because no one really cares about me. I must be incompetent or unexciting." Stop blaming! Catch yourself in the middle of this thought pattern. Suspend your thoughts for a moment: "Oh, I'm in it again."

2. Let the experience be the way it is. Let other people do what they do. Let yourself be the way you are right now. "It's OK, even perfect, the way it is—even if I don't like it, even if I can't see why it's appropriate yet."

3. Own your reaction and make a factual description. "Joe said he'd be here at 7:30; he never showed up. I feel humiliated, afraid I'll be judged negatively by my colleagues, enraged at his lack of support for me and the fact that he lied. Maybe something harmful has happened to him. I am angry, hurt, afraid, jealous."

4. Get centered and remember who you are. Bring your attention fully into the now, into your body. Tell yourself, "I exist" and "I'm full of divine presence." If you need to, ask for help, either from another person or from spiritual sources. Remember you've chosen to grow, face fear, and integrate your soul's knowledge. Say to yourself, "I'm bigger than my emotions," "Some part of me knows how to heal this situation," and "I am one with the flow of grace in the world." Reclaim your authority. You determine the quality of your experiences.

5. Unlabel your experience and go deeper. What's really happening below the words *anger, hurt, afraid,* and *jealous?* Notice the simple animal-like sensations in your body. Let your body do what it's doing. If you're

In mysticism, knowledge cannot be separated from a certain way of life which becomes its living manifestation. To acquire mystical knowledge means to undergo a transformation; one could even say that the knowledge is the transformation.

Fritjof Capra

uncomfortable, your body is probably trying to balance itself the best way it knows. Give it a chance. Be with your body. Breathe. Don't try to escape. Feel the nuances of energy jiggling and moving. Describe the sensations to yourself: "I feel a contraction in my solar plexus, a shaking in my heart; my throat is tight, I want to cry, I want to run."

6. *Enter the physical sensations with your attention.* Bring your soul's wisdom and love into the physical sensation and let each expansion or contraction show you what it wants to do next. Does the contraction in your solar plexus want to release outward, through dancing, mingling, or going outside for a break? Maybe the tension in your chest wants to flow up into your throat so you can say something out loud? Extend each sensation to its next natural expression.

7. *Notice images, ideas, and associations that spring to mind.* As energy starts to move, it may release information about previous similar experiences stored in your subconscious. Catch the connections. Maybe your mother lost you at a shopping center when your were five, or you were betrayed by a friend ten years ago. Become aware of what comes to you as a curiosity or motive now, and follow it naturally.

8. *Ask for understanding.* Pay attention to your heart and ask for its gentle wisdom. How is this experience giving you back a part of yourself? How can it empower you and others? What were you depending on—that you had thought was outside yourself—which you can now see is within you? Instead of trying to change other people, how can you improve yourself? Did your mate give you an opportunity to express yourself uniquely by not showing up? Were you forced to shine as a result? Did you learn how flexible you could be?

9. *Validate yourself for turning the situation around.* Notice how it feels to come from a place of understanding, healing, and generosity rather than a place of punishment and blame. Recognize the quality of your body when it is one with your soul so you can return to it more quickly in the future. Your body will soon learn to prefer the new, open way of being to the old, contracted way.

The "Wilderness Experience"

You've faced many layers of chaos and confusion and have learned from them. You are now a relatively wise and loving person. The balance

REMEMBER
▼
You never give yourself more than you can handle.

of power has shifted—you're much more superconscious than sub-conscious, and it's easy for you to remember to choose the intuitive way. Now the last stage of the enlightenment process is set to occur.

You've reached the bottom of the bucket of the subconscious mind. What's left are your powerful baseline beliefs about the negative nature of human beings, physical life, and God. Here are the deep, most dreaded experiences of human suffering, our root assumptions about the physical world as a place of sacrifice and agony. And these beliefs are inter-connected in a snare of ignorance. Like a fishing net, when you lift one edge to start to deal with it, the entire thing comes out of the sea. The intensity of these deep emotions hits you like a heavy swell.

When water gets caught in habitual whirlpools, dig a way out through the bottom of the ocean.

Rumi

Talking to Your Shadow Self

1. Sit quietly, close your eyes, breathe evenly, and bring your attention into the center of your head. Imagine that the inside of your body is a shadowy field of energy. Let it gradually move outward, through your back, inch by inch, until it is separated from you. Let your shadow self stand directly behind you. Become aware of your hearing, and let your shadow self talk to you in a seductive or an accusatory voice. What does it say? What does it seem to want?

2. Turn around and face your shadow self. What does it look like? Say to it, "Show me something about myself that I haven't wanted to know." Let it change shape, become various per-sonas, hold out tantalizing objects or scenes. Describe what happens.

3. Ask your shadow self to show you the images it holds about the worst possible scenarios for your life. Write them down. Then ask it for the "gift in the garbage," the hidden lesson you might learn if you followed each scenario to its outcome. (Hint: If you learn the lessons, you won't need to live through the situations.)

4. Have a dialogue with your shadow self. Ask it what information it can access. Then ask it what it needs from you. Ask it, "How will I know when you want to talk to me?" Describe the cue(s) your subconscious will give you when it wants you to stop and listen to something important. Come back and open your eyes.

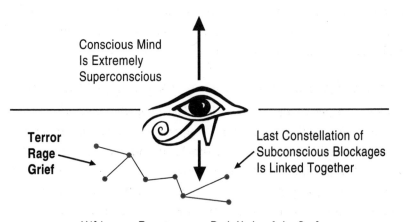

Conscious Mind
Is Extremely
Superconscious

Terror
Rage
Grief

Last Constellation of
Subconscious Blockages
Is Linked Together

Wilderness Experience, or Dark Night of the Soul:
The Last Remnants of the Subconscious Rise

This last confrontation with the subconscious is something that every seeker passes through, and it occurs because the power of our love can now summon and match our most intense fear beliefs. When Jesus was near the completion of his process, he went to the desert, where without external distractions he faced the demons of the underworld. He was taunted and tortured relentlessly during his "wilderness experience." Similarly, Buddha under the bodhi tree was beset by the devil Mara and his minions who tried to humiliate, ridicule, seduce, and destroy him.

These are the hell realms where we encounter terrifying images of cruelty, incarceration, and apathy. It is here where we feel an atomic blast of rage at the insanity of the world, the apparent uselessness of life, the frustration of being limited by the physical body. And we also encounter oceanic grief and despair: the uncried tears of ages of disappointment and unexpressed love. We realize we have wasted so much precious time in anger, fear, and pain.

The more we indulge in the intensity of these insane baseline emotions, the more we will be thrown around. There is no way to pass through to the end of this kind of grief—it has no end. There is no way to hate enough to finish with hatred—it feeds on itself. But you can only keeping raging, grieving, and hating for so long before a realization dawns: "Hey, I don't have to keep doing this! What am I resisting? It's *me* who's choosing to be frustrated. Nature isn't frustrated. Nature isn't grieving. Nature isn't full of hatred. I forgot that I'm an eternal soul, and harmony is my natural state!" Finally! You have entered the last phase of the process.

Phase Three: Being Consciously Superconscious

Now you get it: the cosmic joke! The final *aha! Everything's been working perfectly all along.* Even if life appears horrendous, you sense the deeper compassion and natural order balancing the flow of creation. You were pretending something was wrong and making yourself suffer. You were creating dramas to entertain yourself but getting caught in them. You thought you owned the concept of pain, that your suffering was worse than anyone else's. You were taking it all personally and very seriously.

But now you've awakened from your self-imposed hypnosis. You know now that to end suffering you must work entirely with your own viewpoint; you have only to stop wrestling with ignorant ideas and be your true self. Trust that you are 100 percent love. Finally you have no more doubt. You have the power to choose superconsciousness as your real identity—permanently. Intuition now *is* your way of life.

But do you suddenly become so light and clear that you ascend in a poof of spontaneous combustion? Or disappear during your sleep, carried off by angels? Chances are you'll be here tomorrow, looking much the same but feeling a whole lot simpler. Zen practitioners say, "Before enlightenment, chop wood, carry water. After enlightenment, chop wood, carry water."

You usually hear one last gasp from the dying subconscious blocks, however. Once you've released your personal ownership of pain and suffering, your physical body must also "get it" at a visceral level. Our genetics have evolved over generations, steeped in a culture of fear beliefs and contracted emotions. The cellular consciousness of your body is conditioned to manifest itself continually according to these "rules" of limitation and to expect events such as illness, degeneration, and death.

As you move permanently into the superconscious world view, your body will send up a flag. "Wait a minute!" it shrieks. "Can you really mean it that I am supposed to live without contraction, self-protection, and fear?

⚡
Fear and pain are not my
true nature.

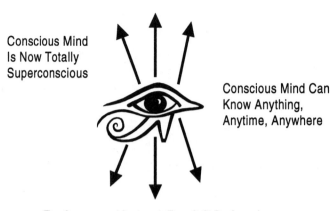

Conscious Mind
Is Now Totally
Superconscious

Conscious Mind Can
Know Anything,
Anytime, Anywhere

The Conscious Mind with True Self-Realization

Are you really convinced about this? I've always done it this way; do you want me to change permanently?" You may experience one last test, a reenactment of a situation you thought you were finished with. Just be patient and choose to flow again.

Mirra Alfassa, otherwise known as "the Mother," who headed Sri Aurobindo's ashram after his death, spent many of her ninety-five years penetrating the consciousness of her cells in search of a new form of enlightenment. She said that "the physical consciousness—the one that regulates the cells' functioning—is used to exertion, struggling, misery, defeat; it is so accustomed to it that it's quite universal."[1] In her experience the biggest problem in allowing "the force, the light, the power" to penetrate the cells is that their ignorance first has to be dissolved, and the only way to accomplish this is through repeated contact with the superconscious realm. At first the cells resist, but eventually they cooperate. Keep running love and trust through your body. Soon even your cells will believe this is their true nature.

Part of using your intuition to dissolve blockages and create illumination is learning to feel and sense the subtle vibrations in your body, to allow the nonverbal information from the cells to move progressively up through your spine and brain until it becomes conscious and verbal.

In Part 2 you will learn to pay attention to these intangible intuitive cues coming from your body, encourage them to flow, and begin to interpret them.

BE INTUITIVE TODAY!
Tune in to people at a distance.

Think of three friends you haven't talked to in a long time. Sit quietly, close your eyes, and picture each person in front of you, one at a time. Receive impressions about their facial expression and body language. What sort of mood are they in? In your imagination, ask them what they're concerned about. Ask what they need help with. Let them show you a symbol that represents an issue they're dealing with. Write down your impressions in your journal.

Now call each one and casually bring up the information you received intuitively, working it into the conversation: "I'm doing this experiment with my intuition, and I got these impressions when I tuned in to you. Does any of it mean anything to you?" Make a note of any "hits" you had.

Direct Writing Questions

Sit down with your journal and get quiet. Empty your mind. Pick one of the following questions and be with it for a few moments. Ask that you be able to receive creative insights from your deepest level of truth. Let the question serve as a magnet. Allow the first word to pop into your mind. Write it down. Let another word pop in. Write it down. Let words proceed forth, without judging them, without second-guessing where the answer is going. Don't jump ahead. Don't stop and read back over what you've written until the writing stops of its own accord. Helpful techniques: write as your own soul, innocent child, or future self; address your personality in the second person, by name; don't try to be too significant! Let your handwriting change shape. Change your speed and your rhythm, or write with your opposite hand.

- Complete an incomplete project, deliver an undelivered communication, keep an agreement, release an expectation about yourself or another. Write about why you stalled so long. How do you feel now?

- Write as your body/emotions: (1) "What kind of situations create stress for me?" (2) "Where I feel stress is _____. It feels like (use all the senses to describe) _____." (3) "I get stressed because my subconscious mind believes that _____." (4) "I deal with stress in an unhealthy way by _____." (5) "I release stress in a healthy way by _____."

- Write as one of your fear beliefs: (1) "I can't let _____ happen because _____." (2) "I need help with _____." (3) "I need to understand _____."

- List your physical, emotional, and mental "weaknesses" from the view of your subconscious mind. Write from the viewpoint of the weakness: "What am I temporarily doing for my personality? What am I preventing my personality from knowing about my true self?"

- "What do I need to understand about the time I was betrayed, lost a loved one, failed to achieve what I thought I wanted, etc.?"

- "Where am I right now in my own process of enlightenment? What have I accomplished? What are my next few lessons? What should I pay attention to now?"

- "If I were enlightened right now, how would my life be different? What would I want to do?"

Part 2

Accessing Subtle Information

In the second phase of the intuition
development process you'll learn to access
and interpret intuitive information from
the intangible realms. You'll learn techniques for
becoming receptive and neutral, and for
maximizing your sensitivity to subtle information.
You'll learn to use your mind to travel
into your body, where intuitive information
first makes itself known.

5

Becoming Aware of the Invisible

There is a quiet place in us below our hip personality that is connected to our breath, our words, and our death. . . . This place exists as we exist, here on the earth. It just is. This is where the best writing comes from.

Natalie Goldberg

The Importance of Environment

I was in Lincoln, Nebraska, to teach a weekend workshop on intuition development. It had been a week of severe late-spring thunderstorms. The rivers were overflowing their banks and the cornfields, yet unplanted, were sitting in lakes of water. The weather was affecting people, creating vague feelings of oppressiveness, and overwhelming them with the invisible currents of the subconscious mind. Heavy issues lurked below the surface of people's personalities. After counseling people all week, I could attest to the fact that many residents were worn down and starting to personally leak and flood. I would never have chosen it as the catalyst, but the hypersensitivity caused by the weather lended itself perfectly to opening intuition.

My group and I were working in the back room of a spiritual bookstore. I had come early to arrange the space so it would help the students stay alert and open. How the energy flows and how the insights come are determined largely by the cohesion of details in the environment we occupy. Each object in its right place; light, air, color, sound, temperature adjusted just so. Context helps shape content. Intuition is fluid and highly personal. To learn about it, you must be open, relaxed, informal, and

Chapter 5 presents techniques to prepare your consciousness to be both fertile and alert, relaxed yet anticipatory. The most beautiful song can sound cacophonous when played on an untuned instrument. So it is with intuitive knowing. To get the most accurate results it pays to take time developing the exquisite attention of the spiritual warrior. This chapter teaches you to find a neutral, calm focus and to improve your sensitivity to subtle, seemingly invisible information.

trusting. To encourage the emergence of intuition, the front of your body should be unobstructed. Nothing around you must remind you too much of the square structured world of logic. You must feel safe and connected to your body, your classmates, the instructor, the surrounding field of energy. Then your mind can extend naturally to new realms of knowledge.

We began the class, chairs in a semicircle, no podium between us, door closed to the bustle of the bookstore. Even so, I knew the room, which doubled as overflow inventory space, presented a challenge. Before we started I raised the issue of the environment.

"Do you feel 100 percent comfortable in this room? Are you sitting exactly where you want to sit?" A couple people scooted around. "Get quiet now and notice what parts of the environment are drawing even the smallest part of your attention."

"The ceiling is very low, and these exposed air ducts are protruding down toward me," one woman said. "They're ugly and they worry me vaguely, like I might stand up and hit my head."

Another woman said, "There are no windows. And the lights are kind of blue and cold, and they're buzzing."

"Yes, and the roof is leaking into those plastic dishes—I know we need to leave them where they are, but I feel I need to check if they should be emptied."

"I'm aware of clutter in the corner of the room," someone else added, "and the concrete block walls and the stains on the carpet. It doesn't feel very cozy."

"Exactly right," I said. "We're dealing with a space that's challenging, to say the least. Each of these environmental oddities will absorb some of your attention if you're not alert. And to the extent that you don't notice, you won't be fully available for learning." About that time, to add to everything else, the heating for the bookstore came on, and we all laughed as I tried to talk above the din of the furnace.

Becoming Conscious of Your Environment

Write about your house. What area of your home is your most sacred space? What do you do there that helps you feel centered and aware? How could you make your sanctuary more conducive to

⚡

I can be aware of two opposites at once.

intuitive knowing? Which area(s) of your home do you avoid? Which areas are gathering dust and clutter? How could you revitalize those areas of your home?

Your Body as "Body Guard"

I explained that as soon as you wake up, your antennae rise and your reptile brain is on the alert for clues about how to navigate the potentially dangerous waters of your day. Your body constantly picks up data from the environment and reacts unconsciously to it to keep you safe and alive. As you commute to work, for example, your body takes readings on the emotional tones of the people driving near you down the freeway: "Red alert!" it warns you. "Woman in lane number two, sad because her husband left her. Should we be concerned? Man ahead, talking on cellular phone and combing hair at same time. Are we in danger?" But perhaps you're spaced out, thinking about what you have to do when you arrive at work or listening intently to a radio talk show.

Your body is trying to get your attention. "Are these situations critical? Should we change lanes, slow down, speed up?" But you're not receiving the message because your mind is elsewhere. Tension builds, maybe in your stomach or between your shoulders. The red light flashes faster. Then at work, in a meeting, you're having a hard time paying attention. Your body again is sending you signals: "These fluorescent lights are making a persistent, high-pitched scream. It sounds like someone in distress. Do we need to do something about it? Fred, on your left, is daydreaming about his vacation in the Rockies coming up in two days. Those images look intriguing. Should we peek into his fantasy? Susan, across the table from you, really wants to express herself but is getting frustrated because she can't get a word in edgewise. She's not paying attention. Can we count on her if something unexpected happens?" Your telepathic, empathic body is feeling restless. So many things need answers, but you're doodling on your yellow pad. The red light is flashing more intensely.

At lunch with your colleagues, your body gives you even more data. The waitress is short with you because the manager changed her hours. "Should we be concerned about her anger?" your body wants to know. But you gloss over it, embroiled in a lively discussion about your current

There are voices which we hear in solitude, but they grow faint and inaudible as we enter into the world.

Ralph Waldo Emerson

project. By late afternoon, you realize you're tense. You've got a pounding headache starting in the back of your neck and wrapping around your temples; you're bordering on a foul mood. You feel like having a drink after work. What happened? You started out quite cheerful this morning.

You haven't been listening to your own information. By this time you have a huge backlog of environmental data, much of it with emotional overtones, and it's stored in the reptile brain, just waiting to pop through into your conscious mind. Some cues you've picked up have probably triggered your adrenal gland reflex as well, and for hours your muscles have been poised for fight or flight. You need a debriefing.

Physical Needs Absorb Attention

Coming back to our seminar room, I explained that even the slightest quandary about things in our immediate environment can cause discomfort for the body. If you subconsciously feel you might be in danger because you need to make a decision about a faint screaming sound you hear, no matter that it's just the fluorescent lights, you will develop a mild tension. If your body is overwhelmed because it's trying to discriminate between what the teacher is saying, what two students are whispering in the corner, and the sound of the barely audible music in the next room, you may build up subliminal frustration—which might make you irritable, which might influence your attitude, which could prevent you from learning. If the temperature in the room is too cold or too hot, or if you're hungry, your body will attend to its survival before it allows any other information to flow. First and foremost, your body must feel safe.

What do we do with the buzzing lights, the clutter in the corner, the dripping ceiling, the din of the furnace? The first step is to recognize consciously what makes you feel uncomfortable and distracted. If you can, change the environment to suit your preferences. We moved our chairs, unified the piles of clutter, and asked that the furnace be turned off until our lunch break. But if you can't change the environment, admit out loud what's bothering you. Name it. Tell your body it's OK: "Yes, body, I'm aware of the water dripping through the ceiling. But it's not overflowing from the pan. We can be in this room with water leaking and still be able to pay attention to the class." Include the environmental oddity, and let it be the way it is. Then consciously recenter yourself on the task at hand. There is room enough for you *and* the drip.

Taking Responsibility for Your Own Comfort

Make a commitment to be deeply comfortable today. Either change your environment wherever you go to the extent possible, or change your attitude about what bothers you. Name the things that are absorbing your attention unconsciously. Notice tension that builds up in your body and do what you can to release it. Write about how your day went, how you felt when you took responsibility for your own comfort. Did your productivity improve? How about your mood?

Name the Problem

Just naming the problem can often dissolve it: "I just realized that I'm irritable because I haven't eaten anything but a piece of toast today!" or "I can't concentrate because three hours ago Frank made some offhand comment about my outfit, and I realize it triggered some pretty deep feelings of self-doubt. I've been stuck on it ever since."

Your body just wants to know what to do next. When you name a situation, you bring it from the recesses of your reptile brain into your conscious mind. Now you can make a choice. Change it or live with it. Your body experiences a big sense of relief. You finally got the message. Now you can let it know what you want to do. When you clear backlogs of environmental data by naming things, your body opens and learns to trust you. Then you can ask your body to bring you just the crucial information: "Yes, the guy in the next car really is ready to blow. Get out of here fast!" When you can consciously receive critical survival information, your body can bring you more refined data—useful insights that pertain to learning, personal guidance, spiritual growth, and creativity.

REMEMBER
▼
You can change the world or you can change your attitude about the world.

Softening Your Awareness: The Feminine Mind

Once you've made peace with your surroundings and assured your body that it will be safe, it's time to activate your intuition. The process starts with a shift into softness. First, though, think how you feel when

Mysticism is the art of union with reality.

Evelyn Underhill

you're concentrating on pushing hard to meet a deadline and do an excellent job. Your brow is probably furrowed, you're bent to your task, and all distracting input has been shut out. This is what I call the "masculine mind," because to accomplish specific goals, both men and women must use dynamic male energy. We're in our left-brained masculine mind so often that we've come to identify it as normal. We forget there is an equally powerful, complementary state of consciousness that is tension-free: the "feminine mind."

Here's how you can tell if you're using the feminine mind: (1) you're not in a hurry; (2) you don't have an opinion; (3) you don't need to change anything; (4) if it changes, that's OK, too; (5) you're willing to wait and see; and (6) you're content with yourself. How often do you intentionally enter this state of mind?

Lao Tsu says, "Be aware of your masculine nature; / But by keeping the feminine way, / You shall be to the world like a canyon, / Where the Virtue eternal abides, / And go back to become as a child." Intuition starts when the masculine mind stops. Since we push ourselves relentlessly to maintain focus and goal-orientation, when it's time to shift into softness, it often happens unconsciously. Something just comes over us and makes us space out and temporarily turn into zombies. With so many deadlines to keep, the unconscious shift toward intuitive knowing can at first feel like sabotage or the early onset of senility! We can avoid this blurry "nobody's home" feeling by becoming conscious of the stages of feminine awareness. Next time you're wound too tight or you're too far ahead of yourself, try the following techniques.

Be Present and Notice What Is

Relax your brain-mind, then draw your attention back to your body, redirecting it to start noticing details of your current physical state. Follow your breath in and out. Come inside your skin. When your awareness is inside your body, you'll also be in the present moment. Slow down enough to describe in simple terms the things you feel, as though you're taking inventory. "I notice I'm sitting in my desk chair; there's tension between my shoulder blades and my feet are crossed at the ankles. I notice a slight nervous feeling at the base of my sternum. I am hungry. I can feel my pulse in the bottoms of my feet." By noticing things, you connect with your world. Connectedness spawns intuition.

Noticing

In your journal, make a "Five Senses" list with separate pages for Sight, Sound, Smell, Touch, and Taste. List your most interesting internal and external perceptions today according to which sense was dominant. Did you become aware of someone at a restaurant because of a strong perfume? Did you decide not to eat all your lunch because of a strange flavor in your chow mein? Keep listing sense perceptions for the duration of the course.

Include and Expand

Move out to the layer of reality beyond your body and start noticing and describing the details you find there. Imagine that your awareness is a big ball. Become aware of things three feet in front of you, in back of you, above and below you, and to both sides: "I observe that the air is slightly stuffy and warm. The color of the light is pinkish. I see the pencil and papers to my left, the bookshelves against the far wall. I'm aware of the smell of coffee coming from the next room and the buzz of the computer." Include more and more space into your "movie bubble," letting your awareness extend out ten feet, thirty feet, one hundred feet: "I'm aware of the trees out in the backyard and the birds singing. I notice the sun is now at a low angle. I am aware of the town I live in, the river nearby, the fields at the edge of town." Everything you include in your awareness becomes part of the bigger you, part of the resources you have access to. Say to yourself, "Everything I am aware of is in me, of me, by me, and for me."

Mystic Alan Watts writes, "I am unusually aware that everything I am sensing is also my body—that light, color, shape, sound, and texture are terms and properties of the brain conferred upon the outside world. I am not looking *at* the world, not confronting it; I am knowing it by a continuous process of transforming it into myself, so that everything around me, the whole globe of space, no longer feels away from me, but in the middle." [1]

The new physics says, in effect, that it is impossible not to be involved.

Lyall Watson

Be with What Is: Don't Vote on It!

You don't need an opinion right now. You aren't required to make a decision, to like or dislike what's happening. No action must be taken. Let it be. You are what you are. The situation is what it is. When you're not busy making a mark on your environment it just might have a chance to educate *you* about a few things. Keep company with each object, creature, and situation you notice.

Find Similarities

The feminine mind always sees oneness. It starts by actively looking for how things are alike: "What do the father and son have in common? Where do the two solutions overlap? What's the connection between the old lady and cats? What is it in me that draws me to Japan?" It is useful to think in metaphors and similes: "Jennifer's personality is like a sunflower. All the world's a stage. Her comment hit me like a ton of bricks. He's a real bull-dog. Katy's hair looks like a shining silver bowl." Each connecting link opens new pathways through your awareness. And every new way you can perceive commonality brings you more deeply into compassion. (Secret: Compassion produces the highest, most efficient level of intuition.)

Seeing Similarities

Make a "Similarities" list. For the duration of the course, write down the ways you see interconnections between seemingly disparate things as well as interesting metaphors that occur to you.

I'm sure you agree, that beauty is the only thing worth living for.

Agatha Christie

Look for Beauty

The feminine mind revels in appreciating what it perceives and how exquisitely conceived our world is. Cultivate wondrousness. Let yourself become amazed at the beauty of a dragonfly, or the intricacy of how your hand works, or the awesome simplicity of how the soul reveals itself when you look deeply into someone's eyes. Appreciate the patterns in the clouds or the papers in magnificent disarray on your desk. Things don't have to be "good" or "useful." Vincent van Gogh said, "It is very beautiful here, if one only has an open and simple eye without any beams in it. But if one has that it is beautiful everywhere." When was the last time you experienced awe?

Be Willing to Be Amused

Every irritating or boring situation can turn funny without warning. If you can find a way to prompt a chuckle out of your experience or tickle yourself when you're in the midst of being dead serious, the feminine mind can break through with an intuitive revelation. Once when I was morose and having a difficult time finding the way out of my bogged-down feelings, I turned a corner I pass every day. As I sped around the bend, in my peripheral vision I saw a man juggling an armload of strange black "sticks" that were poking into the air and waving wildly. It was an unexpected image that popped a hole through my mood. As I looked more closely, I saw that the man held his black Labrador retriever, upside down, cradling and cuddling her lovingly. Their wiggly giddiness rushed into me, and I broke out laughing. I had been touched by a "real moment." Within seconds I could feel my heart again.

When you're inventorying your environment, especially when you're looking for entertainment, even the way a housefly washes its face or a mockingbird brashly rattles off its repertoire of songs or a checkout clerk talks to himself as he works can be the source of a small, private pleasure.

Express Gratitude

As you observe the world expanding in infinite complexity and beauty, you realize there will always be more to know. You feel the power of a greater wisdom that has brought you and your ever-increasing identity and life experience into being. The feminine mind brings you into a sense of beneficence and providence. As you experience this fully, you may weep, overflow with praises, or beam with feelings of ecstasy. Whenever I lose my direction in life, when I find myself complaining or when life seems dull, I make a gratitude list. If I can feel the depth of my gratitude for each item on the list, a glow spreads through my body, and I fill up with a positive attitude, renewed humor, and vigor.

REMEMBER
▼
*Everything is interesting
if you're interested.*

Heighten Your Sensitivity

The more you consciously notice something, the more you'll learn about it and the more energy you'll feel. Sensitivity increases in proportion to your ability to attend to things. What you will discover is that the knowledge and energy was always there. You weren't aware of it because your mind was elsewhere. *Attention reveals energy:* As you hold attention on a part of your body, it may suddenly flood with vitality. *Attention reveals information and knowledge:* You might as quickly understand what foods you need to eat and why, or how deep breathing might alleviate your migraine headache.

The Hand Scan

Hold your hand in front of you and look at the palm. Put your full attention on the top segment of your forefinger. Notice the texture of the skin, the pattern of the fingerprint ridges. Under the skin, feel the nerves tingling, visualize the tiny capillaries wending their way toward the cells, feel the blood moving, the tissues alive with activity. Get a sense of the bone running down through the center, of the nail embedded in the flesh of the other side. Can you feel the joint?

Move to the second segment of the forefinger and include it in your awareness; put your full attention on it. Notice everything, as you did with the top segment. Then move down and include the bottom segment. Your finger is probably tingling and vibrating right now, more noticeably than any of the others.

Next, scan each of the other fingers in the same way, bringing them into your awareness. Do this slowly. Now scan the whole palm.

Quickly compare the energized hand to the unenergized hand. Hold them in front of you and notice the difference in the tingling electrical energy. Now bring the second hand quickly up to the level of the first by including it in your awareness and putting full attention on it. If you would like to transmit this energy into a part of your body that feels tired, simply place your hands on that area and the energy will disperse.

Focusing Your Awareness: The Warrior's Attention

After you've softened and become neutral and sensitive, it's time to bring things into sharper focus. You are now ready to reengage your masculine attention, but ever so slightly, as you would tune in a radio station with the fine-tuning dial. When you activate your warrior's attention, you become like a samurai, alert yet relaxed, prepared yet not initiating needless action. It is now that you establish a clear intent to be in tune with the flow of power and knowledge coming toward you and from you.

⚡

I know what I need
to know right when I need
to know it.

360-Degree Sensitivity

Turn on your 360-degree awareness; open the eyes in the back of your head. Become so sensitive that, like a deer in the forest, you can feel the subtle impress of the hunter's attention as he stalks you. An ancient Zen master, Takuan, describes how the mind of the martial artist functions. In two short essays, "No Gap" and "Mind Like a Spark," he talks about the warrior's fluidity in action, explaining that the spontaneous responsiveness of the warrior is not related as much to quickness of action as it is to immediacy of attention and freedom of mind. He says, "If your mind stops on the sword your opponent is swinging at you, a gap opens up; and in that gap your action falters. If there is no gap between your opponent's striking sword and your action, the sword of the adversary will become your sword. A mind like a spark means the state of mind where there is no gap. When flint is struck, sparks fly at once. . . . There is no interval for the mind to linger. . . . If attention lingers, your mind is taken over by others." [2] Keep your mind rounded and extended evenly through space.

Engaged Indifference

Some years ago I took an intensive training at the Mind Center in Palo Alto, California, with Dr. James Hardt and Foster Gamble, who were pioneering the application of sophisticated biofeedback techniques for success in the corporate world. During this training I sat in a dimly lit cubicle, carpeted on all sides, my head hooked up to several electrodes. I watched a video monitor that gave me computerized feedback on how well I was doing at creating and maintaining a high level of alpha waves in various areas of my brain. During the discussion session after one brain "work-out," Dr. Hardt described the alpha state as "engaged indifference."

He also explained that it was Zen monks who had had the highest test results in controlling not only their alpha state but the deeper theta and delta states as well, not to mention the amazing coherence they could produce between the two brain hemispheres. The Zen master Takuan makes a similar comment: "If you don't put your mind anywhere, it will pervade your whole body fully, spreading through your whole being, so that when you need hands it works your hands, when you need feet it works your feet, when you need eyes it works your eyes. Since it is present whenever you need it, it makes the functions you need possible. If you fix the mind in one place, it will be taken up by that place and thus deficient in function." [3]

The Warrior's Walk

You can begin anywhere, indoors or out. Stand and become alert yet relaxed. Don't fix your attention on anything. Notice everything around you in a full circle. When you feel the current flow into you, let yourself begin to move. Let your body experience the natural shape of the surroundings, using all your senses. Do not describe your experience to yourself. As you pass by the protruding corner of a hallway and change directions, notice the different impressions the old and new space make on you. Feel the impact of the sharp line of the corner coming toward you.

As you walk, notice what your back is aware of. Can you feel an object in back of you when it's ten feet away, five feet away, one foot away? Let yourself feel simultaneous attraction toward and repulsion from objects and directions. Where does the movement itself want to go? If you're walking down a busy street, notice how your body responds to people passing by, to mailboxes, lampposts, and storefronts.

Expect nothing; live frugally on surprise.

Alice Walker

Stop the Internal Dialogue

Carlos Castaneda tells us how his teacher Don Juan insisted that the essential feature of the spiritual path was shutting off the internal dialogue. By doing this, we disengage what he calls the "first attention," or the attention of the external common sense. He says that once the internal dialogue is stopped, we stop the world of phenomena. To Carlos he says, "We maintain our world with our internal talk. . . . We renew it, we kindle it with life, we uphold it with our internal talk. Not only that, but we choose our paths as we talk to ourselves. Thus we repeat the same choices over and over until the day we die, because we keep repeating the same internal talk."[4] By stopping our habitual internal description of ourselves and the world, we can open to endless new possibilities. Don Juan says that when the warrior stops the world, he must be prepared for a monumental jolt. The world of direct knowing suddenly opens to you.

Psychologist Frances Vaughan says something similar, placing emphasis on the importance of a regular meditative practice: "The silent mind, cultivated in many different forms of meditation, is the matrix of intuition. When you are in touch with the stillpoint at the center of your being, there is no need to use imagery or verbal exercises to activate intuition. It flows by itself, unimpeded by fears or preoccupations."[5]

Stopping the Internal Dialogue

Notice your internal conversation. Stop in mid-sentence and go blank. Within a few seconds your internal commentator will make more comments, living out another private stage play with friends, enemies, or both. When you catch it happening, go blank again. Exhale.

Once you can repeatedly enter the spaciousness (even if you can't hold it very long), listen for the silence. At first you may hear a buzzing or be aware of a subtle vibration caused by your physiological organism. Simply intend to listen past that vibration and find the silence, the velvety quiet place of origin. When you first touch it, you may bounce off. Find it and enter it again. Learn to tolerate it, merge with it, become it, desire it.

When you are able to spend timeless time in the silent place, you will be able to trust wholeheartedly the ideas and desires you find occurring to you immediately after you've been there. These perceptions are coming from your direct knowing, from your intuitive voice. Take note.

Set Your Intention

From the sharp-yet-soft focus of the warrior's attention, determine your intent. And certainly the first goal of direct knowing, as Castaneda's teacher Don Juan repeatedly says, is to be impeccable. This implies a deep intent to maintain an alignment with a higher truth and to create integrity in even the smallest details of your daily life. One of the greatest statements of intent came from Jesus, who advised us to treat others as we would like to be treated.

Begin all action consciously from silence. Do you want to start with your right foot first or your left? When Castaneda was learning to navigate volitionally in the dream state, he discovered that nothing could happen without clear intent. He says that "she ordered me to stand up by willing my movement. . . . I tried every conceivable way to get up. I failed. . . . I realized that there was no procedure involved, that in order to move I had to intend my moving at a very deep level. In other words, I had to be utterly convinced that I wanted to move, or perhaps it would be more accurate to say that I had to be convinced that I needed to move."[6] As we begin to use our intuition, we might look more deeply within to find our body's intent to have greater insight and truth, and our "need to move," before rushing forth without cohesiveness.

I wish that life should not be cheap, but sacred. I wish the days to be as centuries, loaded, fragrant.

Ralph Waldo Emerson

Doorway Meditation

The next time you approach a doorway, use it as an opportunity to set your intention. Every door is a passage between experiences, between dimensions of awareness. As you enter the arch of a doorway, pause a moment. Enter the feminine mind and the warrior's attention. Let yourself feel the subtle differences between the space you are leaving and the space you are about to enter. Is there a difference in height? Spaciousness? Color? Temperature? Comfort? What was your consciousness like while you were in the space you are now leaving? Feel into the new space. Prepare to enter the new state of awareness, to welcome whatever it holds for you. When the moment is right, step through.

Get Centered

To achieve clarity, to draw your perceptions equally from body and soul, bring your point of attention, your conscious mind, into the geometric center of your head. There a magical spot seems to function as the center of the self. As you hold attention in this electromagnetic center, you will effectively bring mind, body, and spirit together in one place—the here and now. The insights generated from this convening will be both useful and inspirational.

Activating the Electromagnetic Center

Close your eyes. Take a few easy breaths. As you breathe, draw your attention and energy inside your skin. Imagine that you are looking out from behind your eyes. Stop your internal dialogue. Listen to the silence. Now imagine a point in the geometric center of your head, in the middle of your brain between the pituitary and pineal glands. At that imaginary spot, let a tiny pinprick of light break through. Through that white hole, allow the pure, glossy, diamond light of your own soul to emerge and form a tiny crystal ball. Go into that spot and stay there.

Hold your attention on that crystalline seed. Maintain the feeling of the centerpoint. You may feel it as white-hot or maybe cold and pure. Maintain absolute focus. If your mind drifts and you notice internal talk, stop and recenter. Concentrate on strengthening the purity of the diamond light. Nothing in the outer world demands your attention. Live wholly and fully in the electromagnetic center of your brain for one minute, for five minutes, and then for ten minutes per day.

After maintaining concentration on the diamond centerpoint in your midbrain, you may experience two aftereffects. First, since you are bringing attention, which brings energy, into the area of your pituitary and pineal glands, these powerful "master glands" will be energized. As they are tuned up, the entire endocrine system increases in vitality. You will be able to run more energy and have greater understanding. Second, as you

Attention—yes!
That's present!
And present, you see,
makes past and future.

H. H. the Dalai Lama

hold your focus, energy from body and soul is drawn into the brain. When you finish your exercise, you may feel dizzy, "hot-headed," or top-heavy. A simple way to alleviate this feeling is to bend over and shake out your arms and shoulders: imagine energy pouring off the top of your head into the earth. It is possible, if you don't "drain off" after this exercise, to experience a slight headache or to feel disoriented, especially if you get up and take sudden action.

Hold a Focus

To know, speak, and act from truth, you must first attain one-pointedness of attention. Given the nature of the conscious mind—that it is a freely roving point of attention—you need will and skill to achieve true focus. I can't emphasize enough the importance of learning to concentrate. If you've grown up on a diet of television, remote control in hand, you are probably used to seeing life in two-second sound bites, and your attention span is about as big as a gnat. You'll never learn focus from what's available in the consumer marketplace; you'll have to teach it to yourself.

⚡

I can hear the deep silence any time I remember to listen. It's right below the noise.

Following Your Breath

Become aware that your body is breathing. Stop breathing for a moment, either on the inhale or the exhale. Feel your heartbeat. Then continue, either drawing in or pushing out just a few molecules of air; then a few more, and a few more, ultra slowly, using micro-movements of your lungs and abdominal muscles. Continue until you feel you've naturally reached the end of a breath. Stop breathing and feel your heartbeat. Let the breath reverse and incrementally begin to move the other direction. At the natural end of the cycle, see if there are just a few more molecules of oxygen you could either take into your lungs or let out of your lungs before the breath reverses direction. Each time the breath turns, hold still for a moment and feel your heartbeat. On the inhale, visualize molecules of air moving through the thin walls of the lungs into your blood, and on the exhale, out of your nostrils to merge with the fresh air around you.

Watching an Inner Image

Close your eyes. Focus your attention in the center of your head. Breathe consciously. Put your awareness on the inside of your forehead and imagine a small movie screen there. On that screen allow a symbol to appear. For this exercise, let's use a golden triangle. Picture an equilateral, two-dimensional triangle made of golden light. Hold it on the screen in your forehead. Watch it. If the image changes color or shape, return to your original image and hold it again. If it moves or shifts position, simply recenter and watch it again. Let it be a boring golden triangle. Watch it and watch it. Feel it in your forehead. Hold it for five minutes, then try ten minutes.

Practice the "Presence"

You are not alone. Even when no one is near, you can be in silent conversation with the mysterious Presence that exists in your own body, in the air around you, in the glass of the windows, in the leaves of the plants, in the fibers of your clothes, and in the food you eat. An invisible entity pops up to meet you from every atom. You might be comfortable calling it God, or the Creative Force, or as I often do, the Knower. Imagine that there is a loving, wise being who knows who you really are, accepts you, provides for you, and helps spin out the thread of your life experience by maintaining a constant gaze upon you.

Practice becoming aware of being in the Gaze of the Knower, getting all the attention you need, feeling the warmth of a constant companion, a secret "best friend." It only takes a millisecond to notice that the air, for example, is suddenly full of a smiling Presence engaging playfully yet attentively with you.

As I write I sometimes forget to pay attention and unconsciously assume I'm alone, having to think up all these words and meanings out of my limited reservoir of life experience. And yet, when I remember and feel the Presence, I instantly enter a magical kingdom where a force in each key on my keyboard squeals, "Push me! Now push *me*! Now ME!" Characters appear on my computer monitor as if to amuse and amaze me, and just when I run out of something to say, a thought breezes in and I find words appearing one by one.

There is not a moment when I do not feel the presence of a Witness whose eye misses nothing and with whom I strive to keep in tune.

Mahatma Gandhi

Poet David Whyte says, "One of the main apprenticeships a poet serves is the apprenticeship of attention . . . of paying attention to whatever is there . . . and to let [things] be as they are. . . . Attention is actually a live connection to the world. . . . When you have a live connection to the world, you have to live up to the consequences of what that world brings to you; that the world itself changes through attention. Kukai says, 'All things change when we do.'" [7]

Giving Attention and Being Attended To

1. Make a list of three people you know well or casually who intrigue you and write down something you'd like to ask them. Make it a project to ask them your questions. Write about what they say and how their comments may have triggered new insights.
2. Give three people positive feedback. Let your action be spontaneous.
3. Write about the attention you received today. Was it positive or negative? Can you notice the exact moment you are included in the field of someone's perception?

Tibetan lama Chogyam Trungpa says, "The goal of [spiritual] warriorship is to reconnect to the nowness of reality, so that you can go forward without destroying simplicity, without destroying your connection to this earth." [8] Tell yourself often, "I am here, in my body, 100 percent." Actively be with what's around you. Imbue every object with life force and consciousness. Alan Watts observes, "Going indoors I find that all the household furniture is alive. Tables are tabling, pots are potting, wall are walling, fixtures are fixturing—a world of events instead of things." [9] Physicist Nick Herbert relates the story that when his son first discovered the cell model of life, he was astonished: "'Does this mean I'm made out of little animals?' he exclaimed." [10] Everything is alive in its own way and knows about you at a deep level, and you know about it. Make friends with everything you notice. You may be surprised how much guidance you receive when you believe in the wisdom of the world.

Balancing and Unifying Your Body, Mind, and Spirit

If you can learn to be equally physical, mental, *and* spiritual, you will glide into a new kind of unified perception where the invisible will become visible, the intangible will feel real. You'll gain a stunning insight: you'll understand the paradox that you are simultaneously an individual *and* universal in your identity, with no sacrifice to either. I am "Me," and I am "Us." "I" am part of the "Us" and "We" are part of "Me." This allows you to matter-of-factly draw intuitive guidance from broad, mystical sources: from the collective mind of all people, from the planet itself, and from the past and the future.

But how does this state of balance actually feel? When your body, mind, and spirit become one, you'll feel more authentic, more grounded in your personality, and at the same time you'll move in harmony with the currents of action and guidance generated by the collective consciousness. You'll experience your mind as present within and distributed throughout your body, *as* your body, and you'll discover your spirit is inside your body as well and is guiding you. You'll have access to all of yourself in every moment. No longer will you feel you're partial or missing something.

When body, mind, and spirit are unified, when you direct your attention outward, you'll experience life as a unified field of boundless, free-flowing energy and knowledge. You'll feel your identity as something greater than before, a presence that is everywhere, that is inside everything in the world. "You" won't stop at your skin; your body will feel like the nucleus of a cell whose walls you can never reach. Insight will come from everywhere, from all aspects of yourself, all at once. Life will feel familiar, familial, companionable yet brilliantly spontaneous.

How balanced are you right now? Do you use one aspect to the detriment of the other two? Or do you forget to use one of the aspects, causing a lopsidedness in your personality? Develop your underused aspects.

Earth's crammed with Heaven and every common bush afire with God.

Unknown

Balancing Your Body, Mind, and Spirit

1. Write about your most comfortable mode of expression (body, mind, or spirit). Describe the way you make decisions, organize your life, engage in your favorite activities. *Body:* Are you

instinctual, "grounded," movement- and stimulation-oriented; do you like concrete results? *Mind:* Are you skilled with verbal expression, good at analyzing, organizing, measuring, and conceptualizing? *Spirit:* Are you inspired, a visionary, often "not of this world"?

2. Write about your least comfortable (or missing) mode of expression. What do you avoid and why? *Body:* Do you avoid completing things? Are you afraid commitments or possessions might tie you down? Do you dislike details? *Mind:* Would you rather hoe the garden or ride your bike than read and philosophize? Do you avoid planning things? Do you feel uncomfortable with people who talk too much and "analyze everything to death"? Are you unconcerned with the reasons for your actions? *Spirit:* Do you avoid stopping your work and activities and have a hard time letting go and just being? Are you unsure of your purpose? Do you feel that originality and inspiration are lacking in the things you do? Is form more important than content?

3. From seeing which aspects of yourself are most natural and most avoided, which aspects need more development to balance out your nature? (Hint: If you're uncomfortable with your body, you might do something physical using a familiar mode. For example, do something physical in a mental way, such as exercising and measuring your heart rate, building something, or doing yoga postures, or do something physical in a spiritual way, such as free-form dance, tai chi, or hands-on healing. Use the aspects you know to bridge yourself into the underused one or ones. Write about how you could balance yourself.)

REMEMBER

▼

Identifying equally with body, mind, and spirit immediately opens your direct knowing.

To unify the three aspects of your consciousness, you must first merge your mind and body. The mind must come into the here and now and be alert. If you bring your point of awareness inside your physical body and give total attention to your body's reality, the mind and body will become integrated and you won't be able to distinguish them. *When mind and body become one, you'll experience a surprising and magical result: spirit, the third aspect of self, instantly reveals itself as having been present all along, throughout mind and throughout every atom and cell of matter.* So when you merge mind and body, spirit floods through both.

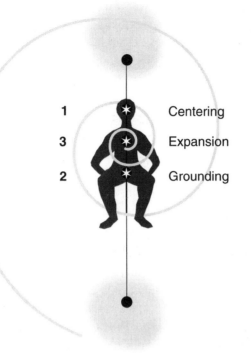

1	Centering
3	Expansion
2	Grounding

The "Three Power Points" Meditation

One of the simplest methods for attaining body-mind-spirit unification is a three-step meditation. In step one, you bring your wandering attention inside your body and place it in its natural "home," the geometric center of your brain. This brings your conscious mind into your body. In the second step, you drop your awareness farther down into your body and establish a conscious link with the earth, integrating the basic life force energy that funds your physical existence. In the third step, you activate your heart, which is the true seat of the soul in the body. As you expand into the world with the soul's awareness, you'll perceive everything from that high, yet neutral, frequency.

I recommend that you use this technique as preparation for any intuitive work. Once you complete the three steps of the meditation, you can continue to meditate quietly or you can begin an intuitive exercise, such as one of the direct writing exercises at the end of this chapter.

The "Three Power Points" Meditation

1. *Centering:* Sit in a chair with your feet on the floor and your palms resting facedown on your thighs. This creates a closed circuit of energy flow within your body. Adjust your posture so your head is level and so you feel evenly balanced between the left and right sides of your body. Close your eyes, breathe evenly, and bring your attention inside your skin. Draw the energy from above your head into the geometric center of your head, and imagine a point in the middle of your brain between the pituitary and pineal glands. At that imaginary spot, let a pinprick of light break through. Through that white hole, allow the pure diamond light of your soul to emerge and form a tiny crystal ball. Go into that spot and stay there. Imagine the glossy light radiating through your brain in all directions, clearing away old thoughts of fear, doubt, and confusion.

2. *Grounding:* Shift your attention now to the base of your spine, and imagine a spot just in front of your tailbone. At that imaginary spot, let a second pinprick of light break through. Through that white hole, allow the pure diamond light of your soul to emerge and form a tiny crystal ball. Feel the vibration, or tingling, which begins in that root energy center. Let the vibration spread in all directions, filling the bottom of your pelvis with a pool of clear light. Imagine that the liquid light becomes "heavy" and starts to drop straight down from the bottom of your spine into the earth below you. Watch it melting through the ground, magnetizing toward the center of the earth, and forming a thick column of shimmering clear light. When the light from the base of your spine merges into the clear light in the center of the earth, you may feel magnetized downward or heavy in your chair, as if it would be difficult to even stand up.

   As soon as the downward connection to the center of the earth is established, an equal flow of energy starts to rise up the column from the earth's core into your body. As you visualize this, relax the bottom of your feet, see them opening, and feel the energy entering your feet and flowing through your ankles, calves, knees, thighs, and hips. As it rises, you may feel tingling or heat. Let the earth energy and knowledge pour into the pool at the base of your spine.

3. *Expansion:* Now bring your attention into your chest, to the heart center. At that spot, let a third pinprick of light break through. Through that white hole, allow the diamond light of your soul to emerge and form a tiny crystal ball. Feel the vibration which begins in that heart energy center. Let the tingling spread in all directions, taking the clarity and compassion of your soul everywhere throughout and beyond your body. As the clear light radiates through you, let it dissolve any darkness, tension, or contractions that might be in your tissues and cells.

　　As the light expands incrementally beyond your skin, include your environment inside the ball of your awareness. Let things around you become familiar and personal. You might say to yourself, "The chair is in me, I am in the chair; the house is in me, I am in the house; the tree is in me, I am in the tree; the city is in me, I am in the city. . . ." Feel the superconscious Presence in everything and look for the light within all matter.

BE INTUITIVE TODAY!

Get impressions about physical places and spaces.

Keep your journal with you so you can jot down notes. Let your body feel relaxed and open as you enter new environments today. Maybe you'll ride in someone else's car or on a bus or train. Maybe you'll go into your garage or out on your porch, or to the market, bank, your colleague's office, or a new restaurant for dinner. In each new environment ask yourself: "What do I know about this place? What kind of thoughts are filling this room? What kind of consciousness does this place naturally facilitate? What happened here before I arrived? Does this space need to be cleaned out energetically? Do I feel safe here? And why?"

Any perception can connect us to reality properly and fully. What we see doesn't have to be pretty, particularly; we can appreciate anything that exists. There is some principle of magic in everything, some living quality. Something living, something real, is taking place in everything.

Chogyam Trungpa

Direct Writing Questions

Sit down with your journal and get quiet. Empty your mind. Pick one of the following questions and be with it for a few moments. Ask that you be able to receive creative insights from your deepest level of truth. Let the question serve as a magnet. Allow the first word to pop into your mind. Write it down. Let another word pop in. Write it down. Let words proceed forth, without judging them, without second-guessing where the answer is going. Don't jump ahead. Don't stop and read back over what you've written until the writing stops of its own accord. Helpful techniques: write as your own soul, innocent child, or future self; address your personality in the second person, by name; don't try to be too significant! Let your handwriting change shape. Change your speed and your rhythm, or write with your opposite hand.

- Write for ten minutes, without actually looking, about what's behind you; keep going farther and farther back through space and/or time.
- Write as your body: "I am aware of _____. If I go into that (sound, smell, sight, taste, feeling) in greater depth, the next thing I'm aware of is _____. If I continue to follow my attention, I discover _____."
- Write several descriptive paragraphs on these topics: (1) "The smallest, most beautiful thing I've seen lately is _____." (2) "The most grandiose, beautiful thing I've seen lately is _____." (3) "The most beautiful thing I've seen someone else do is _____." (4) "The most beautiful thing about my body is _____." (5) "The most beautiful thing about my personality is _____."
- Write about a recent experience in which something serious and troublesome suddenly turned funny or taught you a surprising lesson.
- Write as the Knower about what it knows about your true nature.
- Write as your body and describe its experience doing one of the concentration exercises.
- Write as your body for ten minutes about what you appreciate.

6

Hearing Your Body Talk

You only have to let the soft animal of your body love what it loves.

Mary Oliver

It seems that one can truly understand only when one understands with the body.

Mirra Alfassa ("The Mother")

The Language of the Body

When I was casting about through my memories and client stories for an anecdote to open this chapter, I sat staring blankly at my monitor. Minutes blurred into an hour. Instead of recalling an appropriate story, I daydreamed about a hiking path that wanders lazily between rolling oak-covered hills and a lush estuary near my home. The place has a Shangri-la quality like a secret valley I might discover in my dreams. Finally I turned off the computer, put on my walking shoes, and set off for the trailhead. It was midmorning on a weekday, and I had the trail all to myself. "I must be out here for some reason," I mused. "I should watch for signs and random thoughts."

As I walked, I listened to a running internal commentary. "Why can't my body simply upload the perfect story into my brain, word for word, so I can take dictation?" I brooded. But no, here I am procrastinating again, walking aimlessly, talking to myself. I should be able to come up with something great at the snap of my fingers. I should be working. If I would

Your physical body is the key to unlimited direct knowing. To find out what it knows you must learn to speak the language of the body. Chapter 6 takes you on a journey into your body's world and shows you how to interpret the body's signals. This chapter helps you develop a cooperative, co-creative relationship with your body, so you can know exactly what you need to know precisely when you need to know it.

The body is a sacred garment; it is what you enter life in and what you depart life with, and it should be treated with honor.

Martha Graham

only *think*." So immersed in reflection was I that I experienced a jolt when I almost stepped on a stunning grass snake planted directly in my path. It seemed it might have been waiting for me all morning. I stopped and looked into its eyes. Once again my animal teacher, the earthly luck dragon, was appearing synchronistically to remind me of an important truth.

I noticed that my body, without comment or direction from me, had instantly awakened, was at full attention, and was immersed in an exciting, direct relationship with the taut but sensuous body of the snake. I couldn't think. I had no words. After a timeless exchange of some sort, my little teacher slithered into the golden grasses. Blinking back to reality, I too slithered down my path, feeling more connected to the curving hillsides, the cattails bending in the wind, the snowy egrets winging low over the water.

Still in a daze, I rounded a bend and felt drawn off the trail. I climbed a slope and sat under some shady, fragrant laurel trees. I pulled my journal from my backpack, and as I stared across a wide inlet painted impressionistically with multigreen algaes and rippling reflections of blue sky and clouds, I found myself writing:

> Here at last, around the bend, and in this cul de sac, it is quiet. Walking the first part of the trail was a test because I was unconsciously affected by the whining noise from the freeway and from the Cessnas coming and going at the nearby airport. To find the reality the snake knows, to drop through the surface distractions of my life, I must penetrate into the silence that always abides in the heart of the hillside, in the tiny stand of dry foxtails and in the dragonflies bombing around me now on the breeze. I must walk deeper and deeper into the landscape, walk into the inlet, down through the water, into the center of the pool. I must stand at the bottom of the pool of crystal water, arms outstretched, breathing water, and listen to the Silence. I can feel the stories coming willingly through that glossy smoothness to me, from the depths, without effort or distortion.

Here was the message I had been looking for. I didn't need the perfect anecdote presented neatly in paragraph form. I needed to put aside the mind-set that said I had to start this chapter in a particular way. I needed to burn through the distractions of my daily life, which had overtaken me once again and fixated me in the superficial like a broken record. I needed to attain the great pleasure of direct experience with living things, which my body prefers to all else. I needed the feeling state I had absorbed from the snake's body and from my image of standing at the bottom of the clear pool.

As I reimagined this state of being, I found the image of the bottom of the pool to be a centering device for me, a way I would probably always be able to reconnect with effortless creativity. My body had indeed spoken to me, but not as my mind would have had it—not in words, not with neatly punctuated sentences. Instead, it spoke in its own language, that of feeling, mood, sensation, symbols, and omens. When I let my body give me the answer in its own way, through a collage of vibrations and shapes and a series of interrelated symbols, and when I didn't try to force a mental definition, eventually the pleasurableness of the process itself led me to the final insight. And I realized that the message my body relayed to me came straight from my soul.

Truth and Anxiety Signals

How do you know when something is right for you or when you hear the truth? How do you know when it's the right time to leave the house so you'll be on time for an appointment? How do you know that you want to do something and that you're actually going to do it? Conversely, how do you know when someone's lying to you or when some path of action is wrong? Can you tell when your timing is off? When a situation is being forced? When there's a high possibility of failure or danger?

Your body communicates with you constantly, giving you feedback about the relative safety and appropriateness of every option you consider. Its messages contain either survival information that comes from the body's rapport with the natural environment or higher guidance about your optimal self-expression that comes from your soul and the collective consciousness of the planet. *Most of us never take the time to know how we*

What is Truth? A difficult question; but I have solved it for myself by saying that it is what the "voice within" tells you.

Mahatma Gandhi

know or what we know; we just act. Yet our bodies are speaking volumes—just not in a language we immediately recognize. To develop skill in intuition, we need to decipher our body's information cues, to know quickly and directly, without taking time to figure things out.

The body's language is a binary one—there are only two modes, two words: *yes* and *no.* You will recognize these messages through feelings of expansion or contraction in your body. When a choice or action is appropriate, safe, and on-target for you, you will experience expanding energy: you may sense energy rising and become active or bouncy. Perhaps you'll warm to an idea, get lightheaded, or feel flushed with enthusiasm. Have you ever had the hots for someone, or had butterflies of anticipation, or been up for a new adventure? Have you ever said, "I'm leaning toward this option"? The body's *yes* often feels like health and vitality, even good luck: "I'm rarin' to go; let me at it!"

When I ask people how they know something is true and where they experience this feeling in their body, many describe a warm, spreading sensation across their chest. Others feel energy bubbling from their diaphragm into their chest or from their chest into their throat. Some even feel it bubble up farther, resulting in tears of happiness. Some feel the blood rush to their neck and face, making them blush. Still other people describe a variety of "clicks and clunks" as if something out of alignment suddenly snaps or drops into its rightful place. Most often, you'll recognize your personal truth by a feeling of deep comfort.

These feelings most often occur along the vertical center line of the body and seem related to the sensation of "ringing true," where the body silently gongs like a huge reverberating bell. One of the other most common truth signals is the sudden movement of energy up the spine or along the arms and shoulders, giving the sensation of chills or gooseflesh.

But what happens when something is not true or not appropriate for you? When the body answers *no,* the message is usually unmistakable. In fact, most people are more aware of their anxiety signal than their truth signal. When an option or action is unsafe, inappropriate, or off-target for you, you will experience contracting energy: you may feel energy drop, recoil, darken, or tighten. Maybe you'll act coolly, even coldly, to someone or feel a sinking in the pit of your stomach.

The word "comfort" comes from the Latin words for "with" and "strength" and originally meant operating from a position of power.

Joseph Chilton Pearce

When something is not true for you, your body will try to withdraw and back away. You may feel repulsed, become "leaden," or "turn to stone." Instead of blushing, you may blanch as the blood drains from your face. Your energy level may drop; you may feel gray, blue, or even depressed. You may feel pain in a specific area of your body. Common anxiety signals are a stomachache or nausea, a "pain in the neck," chest pain, headaches, or a feeling like a tight fist in the solar plexus area. Another anxiety signal is a prickly feeling of the "hair rising" along the upper spine and neck.

Why is it important to know your truth and anxiety signals? First, you need a fail-safe way to discern which options in life are best for you, to be able to make authentic choices straight from your soul's superconscious wisdom. Truth and anxiety signals are your pipeline to the highest knowledge. Second, by learning to identify clear answers more quickly and directly, you won't waste so much time and energy and so many opportunities for happiness. Third, by learning to absolutely trust your body's first response, you will find the guidance you get is high quality. Goethe said these deceptively simple words: "Just trust yourself. Then you will know how to live."

Your Truth and Anxiety Signals

1. Write about the different ways you know when something or someone is true, safe, or on-purpose for you. Where in your body do you experience the signal? Does the signal move from one area of the body to another?

2. Write about the different ways you know when something or someone is false, unsafe, or off-purpose for you. Where in your body do you experience the signal? Does the signal move from one area of the body to another?

3. Notice the truth and anxiety signals you get today and write about them.

Making Authentic Choices

Tonight you may make dinner for yourself or go out and choose food from a menu. What will you eat? How will you know what to pick?

TROUBLESHOOTING TIP
When You Doubt Your Signals

1. When you get a truth signal that makes you feel excited and at ease, how do you know you're not settling for an answer that's really coming from laziness? When your body sends you an anxiety signal, how do you know you shouldn't act anyway and that you're not just afraid of something that would be good for you?

2. Make an agreement with your body that you're going to trust the signals you get—regardless of any second thoughts. Even if you might make a mistake, act on what you sense. If the choice is coming from a false place, remember that your soul is ever on the alert. It won't let you stay in the dark for long, especially if you've made a deep inner decision to become conscious. As you try to act on a false choice, you will detect a new and increasing anxiety signal. In this case, choose again in total trust.

Perhaps instead of having what you usually have, you might question your body: "Body, what's your feeling tonight about fresh lettuce? Tomato soup? Pasta with cream sauce? Steak and potatoes?" Let your truth and anxiety signals inform you of your body's preferences, and see if you can pick up the most subtle signals. Maybe your body would prefer a handful of crisp radishes or half a juicy grapefruit.

Perhaps you're thinking that you "should" move from an expensive house you're renting and either find a less expensive neighborhood locally, move out of state, get a roommate, get a studio apartment, try to buy a house, or move back with your parents. As you ask your body about each option, your stomach contracts, you get a headache, you want to nap, you get nervous and irritable. What is your body telling you? Perhaps it's not time yet to make a decision. Can you let it be for now?

Maybe you're job-hunting and you've turned up several possibilities for work. Each one looks feasible in a variety of ways. One job will let you use your people skills, another will pay more but you'll be at a computer all day, and the third will give you a chance to be innovative and work with a team of creative people. When your body responds, it gives you instant feedback: imagining sitting at a computer gives you a pain in the neck. The job with people skills feels lukewarm; there's no tension, yet no real energy is moving. The third choice, working with a creative team, makes your body sit up at attention and salivate. What are you going to do? Will you override your body's direct knowing with "yes, buts" about not making enough money, not knowing anyone there, never having done this before, or not thinking you have enough talent? Or can you trust that your body might know more than your mind right now?

The more you validate your body's answers by acting on its information, the more your body will trust your conscious mind, and the more easily it will provide future expert guidance.

REMEMBER
▼
Your body never lies.

Validating Your Body

Several times this week notice when your body sends a message to your conscious mind. Maybe you instinctively changed to a slower lane on the freeway and just ahead in the fast lane is the debris from a blown-out tire. Or perhaps you got a sense to leave the house ten minutes earlier than you normally would for an appointment and then encountered an unexpected delay on the way—and you were right on time for your meeting. Thank your body out loud, and pat or stroke it tenderly, like you would a favorite pet. Write about what happened.

Discriminating Nonverbal Information

Nothing in life is really that complicated, especially from your body's point of view. For the body, it's always just a matter of one moment, one piece of information, one motivation at a time. And in each moment there is only one choice, one solution that's a perfect fit. In the next moment the selection may be different, so don't be impatient and jump ahead. You're not there yet. Anticipating future choices wastes your time.

When you need intuitive guidance, relax. Ask the body's key question: What's most interesting and crucial for this moment? Let that answer lead to the next most interesting thing. Choosing to work with the creative team might lead you to take a new training program the company offers, giving you a new skill set, making you more confident, leading you to a promotion, and bringing you new clients, who eventually offer you an opportunity to start your own business.

The real thing is when the body realizes that it can see. Only then is one capable of knowing that the world we look at every day is only a description.

Don Juan

Your Body's Key Questions

1. Become quiet, centered, and grounded, and breathe. Ask your body: "What are you most worried about right now? How can I reassure you?" Wait expectantly, and a knowing will begin in you, perhaps with feelings, sensations, and images. In your journal, write about your body's preoccupations and what you can do to help relieve these concerns. In what specific ways did your body make the answers known to you?

2. Ask your body: "What are you most excited about right now? What activities would feel the most rewarding and engrossing?" Wait expectantly, and a knowing will begin; notice feelings, sensations, and images. In your journal, write about your body's most real motivations and what you can do to help manifest these experiences. In what specific ways did your body make the answers known to you?

You may have noticed in the previous exercise that as you paid attention to your body you became aware of subtle sensations and perhaps had fleeting, ghostly images blending into an instinctual knowing that you couldn't trace by logic. The answers popped into your awareness like the answers in the window on a magic eight-ball children's toy: "By all means," "Highly unlikely," or "Try again later." Perhaps your body was concerned about having enough protein to function, since you'd had only coffee and a sweet roll for breakfast. During your morning meeting it gave you an image of a chicken-breast sandwich complete with smell and taste. You got a strong hankering and couldn't wait to take an early lunch break and rush to the restaurant.

Or your body may have told you that it was most excited today about creating a new flowerbed. It released to you a hunger for the feel of soft, well-turned dirt, the moist smell of the nursery where you'd buy plants, the thrill of the colors you would combine, and the simple enjoyment of being in the sunshine. You might even have glimpsed the design of the bed, the placement of the flowers, and how they might look in a year's time. And yet, this came to you in such rapid sequence that it seemed almost simultaneous, with little separation between ideas, sensory triggers, and images. Because of the body's nonverbal way of communicating, we often miss its messages, especially if we're mentally preoccupied. When looking for your personal truth, always trust the sensation of deep comfort.

⚡

I am here and ready for now's word.

Your Threshold of Sensitivity

When your body has an important message for you, it tries to get your attention, usually by getting keyed up or slightly more high-pitched or by making you feel irritated or distracted. And yet it's amazing how long we can ignore the body's attempts to be recognized. We can gloss over the first early vibrations, deny the feelings of urgency that start to build, and suppress the sensations of tension that accumulate as we continue to live only in our head. When the body needs to communicate, it doesn't give up. It whispers to you at first, and if you don't hear, it clears its throat—*Ah-hemm!* Then, if you still don't hear, it knocks at the door, knocks again more loudly, and then bangs wildly. And if you still don't pay heed, your body turns on the red flashing light and the siren—with the volume on high.

The Sensitivity Scale

To improve your intuition, learn to recognize the body's messages at the earliest possible point. If you can become more conscious of greater subtleties of feeling and sensation in your body, you will not only improve the speed and directness of your knowing, you will also spare yourself pain and grief.

Here's the sequence of your body's attention-getting devices.

1. Vibration, resonance, and instinctual urges. If you are sensitive, you may be able to recognize your body's messages at the moment they start to tingle and move at the cellular level. You turn a corner and get a strong anxiety signal—something inside you contracts. You don't think twice; you simply walk away. Or a restlessness may urge you to go to the office-supply store, right *now*, to buy a pen. There you run into a friend you haven't seen in years who has important information for you.

Have you ever noticed a subtle feeling of pressure, as though someone is calling you, but you can't recognize the voice? You become quiet, take your mind off trying to know, and in a few minutes a picture of your sister flashes through your mind. You phone her immediately. She's upset and crying and really in need of someone to talk to.

If you don't pick up your body's messages at this level, the vibrations will intensify, and then you may notice . . .

2. The heebie-jeebies. If you are sensitive, you can receive messages from your body as they gain momentum and start to shake a little more noticeably. This is called "having butterflies" or "creepy-crawlies" or "heebie-jeebies." At this level the vibrations are slightly rougher than at the previous level and have a definite nervous quality. They indicate that a flow of energy and information has started rising from your body into your conscious mind.

Most people consider this uncomfortable, even interpreting the tiny shakings as painful. This is the point at which many unconsciously resort to one of their addictive behaviors and push the disturbing resonance into the recesses of the subconscious mind by eating, watching television, or reading. At this stage, you should determine whether you're picking up an anxiety signal or a truth signal, since there is little difference between anticipating something negative and something positive. Is it fear or excitement?

If you don't become aware of your body's message at this level, you may be more alert when your body activates . . .

3. Sensory information. Have you noticed that what someone said either rang a bell or sounded a false note? Have you ever been hot under the collar or itching to get started? Have you ever referred to situations as sticky or rough, or to people as sharp, dull, tasty, or jazzy? By the time a vibratory frequency becomes sensual, it has risen from the reptile brain to the midbrain and has assumed color, shape, texture, tone, smell, taste, and recognizable detail. If you walk into a new situation and get a cold chill, gag at an idea, or see red when dealing with a colleague, you are focused at the level of the senses.

If you don't notice your body's message here, your body might need to get your attention by building up . . .

4. Emotions. If you haven't paid attention to the subtleties of your body's perceptions, you may reach a threshold where the energy finally breaks into your busy mind in a more recognizable form. Often the first emotional signals will disturb you; perhaps you'll be perturbed, frustrated, and snapping at people. Or maybe your mood will change for no reason and you'll feel heavy or sad.

I experienced a wave of wistfulness one afternoon. It built gradually and soon interfered with the cheerful and industrious state of mind I'm normally in during creative periods. I wasn't writing well, so I asked myself, "What happened today that I didn't pay attention to which could make me feel this way?"

I made a list: I had to call a person who owed me money. A friend told me a children's book I was writing was too long and no one would want it. I was supposed to make a dish that evening for a potluck and didn't have ingredients. As I became conscious of each of these items, I realized there were underlying feelings of rejection and helplessness that I hadn't paid attention to. Those patterns imploded at a deep level and, left unattended, colored my entire day.

If you don't catch the emotions as they arise subtly, they will gather energy and become more intense until you find yourself erupting in a rage or tears. And if you don't register information at the level of emotions, it may take the shape of . . .

5. Physical tension, stress, and addictive behavior. Now the body starts knocking more loudly. You are suppressing the wave of energy, and it becomes more dense. Soon you notice your shoulders are tight, you're developing a tension headache, or your wrists are sore. Maybe you've been living with a situation that keeps you in a constant, dull, subliminal fear of losing your livelihood, and the unacknowledged emotional stress appears in the form of heartburn and indigestion. Or perhaps you've begun a pattern of drinking or frantically looking for an uplifting diversion.

The longer you ignore the underlying emotions and the body's message, the more chronic your tension becomes, until it turns into . . .

6. Physical pain. Now you suffer constant shoulder pain, or your wrists must be wrapped in elastic bandages. Your lower back hurts when you bend over, and your indigestion has turned into chronic stomach pain. You're living with a constant headache and resorting to daily doses of painkillers. Still we set aside these extreme signals from our bodies and plow onward.

Soon the pain roots itself more deeply in your body and becomes . . .

7. Illness or disease. Your body is banging hard on the door to your conscious mind now. The shoulder pain you experienced has spread throughout your musculature as you succumb to a two-week bout with the flu. Your chronic abdominal pain becomes colitis or colon cancer. You have carpal tunnel syndrome and need an operation. The suppressed sadness and pain in your chest becomes a heart attack or pneumonia. Your body is saying to you, "Slow down and look below the surface."

But you *still* don't listen. You breeze through a hospital stay or outpatient surgery and continue until your body in desperation creates an explosion of . . .

8. Drama, shock, or trauma. The illness didn't work. Now your marriage fails, you lose your job, you have an auto accident, a parent dies, or your house is robbed. "Ha!" your body says. "Maybe *this* will make you stop and pay attention!" What's the message underneath this violence?

If you still ignore your intuitions, blaming it all on bad luck, in all likelihood your body will shift into low gear and you will drop into . . .

REMEMBER
▼
Where you make excuses, you're just stalling.

9. Depression, paralysis, unconsciousness, or insanity. Now you are barely able to cope with the world. Your senses have become dull. You lapse into a deep depression, losing interest in life and feeling no sense of purpose. You consider committing suicide. You are overwhelmed and helpless and may even lapse into delusions and break from reality. Perhaps you develop Alzheimer's disease or fall into a coma. You may develop paralyzing phobias or lose mobility and live out life in a wheelchair or on a respirator.

If you don't listen to your body at this stage, the only option left is . . .

10. Death and rebirth. Clear the slate and start again! At this point there is little difference between natural death and suicide. When conditions reach this stage, the soul is blocked by a shut-down body and has no way to break through to the conscious mind. Dying in such density is not much of a relief. We carry our mental and emotional state to the other side and integrate it into our next personality when we reincarnate. As trance medium Jane Roberts commented, she wouldn't want to kill herself because she'd just have to come back and go through the third grade again!

Of course, I've exaggerated, but we all know people who have stubbornly resisted dealing with their inner realities and who have become less pliable and vital and more negative. We also know exceptions to the rule like actor Christopher Reeve and tennis star Arthur Ashe, who appeared to voluntarily take on the most debilitating conditions as a way to teach and inspire humanity—by bringing superconsciousness into their limitations.

How Soon Do You Know?

1. In your journal, write about when you normally notice a body signal. Describe examples of noticing a cue early and of when you were more unconscious or resistant.

2. In situations where your body's message became quite dense, write about the underlying pains, tensions, and emotions that had previously gone unacknowledged. Was your body relaying a message about survival or a message from your superconsciousness, or soul level?

The Sensitivity Scale	
How Soon Do You Know?	
CONSCIOUS Integration of Soul Mind-Body Unity	Vibration — Resonance — Instinctual Urges Heebie-Jeebies Sensory Information Emotions Physical Tension — Stress — Addictive Behavior Physical Pain
UNCONSCIOUS Denial of Soul Mind-Body Split	Illness — Disease Drama — Shock — Trauma Depression — Paralysis — Unconsciousness — Insanity Death — Rebirth!

The Earlier You Notice Something in Your Body, the More Intuitive You'll Be

How Information Emerges

Let's look at the path information takes as it rises from the body into the mind. You may become more sensitive to your body and increase your intuitive flow if you can pinpoint your brain-level activity at any moment during the process. You can learn to track the upward flow of physical vibrations from your cells, up your spine, and through the three layers of your brain. As you become familiar with the progression of data through your awareness, soon you'll know what step to look for next to assist the natural movement and increase the flow of your intuition.

The first, most primal level of the brain, the *reptile brain*, concerns itself exclusively with physical survival. It controls your sensorimotor functions and makes you aware of being in a body and in the material world. It drives you instinctually toward food, shelter, sex, and territory. Without emotion or reason, it interprets sensory stimuli in terms of aversion or attraction. It relates closely to your subconscious mind and your survival behaviors.

Next, around the reptile brain nestles the *midbrain*, or the limbic system, the seat of your conscious mind and personal self. It produces the feeling tones you experience and is involved in creating relationships, emotional bonds, dreams, and inner visions.

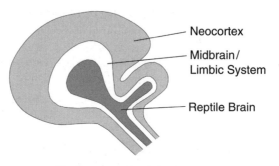

The Three Levels of the Brain

The third and highest level of the brain is the *neocortex*, your intellectual system, which is five times bigger than the two lower brains combined and is divided into left and right hemispheres. It houses abstract thinking, creative thinking, and higher states of consciousness such as compassion and truth. It corresponds to your superconscious mind.

To develop intuition, we must use all three parts of our brain intentionally, interactively, and vertically. All intuitions begin with a physical vibration, whether the stimulus for the insight originates in the world as an event or within your higher mind as an inspiration. Even that light bulb going off in your head is a physical sensation; it's a subtle truth signal. Why do people hit themselves on the side of their head when something finally makes sense to them? Could they be acknowledging the arrival of an ascending insight as it reaches the neocortex?

Can you tell when your intuition is rising? Can you recognize the subtle feeling when something is trying to surface from the depths to be known and gain meaning? Can you feel emotions bubbling up? Can you sense an out-of-reach vision? Each of these sensations is a subtle pressure caused by the flow of your awareness from one level to the next. Your goal is to connect the brains to facilitate a smooth river of awareness through your conscious mind. Let's look at the process of how an intuition rises.

As the body's message moves as an instinctual impulse from your reptile brain into your midbrain, it takes on feelings and is colored by the physical senses. You'll probably recognize that the rising message passes through a sequence of senses, beginning with those nearest the old

How Information Becomes Conscious

▲	**Mind**
Neocortex **Left Brain**	Language — Labels — Verbal Description Analysis — Definition
Right Brain	Abstract Concepts — Patterns
Midbrain	Associations — Meanings
Sensory Information	Vision: Imagery — Symbols Sound: Little Voice — Telepathy Touch: Textures — Impressions Taste: "Can't stomach this," "Can't swallow this" Smell: "It smells fishy," "This stinks," "A fresh idea" Emotions
Reptile Brain	Physical Tension and Pain Heebie-Jeebies Vibration — Resonance — Instinctual Urges
	Body

As Information Emerges from the Body to the Conscious Mind
It Becomes More Visual and Verbal

reptilian way of sensing the world. Smell is perhaps the most primal way to interact with the environment; if you're aware of smells, you are very much in your body and close to the earth. As the data progresses upward, you may notice your sense of taste, which is also deeply instinctual. Then the sense of touch brings you into a more relational way of being, and you become more conscious of the data. After that the information takes on an auditory quality and gathers complexity as you notice the spectrum of sounds. Finally, as the message continues to rise, your vision is activated; you see the light! The information now has shape, depth, color, and nuances. Now you see pictures, symbols, and scenes.

This sensual chain of command is evident in sexual attraction. We may first be drawn to someone by appearance alone, but no amount of good looks will keep us together if our partner has an unpleasant voice, an odd skin texture, or an off-putting smell or taste.

Since the midbrain teaches us to formulate relationships, the message starts to take on a dualistic nature as it rises. We have thoughts like "That dress looks like my sister" or "That painting does not go with this furniture." Here we form associations and find links. When we connect two images in our mind, we create meanings: "I am blonde so I look youthful" or "He is a real tiger." After the sensory experience transmutes into associations, the message moves from the midbrain up to the right hemisphere of the neocortex.

Now our perception becomes even more complex and subtle. We notice many overlapping associations and similarities, differences and contrasts, which create an impression of patterns and give us a sense of abstract concepts. As those patterns register consciously, we are able to grasp strategies, overviews, and visions. We have the dawning of the great *aha!* Quickly the rising information leaps to the left brain. We analyze and define the message, finally putting labels on it. We describe the insight with words. Language is the last step.

If you want to improve your intuition, simply move down the chain of knowing. Go below words into your senses. Close your eyes and tap your imagination. What pictures do you see? What sounds do you hear? If the next step in your career had a texture, what might it feel like? If your dream house were a piece of food, what would it taste like? If your soul mate were a scent, what might she smell like? Think like an animal!

Maybe you're stuck at the level of vision and can only see images in your mind that are related to familiar experiences. Move down through the brain and activate your emotions. If you're considering a move to another state or country, ask your body to give you its first responses as you bring each option to mind. New York: tight throat/anxiety. California: buzzing in your head/curiosity. Japan: soft solar plexus/peacefulness. Mexico: bubbling heart/enthusiasm.

If your emotions are blocked, tune in to the more subtle vibrations in your body. Where do you feel the heebie-jeebies? Are you nervous or distracted? Can you feel it in your stomach? At the back of your neck? In your knees? Once you find the vibration of the body's message, release the energy and move it up through the natural sequence of steps outlined in the table on page 115. If you don't suppress the information wave as it begins at the cellular level, you will not experience tension, pain, or trauma. With practice, you'll learn to consciously use each step. You can jump-start your intuition by dropping to deeper levels and coming up again, or by stretching to a higher level and seeing what your perception tunes in to next.

Describing the Ineffable

Being comfortable with feelings is of prime importance in developing direct knowing. Since language is the final step, being able to describe the nuances of your nonrational perceptions is a powerful method for becoming conscious. Whether you're male or female, turning feelings and sensations into verbalized insights completes the circuits in your brain and allows you to know both subconscious and superconscious information.

One of my clients, Rod, has made a practice of scrutinizing his body sensations and describing what he notices. He defines *describing* as a kind of direct talking, not the usual "talking about." He told me that we shouldn't talk about our experience as if we were translating information for an audience. Instead, we should speak the way lunatics do, directly from the body's knowing, even making up our own words. He describes a powerful physical and spiritual healing experience he had a year after his young daughter died:

> I could feel contractual tensions releasing all through my physical body. It felt as if my body had been dotted and streaked with little alertness-contractions, which had been constantly watching for [my daughter] since her accident. Suddenly I am no longer looking outside myself, rather I am feeling-looking inside myself. Everything is made out of light, bright see-through life. The front of my rib cage has separated and opened like two swinging doors. A rushing out is beginning—I am rushing out very fast—and what's out is opening even more. I can hear the movement. It is fast and high-pitched—almost beyond my sensory range. There's [my daughter]! I can see through her arm—her body's energy units actually separate. She's playing! She is showing me this is her new world! She is showing me how everything can penetrate and move through everything else.

TROUBLESHOOTING TIP
Handling the Heebie-Jeebies
  1. Catch yourself while you're in a distracted state of mind. You may have been telling yourself and others, "I've got a lot on my mind," "I'm angry," or "I didn't eat breakfast or get enough sleep."
  2. Get quiet, close your eyes, and pay attention to your body. Stop describing the way you're feeling—unlabel it, take all the words off. Just be with the sensations. Don't try to suppress anything. This "tension" is not bad; it isn't necessarily even tension. It just is what it is: energy. Where do you feel the most bouncing?
  3. Can you sense that if you give the energy vibrations more permission to be, they might move somewhere? Pay even closer attention and enter the vibrations. Let them move. Where do they go? Let them get stronger. As they increase in power what do they want to do?
  4. If you feel energy in your legs, walk, jump, or dance. If you feel it in your diaphragm or chest, take deep breaths, make animal noises, or move your arms around. If you feel it in your throat, what do you want to say and to whom? Let the energy move through you any way it wants. Let the wave teach you. Don't try to control it.
  5. As the energy moves up through your brain, pay attention to your feelings, sensory data, and associations. Let images appear, and let new meanings simply occur to you.

Remember that *everything is information.* Emotions aren't scary—they're information. Heebie-jeebies aren't threatening—they're a raw form of information. Try to describe the information hidden inside a physical sensation or feeling.

Describing Emotions and Sensations

1. Catch yourself while you're in the midst of having an emotion or a complex sensation, and notice the "label" you've been using to talk to yourself about the situation. Unlabel it. Instead, describe the simple physical sensations you're experiencing. Use images and other sense words: "I feel tingling in my solar plexus, in an area the size of a baseball, as though it were filled with bees. It sounds like a loud electrical hum." Then simply be with the sensations. As they rise further into your awareness, they may change into something else, and you may get insight about why they're there and what they mean. Keep describing them as they evolve.

2. Write in your journal as if you're telling a story in present tense to your best friend: "I have this situation in my life, and it triggers strong feelings that are located in my body _____. The sensations are like _____. I notice that the situation is parallel to _____. It makes me think that I have unresolved issues about _____. The point is _____. If I were going to act from my soul, the way to handle this situation would be _____, and as the situation starts to release, I feel it moving in my _____."

To help make information conscious, you might develop the habit of talking with your friends about "interesting perceptions I had today" or "interesting similarities I found between experiences I had this week," or asking, "What do you think *this* means?" Assume that you have the right to be comfortable in your own body, that you do not have to live with even the most subtle energetic discomfort. You can become conscious of the data in the tissues of your body by simply having imaginary conversations with various parts of your body. Personalize your belly, or the bottoms of your feet, or your thyroid. Let them tell you what they know about life. Make an agreement with yourself that the moment you notice an anxiety signal, you'll stop and discover what the message is. Make it a way of life to keep your body clear of blockages, ignorance, and negativity.

Practice dropping below the surface of your normal daily distractions to find a deeper experience of knowing. Cultivate the habit of including your body in every decision-making process, and feel your cells talking. If you honor your body as a living being, respect its innate consciousness, and talk with it, you'll have a reliable source of intuitive guidance.

BE INTUITIVE TODAY!
Let your body decide what you will do.

When you decide to go to dinner, pick three possible restaurants. Head in the general direction of food without deciding which one you'll go to. Let your body and natural instinct make each choice along the way. If one restaurant is to the north and the others are to the south, when you get to the intersection where you must turn, see which way your body wants to go. At the next juncture point, perhaps you'll find yourself not able to exit the freeway at the ramp that would take you to the Chinese restaurant. Continue, realizing that it's probably the Mexican restaurant downtown that your body prefers. Yet as you park the car, you notice a cozy cafe down the block that you've never seen before, and as you do, your body perks up with enthusiasm. Go for it. And thank your intuition for leading you to a new experience.

Direct Writing Questions

Sit down with your journal and get quiet. Empty your mind. Pick one of the following questions and be with it for a few moments. Ask that you be able to receive creative insights from your deepest level of truth. Let the question serve as a magnet. Allow the first word to pop into your mind. Write it down. Let another word pop in. Write it down. Let words proceed forth, without judging them, without second-guessing where the answer is going. Don't jump ahead. Don't stop and read back over what you've written until the writing stops of its own accord. Helpful techniques: write as your own soul, innocent child, or future self; address your personality in the second person, by name; don't try to be too significant! Let your handwriting change shape. Change your speed and your rhythm, or write with your opposite hand.

- Write as your body about a time your direct experience was so real that your mind became completely quiet. What things have that kind of power in your life?
- Write as your body about the times today when you tried to communicate with your mind via a truth signal and an anxiety signal.
- Describe one example of an experience you've had that falls into each of the first nine categories of the Sensitivity Scale. Write about the hidden message in each.
- Write as your body: "Why am I attracted to the body of my mate or lover? Why was I attracted to a past lover?"
- "If I were (an animal, a color, a flavor, a texture, a sound, a scent, a geometric shape, music, a flower, a food), I'd be _____."
- Write as the Perceiver about a time this week when you were focused at the level of vibration/resonance, heebie-jeebies, emotion, sensory information, the creation of associations and meanings, the recognition of patterns and overviews, and the final description of experience.
- Write as your soul perceiving the world through your body: (1) "The interesting perceptions I had today are _____." (2) "The interesting similarities I found between experiences I had this week are _____." (3) "The hidden meanings in the experiences I had this week are_____." Write like a lunatic!

Part 3
Making Intuition Useful

You've learned to keep your mind clear,

to access intuition from the highest, cleanest source,

and to begin interpreting the subtle, nonverbal

messages arising from your body. Now you're ready

to apply intuition to the activities of everyday life.

In Part 3 you'll learn to use direct knowing to help

increase the guidance you receive from dreams, activate

positive imagination, attain superconscious guidance for

yourself and others, make decisions, communicate more

effectively, open your creativity, heal yourself, and

manifest what you need. Finally, you'll learn to be alert

for the blind spots in intuition development and to stay

in the flow through the ethical use of your

new perceptual skill.

7

Harnessing Dreams and Imagination

The moment one begins dreaming-awake, a world of enticing,
unexpected possibilities opens up. A world where the ultimate audacity
becomes a reality. Where the unexpected is expected.
That's the time when man's definitive adventure begins.

Florinda Donner

Chapter 7 teaches you to trust your imagination and work constructively with your dream world. By learning to be a dynamic participant in your own "other dimensions," you'll maximize your ability to create what you want, understand your deepest growth processes, and access inspiring visions. This chapter helps you achieve 24-hour consciousness and plant and reap great bounty from your inner fertile fields.

Trusting the Power of Your Imagination

Suzanne came to me for a life reading; she'd followed a spiritual path for years but lately was feeling listless and out of touch with her passion and purpose. She wanted to know how to fix what was wrong. As it turned out, Suzanne was a vivid dreamer and used her dreams regularly as a primary source of self-guidance. She told me about a powerful dream she'd had the night before, which she felt had some bearing on her main issue. In it, she was flying across the sky, Superman style, with a young, angelic-looking woman. She said she gradually became aware of a sublime sound, a cross between New Age music and classical, yet with an extra richness. Her angelic companion said simply, "Listen to the music." As she paid attention, the music appeared visually before her, like a billowing cumulus cloud etched intricately with a filigree of fine gold lines. It grew gracefully out ahead of her as she flew, constantly beckoning her toward the heavens. As she followed, she had the strange sensation of actually becoming the sound and the image. As this merger occurred, she knew she was being taught a profound lesson beyond the grasp of her normal mind.

Suddenly the staccato sound of a pounding beat came from below. It too had a shape, this time like short, black, vertical dashes. As she paid attention to it, she started to plummet helplessly. "Listen to the music," her companion reminded her calmly. "Choose which vibration to pursue." As she again listened to the higher spiritual sound, she rose gently on an incline and stabilized. What did this mean in light of her current spiritual crisis?

Suzanne and I agreed that this was indeed an important message from her own soul. She was at a critical juncture in her life where she needed to commit to her inner voice and not be distracted by the conflicting voices from friends, colleagues, and the media that she heard every day. If she continued to split her attention, she might fall into a period of depression and negativity. Yet if she could concentrate on the feeling she desired and see and feel it in herself and her surroundings, the vibration of that feeling would guide and lift her closer to her own "heaven on earth."

Suzanne exemplifies how the power of imagination, especially as it manifests through dreams, can bring intuitive insight to teach and guide us. In the world of imagination the messages from your subconscious or superconscious mind can glide effortlessly into meaningfulness. They might assume an angel's shape and talk to you. Or they might superimpose several body senses, giving you the powerful reality of a particular state of being and knowing.

In your imagination anything is possible. It's easy to access information from any level, rearrange a configuration of ideas and beliefs, plant seeds of intention that will later grow into manifested reality, or even dissolve a reality that's interfering with the birth of a new experience. In this chapter, you'll learn to open and loosen your imagination and work with imagery and symbols—the language of your imagination. Then you'll see how your dreams are a method for talking to your subconscious and superconscious minds so you can be more aware of life.

Imagination is more important than knowledge.

Albert Einstein

Imagination Is Your Ally

People often ask me if they can trust their imagination. They assume that there is some kind of evil twin lurking beneath the surface, bent on sabotaging the good twin on the outside. It's as though imagination is an insidious force, which, given even the slightest foothold, will trick your logical mind into losing control or acting foolishly. I remind them that the logical mind would have nothing to do but repeat itself ad infinitum if it weren't for the creativity and genius of imagination. Life would have no juice, no zest.

Imagination fulfills a bridging function in your mind by helping to link your lower and upper brains. As you have learned, an impulse rises from your reptile brain into your midbrain and there takes on sensory texture, tone, flavor, and feeling. The message comes alive and starts to become meaningful. But right before the message pops into the highest part of your brain, the neocortex, it becomes visual. So symbols exist halfway between the reality of the body and the reality of the spirit. They are the universal language of intuition, served up to us via our imagination. They act both to ground abstract inspirations into the body and physical manifestation as well as to raise instinctual knowledge into conscious recognition and meaningfulness.

For an intuition to finally become conscious, you must interpret the images or symbols presented by the midbrain. Everything you have and know now was previously presented to you as a picture or a pattern in your imagination. How did you pick what you're wearing today? Why did you arrange your furniture the way you did? How did you know where to plant the flowers in your garden? Can you remember the moment you got the picture or had a sense about what to do? If you look for and treasure those moments of revelation, your imagination and intuition will increase.

Imagination determines the quality of our lives since what we can imagine is as far as we'll let ourselves go. We rarely pursue something unless we can imagine it first and get a "felt sense" of how it might unfold. Vivid imagination, with its rich sensory input and endless variety of emotional tones, makes ideas more real for us, and thus realizable. For example, at one of my seminars I asked participants to list five things they'd love to do if money were no object. Since most people's lists can fill pages, I was shocked and moved when a middle-aged woman said in a soft voice that she had only been able to think of two things, and she'd just realized that her boring, small-town life was the result of her dearth of choices.

Imagination is your friend and can flesh out your life, bringing messages from your soul about how to increase creativity, self-expression, and possibilities.

The Sky's the Limit

1. List at least five things you'd like to do and have if money were no object. Describe each activity or object in vivid detail.
2. List at least five things you'd like to create if talent were no object. Describe each thing in vivid detail.
3. Describe in detail at least five anonymous good deeds you'd like to do if resources and logistics were no object.

Your Subjective Experience Is Reliable

I know the way of all things by what is within me.

Lao Tzu

Your entire personality, both your innermost and outermost self, is your soul taking shape. No part of you is false or unworthy. If you trust your imagination to be the voice of your soul, then the greater your imagination, the more your true self can become real. You need not look to other people's lives for ideas. You have enough originality within you to last for as long as you live. Consider how we manifest such wildly different realities. Isn't it amazing that some people marry five times and others can't find anyone they're attracted to? Or that one person is scrupulously honest and someone else learns by getting caught stealing a car and spending time in prison? Is one right and one wrong? Not at all. Each person's subjective experience is just right for him or her.

We find our way through the sequence of experiences and perceptions that create the learning impact we need by being captured by our imagination and emphasizing one idea versus another. One person needs drama to wake up, so he underscores the reality of betrayals, conspiracies, and losses. Another needs opportunities for creativity, so she turns toward the myriad possibilities for images she can make with her camera. *Trust your own needs, timing, and sequence of insights.* The game is to welcome what first occurs in your mind as an image and a yearning. Accept that each awareness of need, each impetus to act, is given to you purposefully by your soul. No images are there by accident. Your personal process is your guide.

Intuitive information can show up in your inner mind or in the outer world via another person, a book, a movie, or an omen. What's the difference? No matter the origin, it's you who notices an idea and gives it weight; the perception is always happening in *you*. Everything occurs in your imagination. Why not be entertained by its unlimited scope?

The next time you're stuck in rush hour traffic or you notice a lady-bug, think, "Look what I've imagined into being!" Whether your inner voice tells you to do something or you hear it through the voice of your boss or best friend, register the message as the voice of your intuition. Whether you see a vision of a house you want to build in a dream or you just happen to run across your dream house for sale down the street, it's the product of your open imagination.

Expanding Imagination

1. List five fantasies you've had in the past few years that became real. Describe how your imagination made you feel about each idea when it first occurred. Why did you trust it?
2. List five current fantasies that have the special energy which indicates they are likely to become real. Describe them in present tense as if they're happening now.
3. Describe in detail five things you want to do in the next two days that involve playfulness and sensory stimulation and that activate your creative process.

Be Wild, Innocent, Positive, *and* Practical

Imagination is fluid and flourishes in a playful environment. To be playful, you need a positive attitude—and a truly positive attitude is natural to the soul and requires no will power to maintain. Like a beachball in the water, it cannot be forced to remain under the surface for long. It comes from a willing-to-be-amused, willing-to-feel-something-new, willing-to-flow attitude. Children are examples of the joyful use of the positive attitude: naturally innocent and self-centered, drawn to experiment with new experience, able to listen to all points of view, and able to get bored and move easily on to the next interesting thing.

Imagination incorporates all the senses in a fertile, creative process. In your imagination, you can try many paths of action without being limited by the earthly restraints of time, space, stress, uncooperative partners, or limited financial resources. You can be outrageous, play with any emotion in any intensity, or change your morality, your gender, or your body type.

Artist and creativity teacher Michell Cassou once told me, "Your whole being wants to lose control, to be daring! It wants to be wild and get

⚡
I am easily entertained
by life.

away with things." In her Painting Experience Workshop, Michell advocates absolute trust in our intuition. She says, "If you feel like you want to make a big brown mess, but you thought you were going to paint a sunset, you *must* make the mess, immediately. If you say, 'I'll make the mess later, after I've painted the sunset,' it will be too late. If you ignore your intuition, it will go to sleep. And later, when you want it, it won't be there." [1]

Reinvent Yourself

In your journal, invent a new personality for yourself. Give yourself a new name, personal history, character traits, clothes, good and bad habits, voice, body, gender, motivations, goals, location, skills, relationships, successes, and failures. Write out your new story and describe your new self in vivid detail.

To make the most of your imagination, make an agreement with yourself that you'll apply your first thoughts, innovations, and creative *ahas!* to daily situations. Your body loves putting imagination into action. Nicola Tesla, the inspired inventor, designed machines in his head, visualizing all the parts and how they were to fit together. Then he operated each machine over various time periods in his imagination and "saw" how it held up. If problems developed, he revised his design and tested it again. Finally, after he'd tested the device thoroughly *in his imagination* and his body was intimate with it, he would proceed to construct it physically.

REMEMBER
▼
Applying your imagination creates motivation.

We truly adore the feeling of materializing a revelation. When you make a sketch with charcoals, write a letter with an antique fountain pen, or bake a cake with blue icing, your body feels deeply alive and excited. Life turns you on.

Loosen Up Your Fantasy World

Emily Dickinson said, "The soul should always stand ajar, ready to welcome the ecstatic experience." Intuition thrives when you're connection-seeking, diversity-appreciating, eccentricity-enjoying, and surprise-cultivating. To help your intuition and imagination flow like water from a faucet, vary the way you normally do things. Change your habits, try new words, use your opposite hand.

Varying Your Routine

1. List five things you do the same way every day. Then list three ways you could do each one differently. Wash your face before you brush your teeth, put on your right sock before your left, take a different route to work, read instead of watching television. Do things differently this week.

2. Change one thought midstream each day for a week: "Oh, I can't go out for a walk with you, Joan. I have to clean my garage—no, wait, I can organize my time so I can fit it all in." "I hate driving on the freeway—no, wait, I might find it interesting if I pretended to be a chauffeur, a bus driver, or a race car driver." "I always have my sweet roll in the morning—no, wait, maybe I'd enjoy a fruit salad."

In my workshops we do an experiential exercise where people make up fantasies about each other. I emphasize that what the participants share *must* be frivolous, irrelevant, and impulsive. *No meaningfulness allowed!*

Brenna, who considered herself a realist and unable to accept facts without proof, turned out to have a colorful experience. I asked the students to clear their minds and allow the energy of their partner to fill the space in front of them and help provide them with the answers they needed. As I prompted them with suggestions, they were to share the first response that came into their minds—the sillier, the better.

I started with questions like "What does your partner's bedroom look like? Where would your partner like to go on a dream vacation? What kind of car would your partner like to have? If your partner got up in the middle of the night to have a snack, what would it be? If your partner dressed up for Halloween, what would they go as? If your partner had another first name, what would it be?"

Brenna protested at first, saying she couldn't possibly know what her partner liked to eat or what car he had.

I said, "Well, if you had an opinion about it, what would it be?"

"Oh, an opinion!" she said. "I have lots of those!" And she proceeded to talk animatedly with her partner Bob for half an hour.

When it came time to see if her answers were valid, she was shocked that almost everything she'd said was accurate. Brenna had laughingly described Bob as wanting a chocolate brown Jaguar with leather upholstery and a vanity license plate; his favorite midnight snack was toast and peanut butter; his Halloween costume was a wizard; and his alternate first name was Carlos. Amazingly, Bob actually had owned a Jaguar, and his current license plate said ALL41; he did eat toast with peanut butter—and jelly; he loved the King Arthur and Merlin mythologies; and as for "Carlos," he was planning a vacation to Mexico in a few months. When she shared all this with the group, Brenna exclaimed, "You tricked me! Now I can't pretend that I don't know things!"

Making Up Fantasies

1. Ask a friend to give you the name of a person they know well but whom you don't. Using your journal, concentrate on the person's name, and become neutral and receptive. Allow the person's energy to fill the space in front of you. Write your impressions. Add to the questions listed above: What mood is this person in right now? What issue concerns him/her the most? What job would this person be best suited for? What is the person's current relationship situation? Does he/she have a pet? What kind of living situation would be best for this person? What are your physical impressions about his/her body or appearance?

2. Check with your friend and see how many of your impressions were accurate.

Working with Symbols: The Language of Imagination

Symbols contain volumes of encoded information and are incredibly powerful in an understated way. They convey meaning directly and intuitively without words. Symbols can lead and focus us. We have gone to war behind banners bearing crosses, stars, and magical beasts like lions, eagles, and dragons. Corporations, even nations, represent the essence of their identities with logos. Think of the United States and you focus on the nobility inherent in the Statue of Liberty. And of course there's nothing like a snazzy business card or a new hairstyle to give you greater confidence and credibility.

Designs, whether a Frank Lloyd Wright house, a Ralph Lauren jacket, or the latest sleek coffeemaker, are symbols. A design is "good" when it simplifies life into classic patterns of beauty and harmony. Through this symbolic distilling, good art and design promote clarity and functionality and give people a sense of personal dignity through the embodiment of sacred geometry. Why do we never tire of gazing at a Monet painting, the Ronchamps chapel by Corbusier, a Shaker rocker, an Amish quilt, or the Zen garden at Ryoanji? Simply because these images return us to our souls and transport us naturally back into an experience of what is most fundamental and real.

Symbols can make our hearts soar and can serve as pathways to higher consciousness. Sacred art, like the colorful Huichol Indian yarn paintings or elaborate Buddhist mandalic thangkas, gives us a detailed road map into divine states of mind. These images have the power to transmit higher experience. By meditating on each layer, each mazelike pathway, and entering each symbol in the painting, you can pass through a process that re-creates the stages on a spiritual path.

Symbolizing Your Experience

Playing with symbols can increase your "intuition muscle." Try this: Design a logo for someone you know. If this person were an animal, what would he be? If he were a flavor, or a texture, or a color, what would he be? If the service this person offers were a geometric shape, what would it look like? If his company had a rhythm, a speed—what would it feel like?

Huichol Indian and Tibetan Buddhist Sacred Mandalas

Or try this: What does humor, incisiveness, industriousness, or tenderness look like when symbolized? If you could draw your favorite song, what implements, media, and colors would you use? Perhaps the Egyptians asked similar questions when they devised their system of hieroglyphic writing. Can you sense the intuitive leaps that caused them to invent the following glyphs?

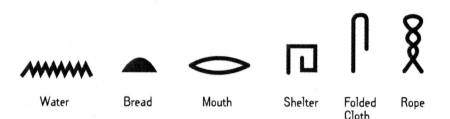

Water   Bread   Mouth   Shelter   Folded   Rope
                                                     Cloth

Symbolizing

1. Make a list of ten people from the media. Write the first and last name of each one in your journal. Then ask your intuition and imagination: If this person had a different name, one that conveyed their essence or some important quality of their personality, what would it be? Don't be logical. Take the first impressions you get. List their pseudonym next to their present name.

2. Pick a person you know. Ask your imagination: If this person were a plant or a tree, what would he or she be? A kind of music? A car? A geometric symbol? If this person had a secret fantasy, what would it be? What does his or her bedroom look like?

You can use this same kind of "what-would-it-be" imagination exercise to describe the subtle sensations in your body. In fact, describing sensations thoroughly is an effective technique for reducing, even eliminating, pain.

Is It Bigger Than a Bread Basket?

Tune in to your body, especially when you are tense or ache or are in an odd mood. Ask your imagination: If this sensation had a size, how big would it be? A shape, what would it look like? If it were an actual object, what might it be? A color, what would it be? A noise, what would it sound like? If it were smaller in size or changed into something else, what would it be? If it got even smaller or changed again into something else, what would it be? Continue describing ensuing symbols until the feeling and symbols disappear. Notice the correlation between the symbol and the actual sensation.

At the beginning of this book I described how the image of the luck dragon synchronously appeared from deep in my mind, showing up again and again in front of my nose. It's been more than a year, and my personal symbol for the intuitive process still appears. I just shake my head and laugh. Obviously I am supposed to internalize something about that symbol. What symbol represents the intuitive process to you? And what does it want to show you?

Symbolizing Intuition

Close your eyes. Become centered and neutral. Ask your body and superconscious mind to bring you a personal symbol for your own process of intuition development. What speaks to you? What image wants to teach you? Let it come into your mind. Develop a personal relationship with the symbol. Start looking for it in the world. Collect images of it in your journal.

Interpreting Symbols

Another way to work with symbols is by playing the game of "crack the nut," or penetrating to the core of a symbol to extract its meaning. When you begin, your conscious mind might have superficial theories about what the image means, but those ideas are only a first step.

Interpreting symbols effectively is a matter of entering them, then becoming them, much as Suzanne's dreaming self entered the sound and shape of the celestial music the "angel" pointed out to her. If you stare at a symbol long enough, focusing your attention into it, getting more and more involved with it, you'll begin to get bleedthrough from the image and actually feel its structure taking shape in you.

Perhaps you and the symbol are exchanging energy and knowledge. You give yourself to it, and it reveals itself to you. As you meld totally into the symbol, the knowledge it represents downloads into your body, and you can feel the living patterns and dynamics the symbol preserves. This is when you get flashes of insight, an all-over feeling of instant understanding. The deeper meaning you discover this way is usually a far cry from the shallow theories of your logical mind.

When Lisa dreamed about a leopard whose spots started flashing on and off and which eventually turned into a lion, she theorized it might have to do with her being a Leo or with her interest in shamanism. But during a meditation, as I helped her focus into the leopard and enter its experience, she spoke as the leopard and said that "my spots are there because I'm scared and I need them for camouflage. I can feel the fear pooling on the surface of my skin and my presence backing away in those places—it's as though I have 'black holes' there. But now, as I relax and start to feel safe, my energy comes back to the surface and the spots fade away. Yet I can feel how any rush of anxiety will bring them back."

Together we realized that Lisa was becoming more public in her career. Her dream was telling her that she needed to trust her own process and give up her need for protection. Then, when she was calm, her true nature would show through, and she'd convey a unified tone and image to her audience.

Decoding a Symbol

Imagine that you are walking along, happen to look down, and find (1) a colorful plastic lizard, (2) a diamond ring, (3) a fortune cookie that says, "You will step on the soil of many lands," (4) a small key, and (5) a perfect red feather. First notice your mind's theories, your body's first impressions; then focus attention on the symbol, give your energy to it, and let it give its energy to you. Enter the symbol, become it, and speak directly about what you represent and the meaning of why you appeared at this time.

Here's a technique you can use when working with dream symbols or other curious images to get as many related associations as possible out of them.

The Lotus Petal Technique

In your mind's eye, imagine a large, open lotus flower with many petals. In the center of the flower, place a symbol you'd like to decode—a snake, for instance.

Go out to the first petal, and imagine another image—an idea or a word—on that petal, something that is related to the symbol. For a snake, the first thing you get might be *poisonous*.

Note this idea, then go back to the center and contact the symbol again. Go out to the second petal and see what idea or image is there. Maybe this time you get *sexuality*.

Return to the center, and feel the symbol. Go to the third petal. This time you get *ancient wisdom*. Continue going back to the center, then out to a petal, until you have exhausted the associations. Don't jump from petal to petal, or you might start associating the associations with each other. Soon you should have an intriguing list: *poisonous, sexuality, ancient wisdom, dangerous, sensual, lizard, dragon, cold-blooded, sacred, feminine, eel, sinuous, silent, teeth, sheds skin, constrictor, viper, rattles, transformation, kundalini, in the grass, hiss, forked tongue, sidewinder, Quetzalcoatl.*

Your Dreamworld: Gateway to 24-Hour Consciousness

Do you remember your dreams in technicolor and vivid detail? Or do you dismiss them as the meanderings of your subconscious and let them slip away as soon as you awake? If you fail to bring them back to consciousness, you're losing a huge part of yourself and not benefiting from your activities in the other dimensions of your awareness.

Dreams provide us with intuitive guidance, but they are also the gateway to a true understanding of our universal nature. Our life, our world, extends far beyond the superficial reality we identify with wakefulness. Just as our conscious mind dreams at night, so our superconscious mind dreams our entire waking reality. Many books on dreams are available, so I will give you only the most important aspects of working with dreams to expand your intuition and live more superconsciously.

To become conscious in the highest sense, we not only need to become centered, alert, and intentional during our waking hours but must also

Dreams offer themselves to all. They are oracles, always ready to serve as our silent and infallible counselors.

Synesius of Cyrne

become aware of the many other activities and parallel worlds we occupy during our "unconscious" hours of sleep. There are twenty-four hours in a day, yet we assume we're living only the two-thirds when our eyes are open. What if you assumed instead that you were conscious all the time? Purposeful all the time? Learning all the time? Creating all the time? *Wow!* What sort of self-image might you develop? When you stop believing that part of yourself is "empty" or unconscious at night, you'll start to feel the positive, limitless nature of your true self. Your soul doesn't get tired and need to rest; it's 100 percent alive all the time.

Weaving Together Day and Night

To increase your intuition, think of your sleeping hours as a highly productive time. Some of your greatest lessons are learned here. But what are they? Program yourself to become curious. Stop thinking of sleep as a black hole separate from your "life" and practice connecting your daytime experience with your nighttime experience. Just as your breath comes in, turns, and flows out, then turns and flows in, so your day turns to night and night turns to day. Find the turn, enter the turn, become conscious of the turn. At the end of each segment, recap what you did, consciously completing the experience of either day or night. At the beginning of the next segment, practice setting your intention and aligning yourself for the kind of positive, growth-enhancing experience you'd like to have.

Doing a Nightly Review and Programming Your Dreams

At the end of each day, before you drop into the blackness, make a habit of reviewing your day's actions. In this nightly review you might take

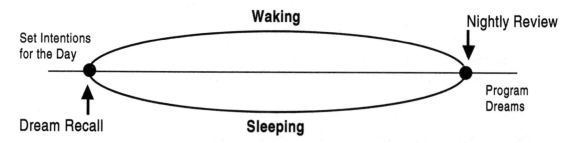

24-Hour Consciousness: Making Clear Connections between Day and Night

stock of what you accomplished and compare that with what your original intentions were that morning. Did you do everything you set out to do? If not, carry a few items over to the next day and don't beat yourself up. Be complete and content with what you accomplished today. Did you behave in a way you are proud of? Did you gossip or think negative thoughts about a friend? Were you kind? Wasteful? Disciplined? Playful? Would you like to do something differently tomorrow? What do you wish you had said that you might say tomorrow? What are you grateful for that happened today? Say your prayers as a way to begin connecting yourself with your nighttime experience, with the higher dimensions of your soul, and with the divine.

As you review your day and find a sense of completion, pay attention to the kind of experiences you'd like to have during the night. Would you like to visit a distant place or touch base with a relative who's died? Heal psychological or physical wounds? Offer a service to others tonight? Perhaps you'd like to visit an inventor's library and learn about future technologies. You could have an adventure with one of your guides or meet souls you will know in the future. Need help solving a problem? Ask your dream self to give you creative insights. Develop the habit of consciously programming your dreams and setting your intention for your "night life."

Programming Your Dreams

Imagine a ball of light about the size of a golf ball. Put a sentence that accurately states your intention inside the ball. Be specific: "I want to visit the Hall of Records under the Sphinx and remember ancient secrets about Egypt" or "I want to visit my dead grandfather and see how he's doing." This technique can be effectively used for programming dream recall as well: "In the morning I want to remember my most important dreams."

Put the ball of light with its message in the back of your neck near the base of your skull. Imagine it releasing its intention all night into your subconscious and the reptile brain. Then go to sleep.

Dream Recall and the Daily List

When you wake in the morning, don't lurch out of bed and rush to the shower. Take a few extra moments to gently rise from the depths of your

The dreamer and his dream are the same . . . the powers personified in a dream are those that move the world.

Joseph Campbell

sleep and to return to consciousness slowly so you can maintain a connection with your dreams. If you jerk awake, it's like throwing a boulder into a pond. The clear reflected images lying on the glassy surface will be shattered. The best way to start recalling your dreams is to have a strong resolution to know your own mysteries. Program your subconscious mind before sleep: "I will remember my most important dreams." Then practice waking up consciously, gently. Ask as the first thought of your day: "What have I just been doing?" Maintain the subtle sensations in your body before your linear mind kicks into high gear. Speak in the present tense: "I am swinging on a rope and jumping from tree to tree. I am aware of water below me. I have the sense I might fall." If you speak in the past tense, you'll distance yourself from the dream experience, and you'll find it more difficult to bring the knowledge back.

⚡

Even if I can't remember right now, a deeper part of me knows.

The best way to recall your dreams is to first make them real and physical to your body. Then your body will know that you meant what you said the night before when you asked your reptile brain to remember your experiences from other dimensions. You can either tell someone right away, describe the dream into a tape recorder, or write it down in a dream journal.

Recording Your Dreams

Each morning write about what you remember from your nightly sojourns. If you don't remember a dream at first, make one up! Or write down the first thoughts or feelings you have upon waking. Write or draw something in your journal every morning. Soon your subconscious mind will get the message that you truly do intend to know your dream world, and it will start giving you the real stuff.

You might leave a margin in your journal so you can come back later and jot down ideas about what your dreams might mean. If you had a precognitive dream that actually manifested, go back and make a note: "This happened three months later when I was on my way to the store and . . . ." You can also read through old journals, highlighting dream images and insights that you might integrate into a painting or a poem.

After you summarize your nighttime activities, turn your attention to the day. Remember what you didn't complete yesterday that you want to complete today. What impact do you want to make on other people and on the world today? What experience and attitude do you want to have? What do you want to give? What are you interested in learning? After you've determined your general intentions, you may want to make a more specific daily list, either in your head or on paper. Collect your energy and center yourself while you set your daily intentions.

You'll find that creating a continuity of flow between your daytime and nighttime experiences eventually helps you identify yourself as a more knowledgeable being, helps you draw from greater, more spiritual sources of information, and convinces you that it's natural and easy to know more.

Categories of Dreams

To help you learn how to interpret the intuitive information in your dreams and to know what you're doing each night, it helps to understand the basic categories of dream experience.

1. Daily processing. Did you ever have enchiladas and jalapeño chili salsa with a glass of fruit juice, two helpings of double-chocolate cake, and a double-espresso right before bedtime and then find that your dream state resembled a ten-car pileup on the Santa Monica freeway? Were you ever so pressured to find a solution to a tricky problem that you dreamed you were tangled up in mathematical equations all night, waking up exhausted the next morning?

If so, you probably didn't do your nightly review and complete the issues from your day. Instead you carried them with you into your subconscious mind and continued to process them. With a little attention at the end of the day, these dreams, which are often a waste of time, can virtually be eliminated.

2. Symbolic, personal process. This was Freud's favorite category of dreams, the kind where you leap into a turgid river, flooded with dark-brown mud, fallen trees, and dead animals. You're swept over a waterfall but halfway down a teradactyl rescues you and deposits you in its nest where you find your long-lost cousin Lenny who is still six years old. Symbolic dreams are always about some personal emotional or energetic process you're working on. Your attention is focused on your subconscious blocks, so these dreams often teem with contradictions, fears, desires, sexuality, violence, obsessions, and power plays. If you can learn to interpret the symbols and uncover the emotional patterns, you'll gain great insight into your psychological process.

3. Visiting other dimensions. Have you ever dreamed you answered your phone and someone you knew, dead or alive, was actually talking to you—and it sounded totally real? Or have you dreamed you saw someone standing at the foot of your bed and felt *sure* they'd been there when you woke in the morning? Have you ever dreamed you attended conferences or classes, or had surgery in a hospital, or met people with real names whom you don't know but suspect are real? Do you play other roles in dreams—a healer or a warrior—or do you have other families and primary relationships at night? Have you dreamed of flying, falling, swimming, riding endlessly in elevators, or squeezing through narrow tunnels? If so, you're moving in other dimensions of consciousness—in which you're freer from the limitations of time, space, and matter—and the people, activities, and movements you remember are *literal*.

When you dream of traveling in cars, planes, or spaceships, you're experiencing various "vehicles" or bodies of information; you're focusing yourself at different frequencies of awareness. A car might represent the information in your physical body, while a spaceship might represent the information in a superconscious collective body of wisdom. If you're going up or down in an elevator, you're changing from one dimension, or frequency of awareness, to another. Flying is the sensation you have when your consciousness attunes to the superconscious self, while falling represents your awareness returning quickly to the physical body.

4. Precognition and past-life recall. Donna moved into a new house that bordered open land. Shortly after moving, she dreamed twelve wild turkeys had gathered on her doorstep. We mused about the possible symbolism. Her inner guidance seemed to be telling her that some sort of abundance was headed her way. But several weeks later, as she approached her car at 6:30 A.M., she was confronted by a surrealistic sight—twelve wild turkeys, quietly gobbling and poking around her driveway.

Often precognitive dreams have an omenlike feeling. Sometimes they seem to be warning us about danger or the death of a loved one. Both my

A dream is a little hidden door in the innermost and most secret recesses of the soul, opening into that cosmic night which was psyche long before there was any ego-consciousness.

Carl Jung

grandmothers came to me with official dream announcements two weeks before they died, and in both cases the dreams contained messages of reassurance. It may be part of human nature to know ahead of time, at some higher level, about the significant punctuation-mark events in our lives and in the lives of those with whom we are intimately connected.

Repeatedly during life readings I find reincarnation to be a fact. Our subconscious mind apparently makes no distinction between the past of this life and experiences in other time periods. And yet, past-life information rarely intrudes unless it is charged with emotion. If you did not understand a traumatic incident from your past, it may surface when the grip of your linear mind loosens, as during sleep. People who died in fear or shock in a previous life may need to relive the memory until they can finally release the emotions. Past-life-recall dreams often appear as nightmares. One of my clients had recurring nightmares of running into a house, clinging to her husband, and knowing they were going to die right before everything went black. When she uncovered more details during a hypnotherapy regression and saw herself and her present husband as pioneers on the prairie dying in a tornado, her nightmares finally went away.

5. Visions and spiritual guidance. On rare occasions we receive direct messages from spiritual teachers or visions about our own future. These dreams often have a special psychic weight. Have you experienced a wise person counseling you in your dream? Have you seen images of a future society or had insight about the way life on earth might evolve? Perhaps you've dreamed you were on a spaceship, talking with intergalactic space commanders or extraterrestrials. When we focus on the superconscious mind, our imagination brings us dreams with a broad overview, great wisdom, and a humanitarian orientation.

6. Abstract, geometric patterns. Have you ever awakened with the feeling that you've just been in a fabulous reality but now it's reduced itself to a strange little cluster of dots and triangles? Or that you knew you were trying to realign your energy but all you can remember is the feeling of having fish scales or having four big black lines at the four corners of your body? And your actions made perfect sense only a few minutes ago!

When you focus your imagination on the highest levels of the superconscious mind, you may have difficulty remembering concrete images when you awaken, since the experience at these higher dimensions is so abstract and mystical. Yet when that learning filters down to your body and your present reality, your conscious mind wants something to grasp—and it creates an abstract symbol. The highest superconscious dreams, therefore, often come to us as memories of geometric patterns or vague sensations in our body. These dreams are so intangible that we often think we haven't been dreaming at all.

Interpreting Your Dreams

To use your intuition in drawing guidance from your dreams, you must learn to decode them.

The first step to interpreting your dreams is to determine their category. You may discover that a dream simultaneously fits two categories, for instance, precognitive and symbolic, as with Donna's dream of the wild turkeys. Even if she had only had the real-life encounter with the birds, the image would still have served as a powerful omen that she could similarly interpret. After Donna encountered the real birds, she felt the precognitive nature of her dream reassured her that her new lifestyle would be abundant *and* that some sort of magic or spiritual presence was close at hand and helping her.

To help find the appropriate category, ask yourself, "Could I really have been there? Could I have done this? Did I interact with real people? Was the motion I experienced actually a movement of my energy or consciousness?" By anticipating when the answer is yes, you'll learn to differentiate precognitive and past-life dreams and experiences in other dimensions from symbolic, personal-process dreams.

Next, make a list of the main symbols in the dream. List the sensations and emotions you had in the dream. Then list the intentions you had, the decisions you made, the actions you took, and the results you manifested. Review your list of symbols and ask of each one, "How does this symbol represent a part of me?"

If you dream your father has ignored your newborn baby, the baby might be a new part of you that's being born, and your father might be the provider and protector aspect of your personality. This dream snippet might be telling you that your new self doesn't feel safe in the world or isn't getting enough direction and energy from your internalized male power.

I can never decide whether my dreams are the result of my thoughts or my thoughts are the result of my dreams.

D. H. Lawrence

From your list of emotions, decisions, actions, and results, you can piece together an understanding of what issues you're currently processing in your subconscious.

If you are stuck, role-play the various symbols, merging with them and letting their life force and message enter you. Speak or write as the image. During a class Pam described dreaming how her black sports car went out of control. When she merged with the car in her imagination and spoke to herself, the car said remorsefully, "I need you to pay more attention to me. We're going too fast and not enjoying ourselves. I want you to tune in to me before you even turn me on, and I want you to stay conscious and be with me while we're moving. I feel abandoned." She realized it was her body's message to her, reminding her that she'd been much too distracted lately.

Look for themes in your dreams. When you review your dream journal, you may notice that you've been visiting old friends and lovers from ten or twenty years ago. This might indicate that you're completing a process, digesting old experiences, and preparing for a period of new creativity. Maybe you've awakened with vague feelings that work was being done on your body at a deep, subtle level. You've felt the strange sensation of balls in your body being rearranged, hands on your head sending in lines of light, a large triangle floating over your chest. You might assume from this that you are involved at the higher levels of your superconscious mind, designing new pathways and blueprints for growth. Results of this "psychic surgery" may show up in your physical world soon.

Is all that we see or seem but a dream within a dream?

Edgar Allan Poe

By this point you should be comfortable with your imagination, realizing that your conscious mind can focus at many levels of awareness and that they're all real in their own way. You should now be able to read the hidden messages inside symbols and be ready to use your intuition for practical purposes. In the next chapter, we'll delve more deeply into ways to access superconscious guidance.

BE INTUITIVE TODAY!
Receive symbols and their messages.
Be alert today for subtle internal pictures and symbols that bring you revelations.
1. Grasp a creative idea by "getting the picture." It could be a

design for a brochure, what to order for lunch, what to wear to a party, or how to structure a business plan.

2. Grasp an insight about your personal growth process. You might see yourself freeze-framed in the midst of an argument and have a sudden understanding. Or you might notice a magazine photo and say, "Gee, I could be more like that!"

3. Grasp an insight about someone else's character. You might see the person symbolically as an animal, or in some kind of pose, or as a child or an old person. Let the image give you its message.

Direct Writing Questions

Sit down with your journal and get quiet. Empty your mind. Pick one of the following questions and be with it for a few moments. Ask that you be able to receive creative insights from your deepest level of truth. Let the question serve as a magnet. Allow the first word to pop into your mind. Write it down. Let another word pop in. Write it down. Let words proceed forth, without judging them, without second-guessing where the answer is going. Don't jump ahead. Don't stop and read back over what you've written until the writing stops of its own accord. Helpful techniques: write as your own soul, innocent child, or future self; address your personality in the second person, by name; don't try to be too significant! Let your handwriting change shape. Change your speed and your rhythm, or write with your opposite hand.

- Take a walk and list twelve images, sensations, or sounds you notice, such as a red candy wrapper, rough board, blade of grass, tweeting bird, or cool breeze. Write a poem incorporating all twelve elements.

- Write nonstop for ten minutes: "What captured my imagination this week, for better or worse, was_____."

- "My wildest, most audacious fantasies, things I'd like to get away with, are _____."

- Describe an eccentric character you've encountered and an absurdly entertaining experience you've lived through. Take five minutes on each.

- Write out your nightly review, dream-programming statements, dream recalls, and daily lists in sequence for one week.

- Pick three dream symbols, merge with them, and write from their point of view for five minutes each.

- Write about five intriguing symbols from your waking life that conveyed information to you directly without words. How did you respond to them? Why did they occur?

8

Receiving Superconscious Guidance

The true lover of knowledge is always striving after being. . . . He will not rest at those multitudinous phenomena whose existence is appearance only.

Plato

If sacrifice consists of thrusting something precious out of the present moment, help consists in allowing something precious to enter. . . . The question of whether or not transformation is possible without help is the key to the whole problem of human life.

J. G. Bennett

Seeking Truth and Speaking It

Several years ago I experienced a period when the world's negativity and density overwhelmed me, and I encountered a crisis in my work as a spiritual counselor and teacher. I wasn't sure I wanted to continue with my chosen path, yet something told me to "just keep walking." I decided to go to the Source and have a heart-to-heart talk with God. I took a notebook and pen in hand, and with a burning need for clarity entered an intuitive state. I prayed, not knowing how the Source would answer. Moments later a vision overtook me, which soon became auditory. This is what I wrote:

I see an androgynous being, full of grace and beauty, and I know this figure carries the weight of Absolute Authority. This is power as I've never seen it, not power "over" but power "with"—the power that

Soothsaying, or truth-speaking, is one of the oldest and highest applications of intuitive knowing. Chapter 8 facilitates your finding clear direction for yourself and others. Here you explore the power of working with inter-dimensional teachers, taking shamanic journeys, and dipping deep into your well of wisdom. This chapter moves you further into the art of interpreting symbols and signs and of making sense of the guru we call life.

comes from living in total truth and total compassion. The being identifies itself as the Spirit of Loving Justice/the Fair Judge, and it speaks frankly.

"In previous lives, you have been impatient with those you taught, not because of their ignorance but because you lost your center and became unconsciously overwhelmed and angered by the fear you encountered. You used personal will to push through your own pain, and through that of others, and lost touch with grace and natural timing.

"As a result, you felt you alone were the mouthpiece of the divine, that by your own means you must raise up the 'unfortunates.' For this you were subsequently stopped, slowed down, even humiliated; sometimes you were punished or became ill until you could once again see how to honor each person's natural rhythm, direction, and timing, which comes direct to each from the Totality. You were forced then to receive the help you had been trying to give.

"As a result of these corrections to your overzealousness, you at times falsely assumed you were unworthy to teach or serve and that you failed God. Your subconscious is currently reviewing this history, so you can find balance and travel the wide path of the heart. Remember that yours is a story common to everyone who commits to full participation, truth, and service in the world. To know the fullness of human experience every person must feel the varieties of darkness and isolation. Only then can they clearly understand and demonstrate communion."

This forthright message, instead of humiliating me, gave me more compassion for myself and my path. Its logic completed some gapped circuit in me, and it was actually a relief to have my truth presented in a whole and merciful way. Afterward, I found it easier to understand others who overshoot the mark and make similar innocent mistakes of perception. Each time I have sought superconscious guidance for myself or others, the experience is always marked by a transcendence of personal shame and negative judgment and the reinstatement of love and beauty.

Often clients are nervous when they come to me for a life reading;

perhaps they fear I'll dredge up secrets from their past or bludgeon them with the truth. No one should fear hearing the truth or speaking it. If presented with the proper attitude and in the right context, superconscious guidance relieves the false pressure of the habitual guilts and "shoulds" that plague us and returns us to the clear straight path.

There are few practical applications of intuition that are as important as obtaining accurate guidance for ourselves and sharing with others our insights about them. As you begin to practice this intuitive skill, make a quick check: How open are you to hearing the truth, either from within or without? Can you comfortably share your personal truth with others? Superconscious guidance is available in every moment, no matter where you are or what you're doing. You must only ask, look, and listen.

If you can't recognize a superconscious message inside your brain, rest assured that the higher powers will use a friend, a stranger, a license plate on a passing car, a billboard, a song lyric, or an actor in a movie to speak what's in your own higher mind. Similarly, you may be used to give messages to others. Guidance is pouring out of all of us, in everything we say and do. We must be willing to share and be alert to notice and respect the ideas of others.

> REMEMBER
> ▼
> *Superconscious guidance is always marked by love and truth and is always empowering.*

Obtaining Superconscious Guidance

The twelve steps to obtaining superconscious guidance are summarized below. The first four steps consist of the preparatory work we've done in the previous chapters. To use your intuition to find guidance you must first set up your awareness to achieve maximum results. Once you've relaxed your body, become alert and aware, aligned and attuned yourself, it's time to get to work. What do you want to know? What do you need help with? The fifth step opens the second part of the process of obtaining superconscious guidance: creating a magnet, attracting an answer, recognizing truth, and validating and completing the process consciously.

How to Obtain Superconscious Guidance

1. Relax your body. Give your full attention to the rhythmic body cycles: your breath, heartbeat, electrical vibration, the vibration of the cells deep within you. Create a feeling of absolute safety within yourself and the environment around you. Center yourself inside your skin. Scan your body from toes to head, relaxing and softening the parts systematically.

2. Become alert and aware. Concentrate on the simplicity of what surrounds you at this moment. Take inventory, allowing both comfort and discomfort in your body and in your emotions. Set aside the need to do something about everything. Make no decisions now. Suspend personal will and notice the presence of divine will within yourself. Everything you notice is part of the Big You.

3. Align. Acknowledge that you (as the point of awareness, or conscious mind) are fully present in your body in this moment. Feel your connection to the heavens (the Father) through the top of your head. Move your awareness to the base of your spine and feel your connection to the earth (the Mother). Bring your body, mind, and spirit into perfect balance. Visualize energy passing through you in even, uninterrupted waves.

4. Attune. Identify yourself correctly as your soul. Affirm your true identity by feeling the quality of diamond light and by contemplating the qualities of the soul, such as: "I am infinite beauty, I am infinite compassion, I am infinite energy." Let the voice of the true self speak within you: "Be still; know that I am God. I am one with the flow of nature and grace. The answers which are appropriate for me, and which serve my growth, already lie within me." Breathe with a feeling of connectedness and oneness with All-That-Is.

5. Focus on your need. Feel your sense of incompletion, discomfort, and need for help or an answer. State your question clearly. Be specific in your request.

6. Ask. Go to the Source and address the higher powers with 100 percent conviction that an appropriate answer will follow immediately and easily.

7. Release. Trust that the great orderliness and wisdom of the universe knows what you need. Send your request. Have no doubts. Be in peace and wait in soft receptivity.

8. Allow the inflow. Do not judge what you receive, how you receive it, or what form the answer takes. Don't second-guess or try to refine the answer.

9. Consciously recognize the answer. The Source may use various means to deliver Its reply. Your answer may come in words, pictures, symbols, or omens; in the inner mind or the outer reality; through any of the sensory modes; from discarnate or incarnate beings; either immediately or in the near future. Use your truth and anxiety signals to determine how appropriate the answer is for you right now.

10. Record the answer. Do something physical with your intuitive response: write it down, tape-record it, speak it aloud to yourself or a friend, or make a piece of art. Make it real to your body.

11. Feel gratitude. Give thanks and feel appreciation for the availability of truth and to the levels of your own consciousness for cooperating with each other. Pat your body; hug yourself. This validates the experience.

12. Implement. Follow and use the information you receive. This completes the experience and frees you to move into a new phase of creativity.

Visualize a Truth Chamber

If you've completed the alignment and attunement exercises and still doubt your ability to receive information from the highest levels, you can reassure your survival-oriented reptile brain that you'll be safe contacting the unknown. Create an imaginary "chamber of truth," and enter it before you begin the second half of the process.

The Dome of Truth

1. Imagine an open space somewhere in nature. In the center of that space, imagine a crystalline dome. Walk up to it, walk around it, and place your hands on its walls. Feel the vibration of the crystal and adjust your body upward in frequency until you match the vibration. As you do, you'll feel your hands pass through the crystal, and your entire body will be able to "walk through walls." Go inside.

2. Feel the quality of the fresh air and clean energy inside the dome. Notice the clear quality of the light. Everything inside this dome reflects your soul and your highest truth. Relax. Orient yourself to the four directions. Imagine a chair in the exact center of the dome and sit in it. Connect to the heavens and the earth and begin the intuitive work.

3. Assume that no one else, unless they match the dome's

vibration, can enter your space. The powerful vibration of your dome must filter any responses, any entities, or any new energies before you can become conscious of them. This way, the visions you receive while inside your dome of truth will be compatible with your highest vibration.

After you've worked with the dome of truth image, you may find that you can carry it around with you, no matter where you are. If you're riding on an airplane or sitting at a dinner table, with a flash of intention you can re-create your clear space instantaneously.

Create a Magnet

We often overlook the second half of the intuitive process. In fact, you may be surprised that there are eight steps to what most people consider the instantaneous flash of insight. You can prepare your awareness to be fertile and receptive, but if you want guidance, you must have a need, an energetic magnet. Otherwise you will continue to sit calmly in the bliss mind of the unified self.

When I do life readings, for example, I take time to go through all the preparatory steps I've listed and to align myself carefully with my client. When the client has no specific questions, I have difficulty generating material to talk about. I am not in my normal inquisitive mind during a reading. Instead, I'm merged with the higher dimensions of my client's soul and my own soul, where we are content, like two old folks rocking on the front porch. At those levels many normally hidden things are known, but there is no great need to isolate any of it. Unless the client's emotions are magnetic with need or desire, no answers will be forthcoming.

A similar process occurs when you're working alone and asking questions of yourself. You must focus on what you want to know, then phrase your question in a way that allows the answer to occur easily. If you say to your superconscious mind, "I'm curious about my mother . . . ," it will not be able to respond since there's no actual question. Being absolutely literal, all it can say is "Uh-huh" or "That's nice." If you ask, "What about my mother?" the superconscious mind still cannot answer because the question is not specific. There's no hook. It can only echo, "Well, what *about* your mother?" If you ask, "Can you tell me about my mother's health prospects?" or "Can you explain the dynamics of my relationship with my mother?" or "Can you give me insight about why my mother's personality is so aggressive?" then the answers spring forth in detail.

So if you're going fishing, be sure to use a hook and bait it. Beneath each question, even under an idle curiosity, lies an emotional need, and under that lies a feeling of incompleteness. To attract answers, you must first get in touch with, and experience fully, the feeling of need, desire, and incompleteness. You must want a response so badly you can taste it. This creates the energetic magnet.

Next, describe your need specifically and form it as a request so the answer will be accurate, appropriate, and complete. If Jane asks, "Will I have a baby?" the answer can only be "Yes" or "No." If her question is blatant, *"When* will I have a baby?" her subconscious mind might block the answer. If she knew it wouldn't be for several years, because she had lessons to learn and fears to clear first, she might spiral into a self-defeating depression or paralyzing panic. But if Jane asks, "What do I need to know to be ready on every level to have a baby?" or "What are the hidden reasons I might subconsciously block the conception of a baby?" then she'll get an answer with meat on its bones.

Feeling a Need and Phrasing Questions

1. List three issues that have preoccupied you for the last month. Under each issue, list three questions you have about it, or three things you need to know to feel complete. Take time with each question and feel your desire to know each thing. Then carefully phrase your wording for each request. For example, your first pre-occupying issue might be "Why am I spending so much time alone?" Three things you want to know about might be "Why did my friend Doug abandon me, seemingly for no reason? How can I meet more people in my peer group? What's the higher purpose of all this free time and open space?"

2. Think of three people you know. Then list three things you'd really like to understand about each person. Phrase the questions specifically. My father: "What is the hidden dynamic under

my father's addiction to alcohol? How can I improve my
communication with my father on all levels? What lessons am I
learning from my father?"

3. List three idle curiosities and feel your true desire to learn
about them. Phrase your questions carefully. "Why does the
aurora borealis create colors and patterns? What causes my
migraine headaches? How will I know when I meet the right
people to work with?"

Direct Your Request

After you've formulated your request, the next step is to ask. To obtain
optimal results go directly to the Source, to the highest power you can
imagine. Then your answer will come to you—surprisingly, directly,
ingeniously, without the distortion of any specific earthly bias. As you ask,
recall the feeling of being a Child of God, and remember that you've been
created for a reason and are re-created moment to moment by the steady
intention of the Creator. If you can feel that the highest power knows about
you, that you are held constantly and lovingly in the gaze of God, you'll
develop a deep conviction that your requests will be answered immediately. Write your request, or better yet, say it aloud.

Next, release your request. Have faith that a reservoir of wisdom exists
where the life purposes and actions of all souls are coordinated, where your
request will be processed and a perfect response sent back. Wait confidently. In the movie *Brother Sun, Sister Moon,* one of the young monks,
who is tortured by lustful thoughts each time he passes the window of a
pretty woman, prays to God to help him over this hurdle. He tells St.
Francis how every day when he passes the window, he asks again for God
to help him, but nothing happens. St. Francis tell the monk, "My son, He
heard you the first time." He urges the young man to let go and trust, and
thus open himself to receive an inner revelation that might shift his
experience.

Releasing Your Request

1. Formulate your question, your need. Imagine placing your question or request in a hot-air balloon. Cut the balloon loose and

let it rise to the highest spiritual dimensions until you can no longer see it. Assume the Source will receive it.

2. Write your question or request and burn it ceremonially. Let the smoke carry your need to the Source.

3. Write your question or request on a piece of paper, fold it up, and tie it onto the branch of a tree. Let it blow in the wind and imagine the wind taking your message to the Source.

Receive Your Answer

Next, allow the answer to flow into you by staying open-minded and relaxed. Take what you get, and make an agreement with yourself that you will not second-guess and try to modify the answer. Allow the Source to use Its creativity and divine timing.

When receiving your answer, watch for God's unique deliveries. Superconscious guidance can show up in a dazzling array of forms. Sometimes it's a picture in your imagination or a gut feeling. Sometimes it's a spiritual guide, an omen, or a symbolic dream. Sometimes the answer comes in something your secretary says or something you hear yourself say to a client. Your answer may come immediately through direct writing in your journal, or it might take a week until you live through a surrealistic episode that highlights the issue perfectly. Be aware. If you're expectant, you'll feel the answer registering subtly in your body. You might include in your nightly review, "Did I receive answers to the questions I asked today?"

When you receive your answer, make it physical so your body will feel included in the process. Write it down, share it verbally, draw it, sculpt it, or act it out. You can even say it aloud with no one around. On the heels of recording your response, express gratitude for the process completing itself. Yes, there really is a higher consciousness out there, and It cares about you and helps you. Pat your body and give yourself a hug. Gratitude sweetens you, opens your heart, clears you, and helps integrate what's just happened. Finally, use the information you've been given. These last steps validate the process, complete things consciously, and open you once again to the possibility of having new questions and desires planted in your imagination.

Improving Self-Guidance

St. Augustine said, "There are many who have sought for light and truth but only outside where they do not exist." You are the expert on you, and you begin within. So you must start looking for guidance in your inner world first.

When you enter the inner realities, your sense of time, depth, and truth changes. An experience such as the one I had with the Spirit of Loving Justice can seem powerfully intimate when you're in your inner world. Yet when you return to the flat daily mind, the things you heard and saw can pale and seem silly—until you settle into the same unified, deep state again. Dreams can seem downright fantastical after you've had your first cup of coffee, but when you were in them, you were hyper-alive. Don't let the shallowness and speed of daily life cheapen your inner wisdom.

Gleaning Wisdom from Dreams

As we look for superconscious guidance, let's return to the realm of your dreams. So much guidance comes to us from this world that we must take our dreams seriously and have a bag of tricks for deciphering them.

Dreams are the touchstones of our characters.

Henry David Thoreau

Redreaming a Dream

Pick an interesting dream with clear images, one where you remember the beginning, middle, and end. In your imagination, run through the entire dream, refamiliarizing yourself with the symbols, feelings, actions, and characters.

Now, as you prepare to run the "film" of the dream yet another time, imagine that you're backing it up so you can see what happened just before your dream began. As you start replaying your dream from an earlier starting point, what do you see?

Run the dream through to the end, and then keep playing the "film" beyond the normal endpoint and see what happens next in your dream.

Write down the new insights about causes and outcomes. These new visions may help you find the deeper message in your dream.

When Laura did the Redreaming a Dream exercise in class, she shared a dream in which she walked on a flimsy rope bridge over a deep gorge. It started to swing in a high wind, and many planks blew away, leaving her with a precarious foothold. She was hanging on desperately when a thin man with a long knife approached the bridge and started sawing the support ropes.

When she redreamed this frightening scenario and backed up her "film," she saw that before she crossed the bridge, she had been lost in a dark forest. Finding the bridge was an exciting next step. When she extended the dream, she was surprised by the arrival of a burly man in a plaid Pendleton shirt who felled a giant tree across the gorge next to the bridge. She was able to step onto it and cross easily to the other side. As she chose the new stronger method for crossing, the old bridge and its saboteur fell into the chasm. She realized she needed to activate her true inner male energy and move confidently into the new phase of her life.

Another technique that works well is to intentionally introduce extra characters into an existing dream. You can start with one and add more.

Introducing a New Dream Character

Pick a dream that you're having trouble understanding—a frustrating dream or even a nightmare will do. Review the beginning, middle, and end of the dream, remembering the feelings, symbols, and actions.

At the point where you get frustrated or terrified, introduce a new character into the dream. Let your imagination make someone up, and continue the dream with the intervention and help of the new person, entity, or animal. What happens next? How does the dream resolve?

How does the new character represent a new part of you that might want to be activated? What is the lesson your soul is trying to teach you?

Don shared a story in class about how he used the technique of introducing a character to deal with a gruesome nightmare. In his dream, Don was being pursued by "Terminator Woman." No matter how many times he shot her with machine guns, threw knives at her, or exploded her, she kept getting back up and pursuing him relentlessly. To calm himself, he imagined that someone else was present to help him. It was Jesus, standing atop a short column. He said to Don, "What do you really want?" Don knew he had to pick *the* thing he wanted most of all. He said, "I want to be like you, with you in your energy."

Immediately, he found himself standing next to Jesus while the column rose slowly. He looked down and saw Terminator Woman crawling pathetically around on her belly, becoming smaller and more shriveled, and gradually disappearing. Instantly Don knew that he'd created her with his own fear and resistance. When Don chose a higher vibration and shifted his attention, the illusion could be seen for what it was. He realized he'd fueled his own "demons" for years.

Working with Your Friends in Spirit

Many enlightened souls cluster around this planet, and they are available to assist you the minute you call on them. Some have lived in the physical world; others, like angels, have never been physical. Nonphysical beings must communicate with you in nonphysical ways; they do that through the medium of your imagination.

⚡

My soul uses any means to give me a revelation when I need one.

Working with spiritual beings is a subjective experience—no one can prove the reality of the entities you see and feel, and perhaps it's not necessary. You will use whatever means you need to get through to yourself. Why not work with imaginal teachers as well as physical ones? Everything exists via your imagination anyway.

When I discuss this subject, I am concerned that some will glorify nonphysical beings as somehow wiser than we are ourselves. I agree with the Buddhist philosophy of "nothing special," and I think it especially applies here; we should not emphasize the superiority of either the physical realm or the nonphysical realm. There are as many enlightened souls in the physical world as in the nonphysical, and there are many derelicts and confused people on both sides as well. I prefer seeing all souls, incarnate or discarnate, as brothers and sisters. If we meet in the superconscious mind, all souls are equal in status.

Before you approach an entity as a guide, I recommend you establish a connection in your imagination with your "spiritual council." Just as dolphins live and communicate in pods of up to a thousand members, we also function on higher levels in groups of like-minded souls who have similar levels of evolution. By taking your place in this group of peers, you'll develop the habit of honoring your own wisdom and that of others equally, and of learning to access the knowledge that comes from the group mind, which I believe will be the skill of the future.

When I first opened intuitively, I rarely saw other beings but usually felt an energetic circle, like a halo or a crown, floating above my head. On closer examination, I saw little people sitting at the points around the crown, like the knights at King Arthur's round table. If I went "into the crown" I was sitting with others at a large conference table in a meeting room. I sensed that my council was composed of people of all ages, both incarnate somewhere in the world right now and discarnate. Working with this group is still my preferred method of accessing superconscious guidance.

Working with Your Spiritual Council

Imagine a round table or a flying saucer above your head. Let your awareness be drawn into that space, and get an image of the circular convening of your council of spiritual peers. Take your seat at the conference table. Notice whom you see. Do you know any of them? Can you describe the other people? Are any historical figures present?

Define your most pressing question. Then join with your council and give your soul's force to the group mind. Notice that everyone else is giving their essence as well, and the knowledge of all the souls from all their lives is blending together.

Place your question in the center of the group and release it. Let the group mind digest the question.

Perfect guidance will be telepathically transmitted back into your mind, and you will know it either immediately or later this week. Return to your body and open your eyes. Write about your experience in your journal.

If you prefer to relate one-on-one with a wise teacher, best friend, or spiritual coach, you might want to access superconscious guidance by visualizing an individual spiritual guide. There are many categories of these helpers: historical figures, mythological figures, ancestors, enlightened masters and saints, angels, archangels, fairies, devas, sprites, kachinas,

When we have an intuition, a mental image of a possible future, we're actually getting flashes of memory from our Birth Vision.... The intuitions we have, the dreams and coincidences, they're all designed to keep us on the right path, to bring back our memory of how we wanted our lives to unfold.

James Redfield

power animals, and spaceship commanders. You can even speak with an archetype, as I did with the Spirit of Loving Justice. As a child, you may have had imaginary friends with whom you routinely talked. Unfortunately, relating to nonphysical beings is an intuitive skill, a normal human ability, that we are told to ignore or even made to fear as we grow older.

When my niece Julia was three, she asked me how she could dream about the angels. I said it was easy; just think about them and they'll be right there. She thought for a few moments and then said, "Oh! Well, if I'm thinking about them, then they must be thinking about *me*!" And she trooped happily off to bed. I believe this is exactly how it works in the spiritual dimensions. Communication is instantaneous, and the calling to mind of Albert Einstein, for example, manifests him in your imagination, and you in his.

Before you set out to meet a spiritual guide, formulate your questions. Know what you want help with. Then it's a simple matter of imagining a setting in which one of these beings can appear to you, going there, summoning your guide, and seeing what happens. If you've studied Sumerian history, you might visualize yourself meeting with Enki or Ishtar on Mount Ararat. If you've been immersed in an exploration of shamanism, you might find yourself in a kiva being taught by a power animal. First lady Hillary Rodham Clinton created quite a stir when, in an exercise guided by Jean Houston, she imagined a conversation with another first lady, Eleanor Roosevelt, as a way to obtain insights about the responsibilities of her position.

Meeting a Historical Figure

Imagine yourself relaxing at a table in a sidewalk cafe where many people are coming and going. Let yourself feel that you'd like to talk to an expert about your most pressing problem.

Imagine that suddenly someone slips from the crowd and sits at your table. He or she says, "I'm sorry I'm late for our appointment. I got word that you wanted to talk to me. I'm _____. How can I help you?"

Notice the person's face, hair, clothes, accessories, body energy, emotional maturity, and the light coming from their eyes. Explain your situation and see what advice they give. Let the

experience unfold spontaneously in your imagination. When it's finished, thank the person, come back, and record what happened.

Why did that particular historical figure appear to you? Is there
a symbolic meaning? Does he or she have a quality you want to
activate in yourself?

Shamanic Journeys

Shamans, like all metaphysicians and psychologists, organize life into
three categories, or kingdoms: the upper kingdom, the middle kingdom,
and the lower kingdom. These three worlds correspond directly with the
subconscious, the conscious, and the superconscious minds. When a
shaman does his or her work, it is usually to journey to either the lower
kingdom or the upper kingdom in order to contact the spirits who live
there for information and to bring it back for use in the middle kingdom—
ordinary reality. Many shamanic journeys to the lower kingdom begin by
entering a tunnel into the earth, while journeys to the upper kingdom start
on mountaintops or treetops. Let's take a journey to meet and work with
one of the shamanic teachers: a power animal.

Working with a Power Animal

Imagine you are out in nature next to a hill. At the side of the
hill is a large opening to a tunnel that goes into the earth. Enter
that tunnel and begin walking. The tunnel slopes gradually and
bends, taking you farther and farther into the earth. Notice the
walls, the smell of the air, the feel of the moist dirt. You might
imagine a steady, slow drumbeat in the background.

Eventually you emerge into a crystalline cave with a fire
burning in the center and a large bowl of water sitting on the
ground next to it. Sit by the fire and wash your face and hands
ceremonially, cleansing yourself and stating your intentions to
receive clear guidance.

When you are ready, stand up and find the exit tunnel that
takes you up and out the other side of the cave. Follow the tunnel
up and up, curving around until you finally emerge into the fresh air
again.

Look around. You're in an entirely new place on the planet. As
you wait by the mouth of the tunnel, an animal with special

significance for you today will emerge from the landscape and make itself known to you. This animal has a teaching for you.

Imagine that you can merge into the animal's body and become harmoniously one with it. Let the animal take you somewhere and show or demonstrate to you something you need to know. Your power animal can talk to you telepathically and can transmit patterns of knowledge directly into your body. When you've learned your lesson, thank the animal, offer it a gift, and come back to your own body. Write about your journey. Why did that particular animal pick you today?

Finding Guidance for Others

The processes you use to obtain guidance for yourself can also give you insight into the lives of others. You can work directly with other people, face-to-face, or tune in to them in absentia. But before you begin, be clear about your motives. Why do you want to know about someone else? By understanding something about the other person, will you be able to be more loving in your own life? Are you responding to a request for assistance? Do you have permission to pry into his or her personal life? If you're going to share the information with this person, can you offer the insights neutrally, without self-importance or the need for a particular response? If so, you're off on the right foot. But if you're curiosity-seeking or if you need ego gratification, you're likely to receive distorted information.

Remote Reading

When you want to obtain superconscious guidance for a person not physically present, you can simply imagine him or her. Sometimes even just tuning in to the person's name is enough to give you the signal to access the energy patterns of that person's body.

Your body is an amazing mechanism. Because it is composed of particles of energy vibrating in a unified field of energy, your body has the capacity to receive knowledge directly from this field concerning any other form existing anywhere in the here and now. To the body, distance is no object. So just by getting the feel of someone in your imagination, your body can give you surprisingly accurate insights.

Quick Body Impressions

Make a list of ten acquaintances or public celebrities whom you don't know well, or at all. One by one, pretend you're inside each person's body. Feel their particular rhythms—their level of intensity, restlessness, calm, and motivation. In between each one, let your body momentarily repattern itself. Stand and move as if they're moving in you. Then come back to your own natural rhythms. Write about what you noticed.

Try the following technique with a friend. Do this little reading for them at an agreed-upon time. Sit in your house and focus on them while they sit in theirs and think about you for five minutes. After you finish, contact them and share the images you received.

Symbols of Guidance

Become quiet, centered, aligned, and attuned to the highest source of love and truth you can imagine. Imagine your friend sitting across from you, and let your body pick up impressions of his or her energy. Imagine that your friend's superconscious wisdom will present you with four symbols describing the current section of his or her life process. Let your mind relax and prepare to receive the first symbol, which will appear in the clear space in front of you.

The first symbol represents the current situation or phase of your friend's life. Let an image materialize from your friend's energy. Take what you get. Examine the symbol closely, turning it around if you need to. Ask the superconscious mind to give you impressions about its meaning. Draw the symbol or describe it in your journal. Then become centered and quiet again. Wait for the second symbol.

The second symbol represents a limiting belief holding your friend back. Let an image appear in front of you, and don't second-guess it. Examine it, ask for impressions about what it means, and then record it. Become centered again and ready to receive symbol number three.

The third symbol represents the action that your friend should take right now. Take whatever image appears, get all the details, ask for possible interpretations, and record the information. Recenter and prepare to receive the last symbol.

The fourth symbol represents the results of the action taken by your friend. Receive the image, describe it carefully, and ask for meanings. Record the information.

Contact your friend and share the results. Together, see if you can interpret the images.

In class, doing the exercise above, Robin's partner picked up the following images for her: (1) current life situation = a cat hanging by its claws on a screen door meowing loudly; (2) limiting belief = a closed jack-in-the-box; (3) action waiting to be taken = a horse galloping with its tail high in the air; and (4) the results of the action taken = a child fingerpainting with Day-Glo paint all over herself.

When Robin and her partner discussed the symbolism and combined the symbols into one process, Robin could connect it to her dilemma of wanting to move away from the small Southern town where she had lived her whole life. Robin, a musician and dancer, wanted to move to a city where she could find more training and friends who supported her interests. She interpreted the guidance as strong encouragement for her to follow her passions, let go of her secure but boring job, and take the risk of "getting wild and messy."

In-Person Reading

When it's possible to sit face-to-face with someone, your body will appreciate the direct contact and increased reality and will often be able to discern greater detail more immediately. You might arrange an hour to practice reading your friend Cindy. To take the pressure off yourself to "perform," explain to her that you will relay the images and insights you receive and together you will determine the meaning and possible application. Assume that Cindy actively participates in the reading, that her superconscious self is actually informing your superconscious self about what to say. Nothing comes to you unless she has given permission for it to be released into consciousness. Cindy must make the intuitive guidance meaningful for herself. When your priorities are straight, go through the alignment and attunement process, and open yourself to her unique energy. Let

---

TROUBLESHOOTING TIP
When Your Inner Critic
Won't Be Quiet

Make an agreement with yourself that you will trust the images you get. Even if you think there's a better symbol or answer just around the corner, take what you get anyway, and let your inner critic be educated for once by your imagination.

If doubts persist, repeat the exercise three times. The response you get on the third try is absolutely it. No negotiation.

the information you receive come from the highest levels of your combined souls.

Conscious Merging

Align yourself with your partner's body and ask permission to be able to "visit" with your diamond-light body.

Imagine separating from your physical body gradually until you are standing behind yourself in your diamond-light energy body. Then walk behind your partner, and gently and lovingly begin to merge into your partner's body from behind, sharing the space with his or her diamond-light body and matching it perfectly. (Hint: When your energy moves in the same direction as someone else's, it's non-confrontational and more harmonious.)

As you become aware of the dynamics of your partner's body, let your attention focus on any hot spots or holding patterns, places where energy is not moving or where confusion or panic exists. Speak directly in the first person as the spot, organ, or body part. Describe how and why you feel this way. What do you need help with? What is your message to the person? For instance, you might be drawn to the person's ankles and feet. You might say, "I feel sluggish and cold; not enough energy is getting through. I can't feel the ground or my connection through the earth to the energy sources I need. I want to feel the heat of the planet and move around more. I want to go more places and jump up and down. I have swelling and too much water in me, and I want to get rid of it. The kidneys have to help me _____."

Move through your partner's body and describe everything your attention is attracted to. When you're finished, thank your partner and his or her body aloud and gently withdraw until you're standing with your energy hands on your partner's shoulders. Leave all your partner's energy behind. Take all yours with you. Return to your own body and rejoin it. Open your eyes and share about the process with your partner.

Seeking and speaking superconscious guidance is an art. It challenges us to stay centered in our own authenticity, checking every piece of insight for its "just rightness" while simultaneously remaining open to the myriad

Be patient toward all that is unresolved in your heart, and try to love the questions themselves. Do not seek the answers that cannot be given you, because you would not be able to live with them, and the point is to live everything. Live the questions now. Perhaps you will gradually, without noticing it, live along some distant day into the answer.

Rainer Maria Rilke

TROUBLESHOOTING TIP
When You're Reading
Someone and You Think
You're Projecting

1. If suddenly you think that what you're seeing about another person might really be true for you, you may have encountered a "matching picture" or overlapping pattern, something you do indeed have in common with your partner but perhaps in a different way or to a different degree. This feeling may also occur if you encounter a negative pattern in the other person's subconscious that you are in denial about and don't want to see. If so, you will react negatively and your perception will be distorted.

2. Become conscious of the issue in your own mind: "I notice I'm talking about distrusting the mother. I know that's something I've been working on. Am I sensitive to it in this person because I know how to recognize it so well in myself?"

3. Check with your intuition specifically about this issue: "Does this person have the issue about her mother to the same degree that I do? Is it based on a different or similar situation? Is there anything she can show me about this issue?" Check that you do not have a negative reaction about your partner or an overly positive feeling of camaraderie.

4. Recenter yourself, become neutral, and look at the issue with fresh eyes.

5. If your intuition doesn't clear the confusion and you're still wondering if you're projecting, speak to your partner directly. "I'm picking up some distrust of your mother, but I know I have the same issue to some degree, and I'd like to double-check. Here's what I'm noticing . . . . Is it true for you?"

voices and facets of ourselves that constantly emerge from the void. Many times you'll feel waterlogged and out of touch with your certainty. No one is meant to proceed totally alone or to be the sole means of educating oneself. At these times it's helpful to ask for a new angle on your situation—then watch who appears as the messenger.

BE INTUITIVE TODAY!
Be aware of internal and external guidance.

1. Notice three pieces of guidance and whether they came to you from your inner voice or via an omen or another person. How did you use the insights?

2. Notice three pieces of guidance you provided to others today, either verbally or symbolically through your actions. Did the others consciously recognize the message? Was there something in the messages you provided that you also needed to hear?

Direct Writing Questions

Sit down with your journal and get quiet. Empty your mind. Pick one of the following questions and be with it for a few moments. Ask that you be able to receive creative insights from your deepest level of truth. Let the question serve as a magnet. Allow the first word to pop into your mind. Write it down. Let another word pop in. Write it down. Let words proceed forth, without judging them, without second-guessing where the answer is going. Don't jump ahead. Don't stop and read back over what you've written until the writing stops of its own accord. Helpful techniques: write as your own soul, innocent child, or future self; address your personality in the second person, by name; don't try to be too significant! Let your handwriting change shape. Change your speed and your rhythm, or write with your opposite hand.

- Write as the Spirit of Loving Justice: "How is my long-term process of growth going? What do I need to pay attention to now?"
- "When I try to tell the truth _____. When other people tell me things about myself _____."
- Think of one of your major life issues. List questions pertaining to that issue. Put them in their natural order and phrase each one accurately. Then, as if you are a master teacher, write an explanation for each one.
- Write as your body: (1) "Letting go is difficult for me because _____." (2) "I love letting go because _____."
- As your future self, write a letter to your present self and see what advice comes through.
- Describe how your personality and the way you do things is inadvertently giving a message to others: "What guidance am I giving to others by being present in their lives at this time?"
- "If I were one of the greatest experts in my field and a young person came to me as a mentor, what would that person ask me and what would I tell him or her?" Write a spontaneous dialogue.

9

Applying Intuition in Everyday Life

We are here to do.
And through doing to learn;
and through learning to know;
and through knowing to experience wonder;
and through wonder to attain wisdom;
and through wisdom to find simplicity;
and through simplicity to give attention;
and through attention
to see what needs to be done.

Ben Hei Hei

Intuitive Life Skills

Recently I asked several people to describe how they use intuition every day.

Jabarra, an interior designer, told me she begins her day by reviewing her dreams to find messages about her inner process on which she should concentrate. Then she tunes in to her body and notices what kind of action it wants to take and what she wants to do first. Throughout the day she takes time to notice the flow of energy around her: What's happening below the surface with the people she's encountering? Is she in synch with her clients and on time for appointments? Finally she takes stock of the remnants of the day and gets a sense of what needs to be changed, what needs a rest, and what needs action tomorrow.

Paula is a healthcare administrator whose intuition kicks in when she

Whether you need a new strategy for your business or want to relieve the pain of a migraine headache, intuition can help you achieve a successful result. Chapter 9 explores five areas where intuition can be used effectively in your daily life: improving communication, making decisions, opening creativity, healing yourself, and manifesting what you need. Remember, intuition is not whimsical. It is a reliable, useful means for living joyfully without friction.

gets a brainstorm about how to improve a system in her organization, how to present a proposal, or whenever something seems too good to be true and cues her internally to rethink things.

Galen, a color and image consultant, practices trusting what often seems to be an accidental "little feeling" about whether or not to do something. She has vowed always to follow through on what her inner voice says, even about the most ordinary details of life. For example, when she's looking for a parking space, her rational voice usually says, "Oh, just park here; you'll have to walk a long way, but this is probably the best you'll get." In the next breath, her inner voice chimes in, "No, go down the block." And when she listens, there's always a better parking spot waiting for her. Galen notices that she assesses others constantly at an intuitive level, receiving flashes about trustworthiness, competence, and compatibility. She also pays close attention to the way things show up in her reality, especially coincidences and the repetition of themes.

Kay uses her intuition to make sure her head doesn't override her body's needs, that she eats the right food, exercises, and doesn't participate excessively in social activities when she needs a quiet weekend. She also employs intuition to help her with personal and business telephone calls. She listens to the little voice that says, "Call so-and-so *now.*" She recently had the feeling to call her pregnant niece, and when she did, her niece said, "I called you three times today but hung up when you didn't answer. I really needed to hear your voice."

George, a psychotherapist, becomes quiet and asks questions like "What's important for me today?" Then he notes what comes into his mind in the next hour. He gets better insights when he shifts modes, like going for a walk after being at the computer a long time, or when he takes his mind off a problem and reads a book. He pursues certain directions with a therapy client when "something doesn't feel comfortable enough."

As you can see, intuition greases the wheels in these people's busy lives, helping them process information quickly, make decisions, interact appropriately with others, and take care of their own well-being. Intuition can help you navigate through your mundane reality in many practical ways. It can make your day more fluid, efficient, effortless, and entertaining. In the last chapter you practiced ways of obtaining superconscious guidance. Now let's bring intuition even further down to earth and see how you can apply it to some of life's most common tasks.

Improving Communication

Has anyone ever looked you in the eye and said, "I'd love to get together with you for dinner next week"—and though they seemed sincere, somehow you didn't believe them? Have you ever given detailed directions to someone, but somewhere in the middle they blanked out and you had to repeat most of it?

One of the biggest problems when communicating with each other is that we forget our communication has multiple levels. When these levels are not aligned in the speaker, the listener will receive mixed signals and is bound to be confused. Conversely, when these levels *are* aligned, communication is smooth, elegant, and even exciting.

Communicating on All Levels

Behind your words are invisible motivations, intentions, goals, and emotions. And mixed with every stream of language is a concurrent stream of symbols and imagery flowing from your imagination. In fact, the more convinced you are about what you're saying and the more real it seems to you, the more all your senses will activate and your body will become a powerful tuning fork, communicating reality to the bodies of the people you're talking to. *We communicate simultaneously with each of the three aspects of ourselves: body-to-body, mind-to-mind, and spirit-to-spirit.*

Communication actually starts at the spiritual, superconscious level with an intention to find harmony, similarity, or connection. Most of us do not take time to contemplate this. Are you aware of communicating spirit-to-spirit with your boss or the bank teller, for example? How often do you pause to become clear about your highest intention before you speak? Do you ever begin with a spiritual statement of intention, such as, "I've given this a lot of thought, and what I'm about to say is meant in the kindest way" or "By saying this, I hope we can become closer friends" or "I'd like you to understand my point of view"? Setting the tone can help streamline your communication process.

Spirit-to-Spirit Communication

The next time you have an important meeting, presentation, or conversation with your mate, become quiet before you speak. Visualize and feel the clear light inside the other person or people. Let your soul approach their soul(s) and declare your truest intention to them: "I want us to be able to work happily and productively together" or "I want to offer information that might help you." Let them share their true intention with you through your imagination: "I want us to reach an agreement" or "I'm open to knowing your ideas." Affirm to yourself that at the soul level all parties are interested in creating "win-win" situations. Write about your intentions. Perhaps use them as introductory statements as you begin your actual communication.

After you're clear about your higher intention, the endeavor becomes more task-oriented. As you think about communicating with someone mind-to-mind, look for the positive goal of your communication. Is it to clarify, educate, entertain, heal, protect, or support? What are your specific points and concerns? How can you make the important points? More significantly, what doesn't need to be said?

Watch yourself this week: How much of your conversation has a positive intent? Do you confuse people with a smokescreen of unnecessary words? Or do you say too little and leave your listener guessing? Do you present information in its most natural sequence? You may notice that a great deal of the "self-talk" that goes on inside your head and what you say to others is marked by negativity. Noticing this can help you locate your subconscious agendas. When you criticize, gossip, complain, or analyze something to death, examine your motives.

Check yourself for hidden agendas, such as, "They *have* to like my presentation and decide to buy 1,000 cases of vitamins, or I'll lose my job" or "I'll spout enough facts to make Wayne's eyeballs roll back in his head" or "If I'm funny and give her plenty of compliments, I bet she'll come home with me tonight." When communicating mind-to-mind, make sure you're free of limiting beliefs and don't impose conditions on the listener.

Next, the communication process drops toward the body and becomes sensory. Take a moment to visualize what you're talking about. Hold the

REMEMBER
▼

Communication that comes from fear only creates more fear. It's a waste of breath.

imagery in your body-mind, and send it consciously to the listener along with your words. If you can't picture what you're saying, can you feel its reality, do you understand intimately how it works, are you in the moment with it?

With body-to-body communication, if I'm telling you how to make chocolate-chip cookies, I organize the steps in my mind, and as I relate that logical data, I visualize and feel myself performing each step. In my imagination I measure the flour and feel its texture; I sift it and help it settle in the measuring cup. As I tell you about creaming together butter, sugar, vanilla, and eggs, I smell the substances blending. If I involve myself in making the cookies as I talk, my body will convey the nuances of the experience to your body. Then my conversation will be filled with rich, sense-oriented descriptions, and we'll light up with enthusiasm. The more real our body's experience, the more immediately we integrate what's being said.

Intuitive Congruence

If you're not saying the same thing at every level of communication, your listener may misinterpret you, not believe you, or not even hear you.

Here's how it can go. Your friend Noreen explains she can't join you for a movie, and you don't know why you're angry. Her reason seems legitimate enough: "My boss dumped a huge project on me, and I'm going to have to pull an all-nighter to finish it on time." If you could peel away the outer layer, you'd see that Noreen actually sent you pictures of her and her boyfriend having dinner at a posh restaurant. Her body sent you exhilarating vibes that didn't match her sob story. At the subliminal level, you knew you were being deceived and rejected.

Or has someone tried to explain something they didn't understand themselves? You probably felt intensely frustrated because your body was telling you, "There's no reality here! We can't trust this!"

It may surprise you that you are among the many who are incredibly telepathic and clairvoyant. Telepathy and clairvoyance are intuitive abilities we use every day in communicating with each other. We can read people and situations instantly. For example, we all carry pictures and patterns in our energy fields that match experiences in our past, even our past lives. If you previously were a politician or a priest or an artist and you now talk about politics, religion, or creativity, people will find you credible even if you're no longer an expert in these fields. An energetic, intuitive congruence will appear between what you say and what you actually are at your deepest levels. On the other hand, if you have a charming public persona but scandalous skeletons in your private closet, when people read you they won't fully believe how you portray yourself.

Around certain people do you become uproariously funny or feel especially comfortable about being your true self? Or conversely do you act out negative behaviors, become subservient, or feel excruciatingly self-conscious, clumsy, or unattractive? Why is that? You're telepathically or clairvoyantly reading and obeying the beliefs and attitudes they hold in their energy field. Some people are loving, tolerant, and believe the best about others. Around these people you have permission to blossom, and you know it immediately.

Other people send out unconscious messages: "I am a princess—give me everything!" or "I can't abide slovenliness!" or "It's totally irresponsible to be late!" Around people like this, if you're not conscious of the hidden agendas, you, usually the most fastidious and punctual person in the world, will unwittingly be late for your meeting with them and will then spill coffee down the front of your shirt. To prevent yourself from unconsciously creating congruence with someone's negative beliefs, say to yourself, "I know more about this person/situation than what appears on the surface. What do I know?" Then take an inventory of the ideas, no matter how strange, that pop into your mind. Once you become aware of another's biases, you can choose to act from a more superconscious stance.

To maximize your ability to send and receive communication clearly, first act as if everyone can hear the comments you mutter under your breath and everyone can see the pictures in your energy field. Let that be OK, and don't think things you don't want others to hear. Create congruence in yourself, then notice the congruence or lack thereof in the other person.

Watch for the same possible sabotages that you look for in yourself. Does the person have an emotional investment or a personal agenda that taints their communication? Are they talking about one issue on the surface and another underneath? What is the intent behind their words? Does what they say match what they're projecting in their imagination? Does their body feel the reality of what they're saying?

Stating Hidden Dynamics Out Loud

As you communicate, you pick up signals from your body about how the other person is receiving you. You must take responsibility for acting on this nonverbal feedback. For example, you're talking animatedly to friends over lunch when you notice that one is fidgeting and another is staring vacantly. You realize you've been talking for five minutes and no one has heard you; you feel like you're speaking in an echo chamber. Perhaps something you said triggered an uncomfortable memory in Joanne; she drifted off and became preoccupied with her old emotions. Mary sensed Joanne's discomfort and she floated over telepathically to see if she needed help. At this point it would be clarifying if you stated the "energetically obvious" out loud in a diplomatic way: "I sense that I've gotten off base here or that something I said triggered another train of thought. You look like you want to say something, Joanne. What is it?"

Or perhaps you're giving a talk at work explaining a complicated process. You're on an enthusiastic roll, but suddenly you hit a wall. When you check with your body you notice that the people in the group are no longer absorbing the data easily. Why? Your intuition tells you that Jim has reached his saturation point and needs to walk around in order to integrate what he's heard, several others need a bathroom break, and Jeanne has questions and won't be able to pay attention until she gets to voice them. If you state the hidden dynamics, everyone will perk up: "Let's stop and take a ten-minute break. I sense that we've reached a saturation point, and several of you may have some questions. Let's address those issues as soon as we reconvene."

When you're the receiver and someone is communicating with you, use this same technique of stating the hidden communication dynamics out loud to help that individual become more conscious of aligning with you at all three levels. You might clarify the spirit-to-spirit intent by saying something like "I really appreciate your intention to help me understand this, Joe." And to create more clarity at the mind-to-mind level, you might say,

"I'm trying to get the overall meaning of what you're saying, but I'm having trouble with the first part. Could you say it a different way?" or "Could you repeat that part and be more specific about the actual steps? I feel I've missed a few key pieces of information." At the body-to-body level, you might ask Joe, "Could you sketch a picture of what the result will look like?" or "Could you give me another example of how it might work?"

How to Achieve Congruent Communication

1. Align yourself spirit-to-spirit with the person or group you're addressing by visualizing the light within each person; stating your truest, deepest intention to yourself; and visualizing a positive result, however that might look.

2. Align yourself mind-to-mind with the person or group you're addressing by being clear within yourself about your positive communication goals (to clarify, educate, entertain, heal, protect, or support) and the points you want to make to achieve your goals. Be alert about saying the right amount—not too much, not too little. Check your audience as you go along to see if you're getting through.

Eliminate hidden agendas or negative motivations coming from fear and insecurity. Don't impose conditions on your audience; let them have the experience and respond to you naturally.

3. Align yourself body-to-body with the person or group you're addressing by visualizing what you're talking about and consciously sending pictures to your audience along with the words. If you can't get pictures, imagine the reality of what you're saying; make it real to your own body in as much sensory detail as possible before you speak. Be enthusiastic as you communicate.

Let yourself show who you truly are with all your natural expertise, all your mistakes and lack of experience. Don't hide anything about yourself.

Use as many sense-oriented descriptive words as possible to help give the other people's bodies an experience of reality.

4. When it feels right, state the subtle, hidden dynamics of the communication process out loud. This can often cut through potential confusion and put everyone back on track.

Telepathic Communication

My friend Larry went to the theater and later described to me how a woman with big hair sat directly in front of him, blocking his view of the stage. He craned his neck, dodged left and right to see, and finally, thoroughly frustrated, he asked her nicely, *inside his mind,* to please scoot down a little. He said he let go of the thought, and in about three minutes she slouched back comfortably and he could see the stage. Try the same technique when you're caught behind slow, unconscious drivers in the fast lane or next to loud diners at a restaurant. It seems we really do know what's going on in other people's minds. If you assume that everyone is telepathic—that we all transmit and receive unspoken thought waves, or even "need waves"—you might have fun playing with pure mind-to-mind communication and perhaps even cut down on your phone bills!

The following technique can bring amazing results by telepathically clearing blocked communication with people in your life. You can even use this exercise to improve communication between parts of yourself.

Tossing the Ball

Close your eyes, become quiet, and center yourself. In the clear space in front of you imagine an empty chair facing you. Let someone you are currently having trouble communicating with come in and sit down in the chair. Make eye contact but don't say anything.

Notice that on the floor next to you is a ball. Pick it up and set your intention to have an easy game of catch with the other person, then toss the ball to that person. Notice how you throw it. How much force do you use? Notice how the person catches it and tosses it back. Is the person cooperative? If not, start again with a clear intention to have the game work smoothly. Continue until the exchange becomes even. Then set the ball back down.

Say something to your partner that you've always wanted and needed to say, and let the person hear you and acknowledge you.

Then let your partner say something to you that he or she always wanted and needed to say, and hear and acknowledge the statement.

Reach down next to your chair and pick up a gift box. Give it to your partner. See what your soul has given this person. Then let your partner give you a gift box, and see what's inside. Thank each other and let the person get up and leave. Open your eyes and write about it in your journal.

Intuitive Decision Making

There always seems to be more than one direction we might take, more than one way to accomplish a goal. We're constantly faced with myriad options in life, and each possibility can have merit, each path can seem somehow attractive. What's an open-minded person to do? As always, with intuition: trust your body.

I heard that the chairman of the board of Sony Corporation had an unusual, highly intuitive way of making important decisions. He pretended the potential solution to a problem was a piece of food, and he tried to eat it. If he could swallow it easily, if it had a pleasant taste or left him feeling satisfied, he took it as a sign of truth. But if the solution stuck in his throat, sat like a rock in his stomach, or gave him a feeling of indigestion, it was a definite no-go. Making decisions intuitively using your senses can give you a quick sense of what's going on.

Intuition is neither the ability to engage prophesy nor a means of avoiding financial loss or painful relationships. It is actually the ability to use energy data to make decisions in the immediate moment.

Carolyn Myss

Sense Decisions

Think of a current problem in your life and make up several potential solutions. Close your eyes, become quiet, and center yourself. Feel the reality of your need to solve the problem.

1.   Imagine that each potential solution is a kind of food, and notice what happens as you try to "eat" each one. Notice your body's comfort level and natural resonance to each. Afterward, make notes about your insights.

2.   Imagine that each potential solution is a kind of music or a sound. Bring up the solutions in your mind, one at a time, and see what each sounds like. Afterward, make notes about your insights.

3.   Imagine that each potential solution is a smell. One by one, bring the solutions to mind and notice the odors they give off. Make notes about your insights.

4. Imagine that each potential solution has a texture. One by one, bring the solutions to mind and imagine feeling them with your eyes closed. What do you learn about each? Make notes.

Another technique for intuitive decision making uses a personal truth symbol. With practice you can learn to make truth checks with your symbol very quickly in the midst of business meetings, at the grocery store, or while you're on the phone.

Truth Symbol

Close your eyes, become quiet, and center yourself. Feel the diamond light inside and all around you—the vibration of your own truth. Let yourself be saturated with that energy.

Now, in the clear space in front of you, allow a symbol to appear—something that represents your own personal truth. Take what you get and don't second-guess your imagination. Examine the symbol carefully, turning it around to see the back, even looking at it from above. Open your eyes and draw a picture of your truth symbol.

Think of a current problem in your life and make up several potential solutions. Close your eyes and become centered. Feel the reality of your need to solve the problem. Bring up the first potential solution in front of you. Visualize it or feel it.

Next, overlay your truth symbol on top of the solution and see what happens. Does the symbol hold true to form or mutate? Does it get brighter or seem even more truthful? Accept the information you get.

Clear the space in front of you, then move on to the other potential solutions, bringing them to mind one by one and overlaying your truth symbol on each. Afterward, make notes about which options seem the strongest.

The following intuitive decision-making technique can give you more detailed feedback about each of your potential solutions. In this exercise you can move down various action paths to see which one makes your body feel most alive and which one stays strong over time.

When I am completely myself, entirely alone, and of good cheer . . . it is on such occasions that ideas flow best and most abundantly. Whence and how they come, I know not; nor can I force them; nor do I hear in my imagination the parts successively but I hear them all at once. The committing to paper is done quickly enough, for everything is already finished; and it rarely differs on paper from what was in my imagination.

Mozart

Potential Action Paths

Think of a problem in your life right now and several potential solutions. Close your eyes, become quiet, and center yourself. Feel the reality of your need to solve the problem. Bring the first potential solution to mind. Visualize it or feel it. Imagine that you are living this solution. Enter the "movie" and feel how your body likes this situation. Do you feel tension anywhere? Do you feel expansion?

Next, project this situation six months into the future. Notice your body's first responses. How does this option feel now? Can you get a sense of whether things have changed? Is it healthy for you?

Next, project this situation one year into the future. Notice your body's first responses. How does this option feel now? Can you get a sense of whether things have changed? Is it healthy for you? Is there tension anywhere in your body?

Clear the space in front of you, get neutral again, and bring the second potential action path to mind. Repeat the steps. Continue until you feel you've exhausted your current options. Don't forget to try the potential path of doing nothing.

Many of my students have successfully used the Potential Action Paths exercise. Dr. Dale Ironson, who taught it to me, told me how it had helped him when he was contemplating buying a house. When he first imagined owning a particular house, his body had a good reaction; it felt like a perfect fit. When he imagined the house in six months, he still got a good feeling. But when he imagined the house in a year, he was shocked: his throat tightened up and he could hardly breathe. His reaction was so severe that he asked his realtor about possible chemical substances in the house. Research revealed that the house had been built on a toxic-waste dumpsite. Clearly in a year's time he might have experienced dangerous leakage. By asking a question that he normally might have overlooked—"How good will this house be for me in the future?"—Dale's intuition was able to truly rescue him.

Enhancing Your Creativity

Julia Cameron, author of *The Artist's Way,* has delightful things to say about creativity and the intuitive "artist brain." She describes this part of us as "our inventor, our child, our very own absent-minded professor . . . .

It thinks in patterns and shadings. It sees a fall forest and thinks: 'Wow! Leaf bouquet! Pretty! Gold-gilt-shimmery-earthskin-king's-carpet!' Artist brain is associative and freewheeling . . . . The artist brain cannot be reached—triggered—effectively by words alone. The artist brain is the sensory brain: sight and sound, smell and taste, touch. These are the elements of magic, and magic is the elemental stuff of art."[1]

To get your creativity going, dare to be slightly silly. In my work in Japan I particularly remember a group of inscrutable businessmen who had surprisingly spectacular results with the Inventor's Library exercise. They came back from the meditation and drew pictures of some amazing inventions: goggles that took instant photos, ceramic pinecones that generated an endless supply of heat, and a blue-green gel that hardened in the sun but turned liquid in the dark.

The Inventor's Library

Close your eyes, become quiet, and center yourself. In the clear space in front of you imagine a huge building on a hill. Walk up the wide pathway to the giant front doors, and the guard will let you in. Enter the great rooms and notice the endless corridors of shelves stretching as far as you can see. On the shelves is an endless array of boxes—all different sizes, shapes, and colors. Some are so big you have to lower them with a forklift. Some are so small you can only see them if you get up close.

Let your body decide which way it wants to walk and when it wants to turn down one of the aisles. Let yourself wander around in the Inventor's Library for a while, looking at the grand variety of boxes and wondering what might be inside each one. Soon one of those boxes will catch your attention in a special way. When you notice "your" box, take it off the shelf and carry it to the end of the aisle, where you will find a private viewing room.

In the viewing room, remove the box's lid and see what's inside. Take the invention out and examine it carefully. Look for the instruction sheet that comes with it. What is the title of the invention? How is it supposed to be used? What components is it made of? If you have difficulty understanding what your invention is or how it's to be used, ring a buzzer and a guide will come in and explain it to you.

Return to your normal awareness and draw a picture of the invention. You might want to write about it: How could this invention be a symbol for something you need in your life right now?

Let's continue exploring our artist brain. Stay loose and experimental. Have you ever wished you could be a great musician, painter, sculptor, or poet? In your imagination, your inner artist is capable of anything.

The Art House

Close your eyes, become quiet, and center yourself. In the clear space in front of you imagine your favorite place in nature and a fabulous getaway house: an infinitely charming cabin in the woods, a mountain chalet, a beach house, a high-desert adobe with rock gardens, or even a penthouse in Paris, high above it all. This is your private place for creativity and self-reflection. Go in and look around.

There are rooms for every kind of creativity: a music room with every fun instrument you can imagine; a kitchen with state-of-the-art gadgets and mounds of fresh foodstuffs and spices; a studio with huge flat tables, easels, paints, pens, and brushes of every kind; and wonderful natural light. There is a place to sculpt, work with clay, make paper, or work with metal and jewelry. There's a dance studio with mirrored walls and a stack of CDs next to a player. There's a woodshop and a darkroom. There's a place to write on beautiful handmade paper with fountain pens and to type on a full-size color monitor. Anything you can think of you can have here in your art house.

Let your body and your artist brain lead you to the kind of creativity you want to indulge in first. Go into that room, touch the tools and materials, smell and feel it all. Surrender to a total involvement with the medium you've selected, letting yourself experiment fully. Concentrate your energy, then release your energy. Enjoy the natural movements of the currents that want to flow through you.

When you're finished with your art play, return to normal awareness and make notes in your journal about what you did and how it felt.

Symbols Convey Concepts, Associations, Feelings, and Experiences Almost Instantly

You can also stimulate your creative process by using symbols to activate the connections between your body consciousness and your higher abstract inspiration. Scan through the symbols on this page, first getting quick body impressions. Are you slightly attracted or subtly repelled by certain ones? Do you feel happy, stressed, anticipatory, reassured, or motivated toward some kind of action?

Making Associations

Explore each symbol in your journal.

Write a string of associated words, as fast as you can, without reviewing the list. For instance: *Camera, lens, shutter, film, eye, click, blink, view, zoom, look, pictures, format.*

Then write a series of words or phrases that convey emotions or a feeling state you associate with that symbol: *Private view, enjoy, preserving a moment, being close to people and landscapes, magical images, loving details, perfect framing.*

Finally, write a two-sentence story for each symbol using some of the associations you listed and perhaps building from that: "My lens shutter blinked rapidly, preserving an intimate moment with the hummingbird. I enjoyed being with her fragile magical body and zooming into her high-speed world."

Another way to keep your creativity flowing in the midst of our fast-moving, logical, stress-filled lives is to write a haiku-style poem every day. Japanese haiku is a lovely form of poetry that captures a thought-provoking, timeless moment in three simple lines.* On my last trip to Tokyo, I made a practice of creativity by writing one haiku per day to capture essential feelings:

diesel fumes and beeping backing
trucks in off-white rain
a flowered umbrella!

battleship buildings layered
grayblue on a grayblue sky
fake bird calls and surf

mountain of fermenting disco club trash
spills across sidewalk by bus stop
fifty commuters, unblinking, on line

on the corner today, fat puppies
for sale, in cages
everyone squats to ooh and ahh

Healing Yourself

Your intuition can be the vehicle to bring you relief and comfort as well as more profound healing at both an emotional and physical level. Once in a dream, I experienced one of the most real and powerful healings of my life. Solely through the vehicle of imagination, I was given a confirmation

---

*Traditional haiku is composed of three lines of five, seven, and five syllables each, and usually makes reference to one of the seasons. I, in typical American fashion, take creative license and don't pay much attention to the strict discipline of the form.

that energy and attention from the divine, superconscious realms were indeed flowing through me.

In the dream, I had coughed up my heart and was cupping it, still beating, in my hands. It wouldn't go back in. I screamed for help, but no one came. And the longer I held it outside my body, the weaker it became until it cracked in two. "Please, someone—help me!" Then, in the nick of time, a magnificent man materialized in front of me—eight feet tall, majestic and full of power, quiet with dignity and the wisdom of the ancients.

His skin was the bluish black of the clear night sky, and he radiated indigo black light, cool and penetrating, which went straight into me. His presence was infinitely calming. His eyes, like still, deep lakes at night, glowed with the black fire of outer space. His black, shiny hair hung straight and long down his back, reaching well below his waist. "I am the Angel of Healing," he told me, without speaking aloud. He bent over and looked into my eyes. I was transported into universes beyond anything I could ever remember and was reassured about who I really am. He wrapped his huge, long hands around mine, gently reuniting the halves of my broken heart.

As the heart knit itself together, he talked casually to my frightened mind: "This is not really your heart. Did you know this? It belongs to God and has been given to you on loan. It is God's force that makes this heart beat and God's truest impulse that makes this heart love. Give your heart back to God now, and it will once again be whole and happy and light as a feather. And God will give you the gift of a full life, and you will give God the gift of living as You. Relax your throat, open your mouth, make the long sound of the universe: *Ahhhhhh.*"

And he slipped the now-perfect heart into its rightful place. With one hand on my chest, he slowly passed the other up across my forehead and over my crown. The indigo black light penetrated my skin, bone, brain, and beliefs. "Here, now. Let me help you forget what you know," he whispered. And I sighed and fell back against him, released from my prison of limited thinking and memories, free from perceptions no longer appropriate for that day. I floated in the dark peace of the cosmic mind, fresh and clean, like a baby waiting to be born, and grateful for the chance to know, and to love, anew.

⚡

Each moment, place, and experience is whole and filled with my whole love.

*What do we live for
if it is not to make life
less difficult for each other?*

George Eliot

Though this healing happened in a dream, it had an almost tangible quality and is still burned into my memory as if it is continually happening. When our inner need for healing becomes great enough and our request for help is deeply sincere, though we may not even know we have sent out the cry, some sort of "healing angel" comes to us, in dreams or in real life, with healing eyes, healing light, healing hands, healing words. Healing! Whole libraries of books exist on the subject. What I say here will be just the barest nubbin, something that I hope will spur you to experiment with your natural healing motivation, energy, hidden knowledge, and heart power.

The most profound healing experiences happen when your intuition is open, when you're receptive but not naive, and when you're on the vulnerable edge of need with a kind of sweet sincerity. It is this state of sweetness, trust, and readiness that brings the "healing angel" into the space with you. In the following exercise, take time to find this mood or healing attitude within yourself.

Calling the Healing Angel

Sit close to a mirror (remove your glasses) and stare into your own eyes. Contemplate: "Who am I?" Contemplate: "What causes me pain?" By delving deeply into the psychic, emotional, or physical pain in yourself, you'll begin to formulate a sense of what in you needs healing.

When you've found a wound, close your eyes and become centered. Concentrate on the feeling, the helplessness, the confusion or lack of clarity, and on your desire to heal this issue in yourself. Feel your need to dissolve this limitation from your being. Yearn for the Healer. With simplicity in your heart and no preconceived ideas about form, ask for help from the Healing Angel. You can specify that you'd like a visitation in the inner world and the outer world.

Let a vision occur in your imagination, and receive the healing in the form of light, touch, words, and teachings. Afterward, write about it. Stay alert this week for a parallel physical manifestation of healing in your life.

Everyone has healing power of one sort or another, which when called into action through need can work wonders. Mythologist/psychologist

Jean Houston tells a dramatic story of how she dissolved a potentially cancerous growth during one intensive weekend of focused visualization and meditation work.

One of my clients, Marybeth, told me how she had cut her finger deeply while chopping vegetables. After an initial shock of a few seconds, she quickly centered herself, brought her superconscious mind into the cut, and flooded the tissues with love and kindness. As she dressed her wound physically, she held the hurt finger calmly with the hand that had caused the wound. She let her right hand apologize to her left hand, saying, "I'm sorry. You were helping me, and I wasn't paying attention to you. I was going too fast. I didn't mean to hurt you, and from now on I'll respect you." She talked to the cells that had been so shockingly separated from each other, saying, "It's OK. You don't have to be scared. Just let go; I'll bring you back together again, and you can find each other." She visualized and felt the energy flowing normally in that little section of her finger. Then she simply relaxed her entire body, affirmed that everything was normal, and returned to fixing dinner. The next day, the cut was almost entirely healed.

Perhaps encoded within your own DNA is the knowledge base you need to heal any ailment in your system. Imagine that the slight turn from alignment and harmony which causes pain and illness in the first place can just as easily be rotated into its perfect position—no extra degree of difficulty involved. Try this exercise to help heal a physical problem in your body.

Happy Cells

Think of an area of your body that feels tense, has pain, or seems to want attention. Close your eyes, become quiet, and center yourself. Sense how large the area is. Send part of your awareness into the area, like an investigative reporter with a camera. Take a picture of some of the disturbed cells in the area and project it on a screen in front of you. Next to this image, let your DNA memory bank project the image of perfect, happy, healthy cells of the same type.

Watch the images for a while and sense how the unhealthy, stressed cells are interacting with each other. Are they cooperating? Are they absorbing and eliminating what they need? Is their vibratory level irregular? Are they complaining about something? Can you hear any sound the cells are making? Now notice how the group of healthy, happy cells is functioning. See and feel the difference in the level of openness, cooperation, trust, giving and receiving. Notice the cells' optimal frequency level. Can you hear any sound these cells are making?

Match your energetic vibration to the level of the healthy cells. As you do, visualize the image of healthy happy cells overlaying and merging into the image of the tense cells. Let the higher vibration flow into the lower and raise it. See the images on your screen blend into one healthy, functioning group.

Send the investigative reporter part of your awareness into the needy part of your body and extend the happy-cell image and frequency throughout the whole field of cells there. Imagine the cells all vibrating and jiggling together, exchanging energy, receiving and giving freely. Imagine that the sound they're transmitting is like a song sung by a chorus. Keep your stabilizing attention on the cells for a while and telepathically transmit to them, "This is your natural state of being. You never have to leave this experience. I will support you in maintaining this state by consciously remembering what it feels like."

Don Juan once told Carlos Castaneda that well-being was a condition one had to groom, "an achievement one had to deliberately seek. He said that the only thing I knew how to seek was a sense of disorientation, ill-being, and confusion. He laughed mockingly and assured me that in order to accomplish the feat of making myself miserable I had to work in a most intense fashion. . . . 'The trick is in what one emphasizes,' he said. 'We either make ourselves miserable or we make ourselves strong. The amount of work is the same.'" [2]

Manifesting What You Need

Some teach that if we control our thoughts and learn to manipulate our energy, we can manifest anything. Certainly there is great power in working in alignment with the principles that govern the descent of creative energy from the blueprints of the higher mind down into the magnetic, coalescing physical world. Follow the steps in the right order, apply the right amount of intention and focus, and—voilà!—you've got what you asked for. But since it's so potentially misleading to think that more money, a bigger house, a more devoted partner, or a thinner body would give us a better life, I've always been leery about "prosperity consciousness" and its have-it-all-now philosophy. Some greater perspective seems to be missing.

So when we talk about manifesting, we must first address the issue of the right use of will. If we impose our will on life and aim to manifest things that strengthen our ego and make us feel secure, we can lose touch with our spiritual identity. But neither should we blindly accept our fate and express no ideas of our own. We don't want to be arrogant, but we don't want to be victims either. We don't want to think that the material world is the be-all and end-all, nor do we want to live as ascetics, denying the importance of our physical humanity.

Many clients tell me stories of magical manifesting, or of failure to manifest, based on these two very different attitudes. Many people learn to rely on their own efforts to make their way in the world, raising themselves up by the bootstraps. This heroic, self-affirming method works for a time, but eventually their focused will power and energy stops getting the same results. People in this category of manifesting are forced by life, often through loss of relationships or health, to surrender their ambition and materialism and to accept help from the unseen realms.

Other clients rely entirely on other people and on "providence" to give them what they need, assuming that whatever comes is what they need. They learn to have few personal wishes, to receptively follow the serendipitous clues, opportunities, and connections that drop into their laps. They take no credit for what happens to them. Eventually, often because the quality of their experience has devolved and they feel unmotivated, depressed, and victimized by other people and by life, they are forced to trust and act on their own desires.

If you've been manifesting your life predominantly from one view, it's probably time you integrated the other view to achieve a more balanced understanding of creativity. We can find a way to move through life that strikes a balance between having to beat down doors and having to sit

Do you know that your fervent wishes can only find fulfillment if you succeed in attaining love and understanding of men, and animals and plants, and stars, so that every joy becomes your joy and every pain your pain?

Albert Einstein

⚡

If an idea comes into my
imagination, there's a way
I can manifest it.

around humbly waiting for word from on high. In this new integrated way, we accept that the ideas we get naturally *are* the word from on high and that if we get a truth signal we should step toward the vision with real action, because no one else will do it for us. By acting in faith, the next thing we need to manifest is drawn into our present reality, and we realize we want it. And as we trust and act, we get all the help we need along the way from both visible and invisible sources.

If you want to manifest more money, to use your intuition to help you materialize that reality, first you must define the dollar amount and make it verbal: "I want to create 50 percent more income this year, or $150,000." Next, drop that conceptual idea from your neocortex to your midbrain and find a way to relate to and bond with the concept. What does 50 percent more of *anything* feel like? How does it translate into your sensory experience? Visualize a pile of fifteen hundred $100 bills. Better yet, get play money and physically create it. Put your hands in it.

Or imagine what kind of experiences $50,000 more per year will provide for you. Use your imagination to flesh out the ideas so they can become real to your body. Will you go on a trip to India? Buy a boat? Refurbish your wardrobe? Can you imagine this much money being normal?

Or imagine the money goal as a quality of energy. If you were being 50 percent more of your true self, doing 50 percent more of the things you love, what would your life feel like? What kinds of ideas might interest you? How would your habits change? What would your attitudes and energy level be like?

Finally, drop the idea into your reptile brain and let your body get excited about how it's starting to have more stimulation, more balance, more energy, more variety, more love, more creativity. Since your body registers only the present moment as real, start acting right now as if you already have this amount of money and these kinds of experiences, and do whatever you're drawn to do *from this reality*. Have the experience of the reality slightly before you have the actual reality.

One note of warning: Before your subconscious will allow you to manifest a different or greater reality, you must give up your complaining and feelings of being unappreciated and deprived. Here's how to optimize the use of your intuition to bring new creations. First, imagine what it would feel like to be fully appreciated by others, and imagine that life actually is fair. Everyone's doing what he or she needs to do. What you have in your life now is the result of the things you were thinking last week. What you're thinking now will create next week's experience. What you have now is what you've allowed yourself to have so far. Second, start appreciating what you have, being with it, and enjoying it without needing to change it. It feels fine, you feel full, you have what you need, and all is well just as it is. Third, let your satisfaction and fullness brim over. Actively express your appreciation to others, to nature, to God. Might you actually *provide* others with the very thing you've demanded that they give you? Once you're clear and ready, here's a technique you can use to help bring something new into your reality.

⚡

What I have now is
what I already asked for.

Mocking Up

Pick something you'd like to manifest soon. It can be something specific and concrete, like a new laptop computer, or a life situation, like a new job or relationship. Before you start the meditative part of this exercise, do some groundwork in your journal. If it's a new laptop you want, get pictures of it, write down the purchase price, go to the store, and see it, feel it, use it, understand it. Write about it and describe yourself using it. Let your body become familiar with the idea that the laptop is a normal part of your life.

If it's a new job you want, outline the way you want to feel at work. Describe the people you're working with as if they're present. Describe your desk and work space in detail. Describe the tasks you get to do, the challenges that stimulate you, the feeling of being eager to get to work in the morning. Create the emotional reality first, then fill it in with body-pleasing sensory details. You may not know the exact job description, but you know at a deep level the kind of self-expression and interaction with others you need to have to feel whole and happy.

Close your eyes, become quiet, and center yourself. Feel your desire for the object/situation—and notice why you need it to enrich your life experience. In the clear space in front of you, visualize the energy body or energy blueprint of the object/situation you want to manifest. Feel its core vibration first. Let your body get to know it the way two friendly dogs become familiar with each other. Let your energy field extend out through the blueprint and embrace it and become intimate and relaxed with it. Let the object/situation become a living part of your energy field.

Get the idea now that the more transparent the energy of the object/situation is in your imagination, the farther away it is in time and space. The more solid and dense it seems, the closer it comes to present time and to your physical body. Concentrate on the energy blueprint and invest your attention and life force in it. As you do, draw in "matching funds" from the higher realms and know that the divine is also investing its attention to help this become real for you. Watch the object/situation flesh out with moving particles, molecules, shape, color, sound, and texture—becoming more and more real looking.

Say to yourself and to the Divine: "I am ready to live with this *now*. I am willing to accept the growth and new experiences this will facilitate. I give permission for my body to manifest this immediately." Take the image of you, your body, and the object/situation all living together and imagine capsulizing it with the command "Get it now/have it now" into a tiny pill and dropping it down a chute from the center of your midbrain into the core of your reptile brain. Let the pill rest there. Your reptile brain will happily launch into action. Take your attention off the process and get on with the next thing in your life. Watch for the realization through your own action or outside action.

> *To be really great in little things, to be truly noble and heroic in the insipid details of everyday life, is a virtue so rare as to be worthy of canonization.*
>
> Harriet Beecher Stowe

I've sketched a few ways you can apply your intuition and imagination to make your daily life more flowing, functional, and enjoyable. And now, squeaking in as I finish this chapter, here's a late-breaking e-mail from Lisa in Tokyo, who is responding to my survey about daily uses of intuition. She says, "My houseplants tell me when they're thirsty. And when I fill my bathtub with hot water, I can't get the knob to adjust the temperature perfectly, so I change it and come back a number of times, and often without even putting my hand in, I just 'feel' when it's ready for me to jump into.

And sometimes I open a dictionary or book to the exact page I need at precisely the right moment! I know this sounds crazy . . . ." It doesn't sound crazy at all—it sounds like Lisa has found a way to make her ordinary life quite self-entertaining.

BE INTUITIVE TODAY!
Activate your telepathy.
Trust your telepathic sense about someone. Notice what they're saying underneath their words, then respond aloud to their unexpressed thought as if they had said it. See what happens.

Direct Writing Questions

Sit down with your journal and get quiet. Empty your mind. Pick one of the following questions and be with it for a few moments. Ask that you be able to receive creative insights from your deepest level of truth. Let the question serve as a magnet. Allow the first word to pop into your mind. Write it down. Let another word pop in. Write it down. Let words proceed forth, without judging them, without second-guessing where the answer is going. Don't jump ahead. Don't stop and read back over what you've written until the writing stops of its own accord. Helpful techniques: write as your own soul, innocent child, or future self; address your personality in the second person, by name; don't try to be too significant! Let your handwriting change shape. Change your speed and your rhythm, or write with your opposite hand.

- Think of a recent communication in which you were misunderstood. Write separately as your soul, your mental body, your emotional body, and your physical body: "What do I really want to say to the other person or people?"

- List words or phrases you use regularly that promote negativity, unconsciousness, procrastination, limited thinking, ugliness, stupidity, or lack of respect for others and yourself. Try to eliminate these words from your vocabulary.

- Pick a person who upsets you and write from your body's point of view about their lack of congruence: "The mixed signals I'm getting are _____."

- Write directions to your house for people coming from the north, south, east, west, and even from above. Be simple, clear, specific; give enough information but not too much. Use good sensory descriptor words, for example, "hairpin turn" instead of "U-turn."

- Write as your future self: "What I feel and know about the important decisions looming before my present self is _____."

- Write as the Healing Angel: "To facilitate healing for (my mother, my father, my child, my boss, my cat, my best friend, and so forth) I would first _____, then I would _____ and _____."

- Write from the point of view of your body: "I'm in the process of manifesting _____ now for the near future, and I'm doing it by _____."

10

Staying in the Natural Flow

Chapter 10 helps you
maintain your delicate
new way of knowing in
a world crowded with
skepticism. It helps you
understand the typical
aberrations in the
development of intuition,
missteps that can distort
effectiveness and slow
down your process of
spiritual growth. If you,
like all of us, occasionally
trip and fall in a hole,
this chapter provides
important tips for dust-
ing yourself off, getting
back up, and entering the
flow again.

I am an experiment on the part of nature,
a gamble within the unknown,
perhaps for a new purpose, perhaps for nothing,
and my only task is to allow this game
on the part of the primeval depths to take its course,
to fulfill its will within me
and make it wholly mine.

Herman Hesse

Congratulations! You've succeeded in covering the basics of the intuitive process, and by now you should be able to trust and apply your intuition in many ways to create a smoother, fuller, more rewarding life.
Having practiced accessing your direct knowing repeatedly for some time,
you must also be aware how effortlessly intuitive help arises when you need
it and how living intuitively can spiritualize your ordinary reality.

Yet at the same time, you've probably experienced firsthand how your
intuition can occasionally be blocked or distorted by subconscious fears
and then just as quickly can start flowing again as you return to compassion and understanding. I hope that at this point you are excited to continue applying your intuitive awareness to all areas of your life—yet are
also mindful that honing your new perceptual skills to a fine edge will take
time and attention.

As you proceed down the river of life, there may be a few rough spots
and obstacles hidden beneath the waters. As I advocated in the section on

The highest point of life may be to live in a state of pure flow, a "now-state" without past or future, in which prediction and control are not factors—a state of continual, instant-by-instant adaptation to the unknown.

Joseph Chilton Pearce

improving communication, stating hidden dynamics out loud can often clear the way immediately. The same is true when dealing with the potential blind spots in intuition development. By talking about them, even laughing about them, you won't waste too much time and energy caught in swirling whirlpools.

Some Things to Watch Out For

As on any path to higher awareness, we are bound to make some errors of judgment while developing intuition—after all, to know ourselves as spiritual beings requires a fairly dramatic shift from our everyday consciousness. That's probably why every spiritual path has had its blind spots; it's hard to see the whole picture all at once. Channeling ascended masters may seem as far off the mark to future generations as vowing to not eat or speak, trying to appease the gods through blood-letting and human sacrifice, and burning women who practiced natural healing and midwifery now seem to us. To err is human, but we can learn to identify our perceptual "mistakes," correct them, let them go, and move on more rapidly.

Really, the worst that might happen if you make a mess of things is that you'll stall your own growth for a while and possibly contribute to stalling other people's growth. You might add some negativity to the world and reaffirm the already overwhelming thought we all unconsciously buy into—that the world is a place of suffering, and we'll never get out of it, and we have to sacrifice our true selves to incarnate. But the more conscious and intentional you become, the less you'll be able to tolerate causing *any* level of pain, confusion, or even inconvenience to others. To speed your process of growth and not get bogged down in mistakes, you need to pay close attention to your anxiety signals and commit to living from a state of deep comfort. Let's look at some of the common stumbling blocks to maintaining clear intuition.

The Quick Fix and the Easy Answer

Today, our generation has been programmed to be consumers and to have short attention spans during which we must respond to intense stimulation. We therefore want our enlightenment to happen instantly, and if one technique isn't interesting enough or doesn't give immediate results, why, we just flip the channel. If you tried one of the intuitive decision-making techniques, for example, but couldn't visualize an answer, or if your truth symbol started playing tricks on you, you may have gotten frustrated and passed over that particular use of intuition. And yet it's fairly common to have ambiguous results at first, or to have one of your non-dominant senses provide the information, or even to have some unfamiliar combination of senses become activated. It could take some time for you to acquaint yourself with these new perceptual circuits.

I see people, particularly in the New Age movement, jumping impatiently from technique to technique—purifying themselves with special diets, chanting, dousing out their decisions with pendulums, smelling aromatic oils, shining colored lights on themselves, journeying to ancient power places, and so on. These tools and techniques worked in ancient times to raise awareness, and they can still help us. But let's remember that tools are simply a means to an end and shouldn't be confused with the real inner work. You yourself are the most powerful tool of all.

Many people are also seduced by paths to higher knowing where a neat and tidy doctrine is laid out for them by a powerful parental figure like a church, a guru, a shaman, a spaceship commander from Arcturus, or a teacher claiming to be a high priest of the Order of Melchizadek. Knowing just what rule to follow in every circumstance is a relief if you don't trust your own intuition. But going too fast, skipping from method to method, and settling for answers you had no part in originating can leave you open for a bad spill.

The first phase of any spiritual path, including the intuitive way, is to subject yourself to a scrupulous and ongoing character assessment. Here's where many of our perceptual mistakes are made. We are tripped up by what we're unconscious about. Removing fear from our thoughts and behaviors is not a particularly pleasant or speedy job. In fact, most people do everything possible to avoid facing their dark side, and when they do, they'd like to think that one quick pass through the underworld will clinch it. If you've been working with clearing your subconscious mind, you know that we cycle around many times to dissolve hundreds of large and small interrelated confusions and blockages. It takes great ongoing compassion for yourself—and patience—to become clear. No amount of magical think-ing, talking the good talk, or blindly following someone else's rules will do the trick.

Control, Hypocrisy, and Ambition

As we open to intuition, if there is still some fear lurking below the sur-face, there will also be some form of ego, some sneaky little way our mind tries to control the world to make us feel secure and right. Hidden ego agendas can produce behaviors that range from relatively innocent per-sonal biases and bids for attention to blatantly arrogant control games. After you learned that you could get information about other people intu-itively, were you tempted at all to show off or to use this new skill to for-tify your position at work or with friends?

As Marge started opening her intuition, she discovered that she had a real sensitivity to the subtle energies in the human body. She could feel hot and cold spots, too much electrical force, and could direct and balance the flow of energy with her hands. So successful was she at healing people that she eventually made it her livelihood. Her confidence grew and she exuded a take-charge attitude. She always seemed certain about what was causing her clients' pain and presented her assessments with great authority.

"You're a mess, but I can help you," she would cheerfully say. Though this reassured many people, her presentation was subtly geared to bring *her* attention, and it actually complicated the client's healing process. To heal, they were now saddled with overcoming a judgment about their basic "flawed" nature as well as needing to realize that, in spite of Marge's tal-ent and engaging performance, all healing still had to occur by means of their own soul and the divine. Do you have an expounder or a savior in your "My Many Faces" list?

You may get a clue about your blind spots by first noticing hypocrisy, ambivalence, or double-talk in others. If you are triggered by issues you see in others, the same thing may exist in you but in a different form. Watch for people who claim to be spiritual or moral yet act in a way that goes against common-sense principles. Notice the man who meditates and reads voraciously about Buddhism yet still demeans women. Or the spiritual counselor who advises people to clean up their lives but gossips about her clients. Or the strict vegetarian who feels threatened by a roommate who eats eggs or chicken. Or the teacher who claims to be the exclusive voice of Mother Mary or who doesn't make a decision unless advised by beings from an advanced star system. Or the Christian who discriminates against gays, Jews, Democrats, and people of color. Do you ever choose role models who display this kind of split in their basic character? Are these people really showing you how to live more skillfully?

Self-Righteousness

List five things that offend you and raise your hackles. As you imagine each thing, notice what you want to yell at the offender. Write down your scathing comments.

How do *you* do each of the things that offends you? Is there another area of your life where the behavior occurs? If you are offended by someone who stole your wallet, for example, might you be stealing attention from your husband when you're out with friends?

Keep your eye peeled as well for inconsistencies pertaining to greed and ambition in relation to your intuitive growth. It's possible to be greedy for information as well as material things. Do you buy piles of books that sit by your nightstand unread? Do you know people who binge on psychological and spiritual leading-edge ideas? If you're overly ambitious in your intuitive growth, you may get too far ahead of yourself and not fully integrate your insights and lessons.

REMEMBER
▼
Each thing you judge (positively or negatively) is you.

Attachment

When opening your intuition you may seek security by becoming attached to a particular spiritual tradition or methodology, as others become attached to their car or mate. For example, you might be convinced about the rightness of going to confession and be totally unwilling to experience the benefits of creative visualization. Or you might have a bias against working with entities.

A Buddhist priest I once knew discounted most of what I said because I had referred to clearing emotions that originated in past lives, which he considered to be a New Age concept and thus inferior to his traditional spiritual lineage. Placing too much value on any one way of being or doing things can blind you and lead to debilitating self-importance. Attachment slows the evolution of your soul and makes it difficult for other options to educate, nurture, and round you out. If you place too much emphasis on form, whether it be one form or many forms, whether it be a technique or a belief system, you will miss the direct, mystical communion that surpasses all the explanations of the mind. What we're aiming for in the intuitive way is a lively balance between the ability to concentrate and the ability to adapt.

Releasing Attachments

1. Give away five things this week. Let one thing be something you really like. Let one giveaway be anonymous. Write about how it feels to let go of things you care about and don't care too much about, and write about how it feels to get credit or not get credit for a charitable act.

2. List five aspects of your identity that you'd like to have recognized by other people. "You're so well-coordinated, have such beautiful eyes, are so eloquent, and _____." Imagine becoming so comfortable and happy with each aspect of your identity that if someone were to compliment you on it you'd feel surprised. Write about how your behavior might change, especially toward others, if you no longer had these particular needs for attention.

Avoidance, Addiction, Denial, and Drama

To avoid feeling fear and to cope with subliminal emotional pain, we create thousands of ingenious distractions. I'm sure you know someone who lives for romance or to be different or dramatic. On the path to intuition, people can avoid the real world by becoming preoccupied with the details of psychology and metaphysics: who abused you in your childhood, your sacrifices and betrayals, past lives, dream realities, parallel worlds, messages from angels, gemstones and gadgets that affect the subtle energy bodies, or even the idea of being abducted by aliens.

Judy was a recent client whose entire reality revolved around the notion of being hypersensitive to negativity and being possessed by negative beings. She complained of going out of control and being helpless to function in normal reality. She was sweet and lovable but her life was a mess. When I told her I didn't see any sign of possession, she said, "So why did I leave for work and end up a hundred miles away in a sleazy part of a big city? Tell me *that*!" Her mind had invented a highly dramatic and oddly entertaining negative reality that kept her from having to face some emotionally terrifying past experiences in her subconscious.

We need to watch for hidden agendas marked by a longing for glamor and romance where we avoid the mundane—and thus miss the guidance coming from our bodies, which are firmly planted in daily reality. I have seen people change their personalities radically when they begin spiritual studies. A rambunctious, funny, outgoing young man suddenly becomes blissful, mellow, mild, and humble, hardly talks, gives away all his money, and reverently raises his hands in prayer to everyone—after joining an ashram. A practical businesswoman changes her name to Mary Lightning Bolt, says "Ho!" after people speak, and starts wearing ethnic jewelry and fringed skirts, burning sage in her office, and drumming with her women's group—after she attends a Native American sweat-lodge ceremony. These total immersions in specific forms of spiritual practice can be educational, yet at the same time they can stop the flow of our authentic expression.

Ironically, even the pursuit of healing and knowledge can be a distraction. "Maybe, if I keep taking workshops, reading the newest books, doing therapy, seeing the latest healers and psychics in town, I'll find the magic elixir." Some people are addicted to seminars, and their social lives revolve entirely around the human-potential movement. Other people are on a mission to perfect the health of their bodies. They have had everything from candida to parasites to chronic fatigue syndrome and are experts on homeopathy, acupuncture, herbs, colonics, aromatherapy, chi kung, Bach flower remedies, and fasting on watermelon. One week it's no red meat, the next, only protein. Then it's no wheat or sugar, followed by no dairy products or spices. If your attention is riveted on controlling the minutiae of your diet, there's not much time to feel deep emotions. Since it's not OK to be addicted to alcohol, drugs, or cigarettes anymore, we've tricked ourselves into justifying our addiction to "good" things that are supposedly growth-inducing.

Since everything is but an apparition, Perfect in being what it is, Having nothing to do with good or bad, Acceptance or rejection, One may as well burst out in laughter.

Longchenpa

We should also examine our need for drama, magic, and miracles. A woman I recently met at a luncheon told me of a particularly dysfunctional relationship she had entered into primarily because she'd been attracted to a house she saw as she walked along a beach. A few days later she met and befriended a girl on the same beach who turned out to live in the house, and soon after that, she met a man at a conference who turned out to be the girl's father. "It's synchronicity!" she thought. "This *must* mean something; it *must* be significant. Why else was I drawn to that particular house? This must be a powerful relationship."

I've also known people who got involved in disastrous relationships and adventures because they had a precognitive, though somewhat vague, dream that seemed to highlight some aspect of the subsequent real-world experience: "But he was wearing a red shirt and his name was Dan—just like in my dream." Perhaps our subconscious mind is drawing attention to the man with the daughter with the house on the beach or to the man named Dan in the red shirt, not because they're our soulmates, but because they represent unfinished business in our subconscious or an example of what *not* to do.

False Humility, Sacrificial Service, and Messiah Complexes

No matter where you are born, as you stretch out to open your intuition and spiritual life, you unconsciously carry your culture's religious beliefs with you. Developing intuition will eventually require you to reexamine your religious faith and reown the parts that align with your own deepest ethics and common sense. You may still prefer to practice Buddhism, Judaism, or Christianity, but the precepts you live by will have been clarified and internalized through your own superconscious choice.

If you have not given your religious beliefs much thought, some of the unconscious assumptions may interfere with your obtaining the fullest experience of yourself as a soul. For example, from our prevailing Western religion we inherit the idea that we are born flawed and incomplete. We are supposed to be abjectly humble with little sense of personal self, and we are taught not to try to find enlightenment through our own efforts but to surrender and let a more divine person do it for us. We are taught that it is noble to sacrifice ourselves and suffer for others. Many Eastern religions, for example, place a high value on collectivity and emptiness, so emphasis on the personal self, even on the soul, is discouraged for a different reason.

As you venture beyond the confines of religion into a study of metaphysics and intuition, you'll discover for yourself that there are universal principles that are inherent in human nature, no matter what our culture or religion. The study of these principles is neutral, almost scientific—and it is what every religion originally concerned itself with. And yet, as you begin practicing alignment with these natural laws, as you apply intuition to daily life, you're bound to come up against this thought: "I'm being too egotistical—who am I to think I could know this information directly? Who am I to think I could heal someone?" Or there's the more passionate stance: "I am nothing; I give myself in service to everyone and need nothing personally! I am just a vehicle for God's will."

This humility often leads to the messiah complex, a deceptive form of ego that comes from trying to be a saint or a savior. Your clarity can easily become distorted when you have to help, when you can't allow others to have their own experiences but instead try to rescue them from their suffering. Some people take on great camouflaged self-importance and a strange sense of worth through self-sacrifice. Yet this kind of covert superiority robs everyone of their unique connection to the divine and drowns clear intuitive knowing in a pool of personal will power.

Sacrificial service doesn't help either the helper (whose capacity to receive eventually dries up) or the unconsciously guilt-laden "helpee." Be aware, then, of the imbalances in yourself and others when there is the appearance of too much or too little: too much personal power, too little credit, too much humility, too little responsibility.

A sobering thought: what if, right at this very moment, I am living up to my full potential?

Jane Wagner

Rescue Behaviors

1. List five situations or conditions you can hardly bear to see other people suffering through. Write in detail about what happens in your body, and where, when you perceive other people's pain. What do you do to minimize your discomfort? In each situation, could you allow the other person to fully experience their pain and get whatever they get from it without your inter-

ference? Imagine that you're not the right person to help them; who or what might be more appropriate, and why?

2. List the situations in your life where you would secretly like someone to rescue you. What would it feel like? What would the rescuer do for you? Now imagine that your own soul is going to provide the means for you to be rescued. What might your soul create? Are you ready to be rescued in each case? Could you receive help equally well either from another person or via your own resources?

Spiritual Codependence

In the early stages of intuition development, it's natural to feel vulnerable and lonely. It is common to want a best friend in spirit or a spiritual family, or to anthropomorphize the nonphysical dimensions as a way to feel safer as you tread the path into the unknown. Sometimes our need for attention leads us to seek specialness by association, as if being the friend and collaborator to a discarnate entity or a spiritual guru will bring us greater spiritual credibility and certainty. Dependence on others, physical or nonphysical, can keep us from our own wisdom and can produce convoluted guidance.

Carla was the secretary to a well-known trance medium and seemed almost in love with the entity who channeled through the man. When there was a parting of the ways between her and the medium, she announced that she would now channel the entity, calling it by a slightly different name. She created a new persona for herself, setting up a situation where she could safely build confidence, have companionship, and draw attention through her association with an otherworldly being while offering clients advice about their lives for which she would not have to claim much responsibility. How much more direct might her growth have been, I wonder, had she returned to school to become a minister or credentialed transpersonal counselor using her own innate wisdom?

Possession and Misplacement of Authority

One of the most common fears about intuition is that if you open yourself to the unknown, you'll become the victim of negative forces and evil spirits. At one point in the early years of my intuition development, when I was experimenting with the idea of discarnate entities, I had a slew of unusual dreams about other planets, ancient libraries, intergalactic teachers, and spaceships. I woke up every morning with reams of totally useless but fascinating information about the names of star systems, strange foreign languages, sacred geometry, and prehistoric cosmic events. I spent hours writing it all down. Soon I began to get headaches and was having long sneezing jags that would go on and on—twenty or thirty sneezes in a row. I thought I was developing allergies. But during my annual "checkup life reading," my teacher clairvoyantly saw that I was "possessed" by some extraterrestrial beings. This sounded strange to me.

"You have made a contract with these souls," she explained, "and have agreed to let them experience your personality, which they are curious about. In exchange, they're providing you with information from the other dimensions, which you are curious about. It's an even trade, but I'd suggest you take a look at providing yourself with your *own* information. Your body is instinctually trying to throw them off, to get them out of your energy field, by sneezing repeatedly, as if this will jar their connection. You're experiencing headaches because they are telepathically linked to you through the back of your neck and the reptile brain. The headaches are originating near the base of your skull. Are you sure the information you're receiving is worth the energy drain you're experiencing?"

She let me make up my mind, and I decided I'd rather go straight to my own superconsciousness for guidance from now on. Together, we "intended" a message to the entities saying that I was now taking over my own space again, 100 percent, and thank you very much but the contract was now complete. Immediately following the reading, my sneezing and headaches stopped. That night, no titillating otherworldly data appeared in my dreams. I was clear again. As a result of my own experience and of having seen clients who had similar "possession" problems, I realize there are some situations where discarnate entities do resonantly share your emotional and etheric experiences to some extent. There are several important things to know concerning this phenomenon.

First, possession is always an agreement, or contract, between both

⚡

I always return to the truth.
I never leave it.

parties. I do not believe it is a sinister plot to rob us of our personal sovereignty as Hollywood would have us believe. You can end the contract whenever you want. Second, no one—not even discarnate beings—can do your spiritual work for you, nor can you do theirs for them. The fastest spiritual growth occurs when you go directly to your own superconscious mind for guidance. Third, there is very little difference between possession by discarnate entities and possession by incarnate ones. If you attract every homeless panhandler and stray cat within a 100-mile radius or if you constantly find yourself enmeshed in dramas with friends and family, you might be open to the same confusion in the nonphysical realms. You may need to center yourself more often and pay attention to your boundaries and your own opinions. Fourth, if you place authority outside yourself and assume the outer world is bigger and more powerful than you or is a hostile place, you will tend to attract dominators and leeches, be they physical or nonphysical. Practice feeling connectedness and oneness. Fifth, there isn't much difference in outward appearance between possession and obsession, which is an extreme variety of attachment. This automatic, stubbornly one-pointed focus of your mind can block your clarity the same way giving your power away to others can. Finally, and ultimately, you are the authority in your world. No one can influence you unless you say so. If you tell someone "No" and mean it, energetically they cannot remain in your reality. Practice making conscious choices from the superconscious point of view.

The placing of and witnessing of authority is a powerful spiritual act and one of the main keys to keeping your intuition open and functional. Authority is sacred; it is the godforce, the creative wisdom that brings forth new life. It exists in everything equally and appears to you whenever and wherever you place your attention. Attention contains and reveals authority. Authority appears in only one place and one moment at a time, because that's the way your conscious mind works. Don't make the mistake of dualistically thinking the authority in your life is either in you totally or in the outside world totally. That can lead to dominator/victim authority problems. Authority is everywhere, but it is you who have the capability to bestow the respect due this awesome force of life and love. Wherever you see it, guidance can originate.

Vesting Authority

1. Make a list of five people to whom you give a lot of authority. How do you let them influence the quality of your experience? How do you let them dictate your actions? If you took your authority back from them and let them just be who they are, how would your relationship change with each one?

2. Make a list of five situations or cultural beliefs in which you invest a lot of authority. How do you let these conditions or beliefs influence the quality of your experience? How do you let them dictate your actions? If you reclaimed your authority, how would your life change concerning each thing?

Boundary Problems

If you pay too much attention to others and the outside world, and if you constantly compare yourself to others, you won't be in the habit of feeling your body or recognizing the tone of your own particular energy. Then you'll be plagued with self-doubt and will have problems defining who you are and recognizing what's inappropriate, or even dangerous, for you. If the boundaries of your personal self are not firm and you don't occupy your own space fully, psychic, emotional, and physical invasion can occur. This is not as scary as it sounds, but it can be troublesome because you can confuse other people's needs and agendas with your own.

Always be a first rate version of yourself, instead of a second rate version of somebody else.

Judy Garland

If you're unfocused and not present in your body, when people read you telepathically, they will clearly pick up that your body is there but you're not. This unconsciously worries many people; they wonder, "Where is she? I don't know how I'm supposed to act with her; is it safe to be around her?" They come forward then, looking for you, pushing you, trying to get a rise out of you. They'll close in until you finally show up and push back, until you become definite and recognizable. Then they relax, because they know where you stand and can have an actual interaction with you.

You may also develop boundary problems as you become receptive to subtler forms of information, because as you look for these intuitive insights your conscious mind feels like it's stretching outward in search of finer and finer levels of data. It's easy then to think that you're flowing into various situations or people to get an intuitive sense of them. If you flow into them, you will also unconsciously assume that you're flowing out of yourself. This can cause you to feel empty and inadvertently misidentify yourself with whatever you flow into. Then you become the human chameleon. You'll be articulate around highly verbal people, defensive around defended people, and self-expressive around animated people. If you spend too much time with complainers, victims, and depressed people, you'll feel like a stone. This shape-shifting tendency eventually stops the flow of your creativity and can lead to severe energy drain as well as mental problems. As one of my friends told me the other day, "You know what killed the chameleon, don't you? Sitting on plaid!"

The Ethics of Intuition

For your intuition to function in an optimal way, it helps to practice a simple code of ethics. As the Buddha taught, it is skillful to live in a way that completes old karma and doesn't create any new karma. If you choose this ethical way, you will not only clear up your own life but will also contribute to the clarity in the world. Let me recap a few of the principles that will help keep you on track.

1. Be clear about your deepest motives and act accordingly. Your real motive comes from your superconscious mind and usually has a threefold expression: (1) to embody your soul, (2) to experience the pure joy of creating, and (3) to help others overcome their blind spots and blockages so they can do the same three things.

2. Honor the wisdom of your own process. Surrender totally into the wisdom of your life. No one else's path is right for you. You have your own life plan, your unique talents, your special style. Be true to it and don't copy anyone else's pattern. If you were supposed to do it their way, you'd be them. So when you encounter ridicule, skepticism, and superstition in others, just smile and keep believing in yourself.

3. Respect all souls and all forms of life. Grant each created being the same beauty and right to be. Look at your fellow men and women, your animal and plant brothers and sisters, your insect and rock relatives—no matter how misshapen, ignorant, or sickly—as being worthy in the Creator's eye. With our puny brains we cannot know the full reasons that our nemeses and heroes exist. Perhaps angels and ascended masters walk among us in disguise. When in doubt, ask yourself, "How would Jesus, Buddha, Krishna, the Guadalupe Virgin, the Dalai Lama, Mother Teresa, and other enlightened beings act in this situation?"

4. Always ask permission to help others or to look into their private lives. While all things are known by all souls in the higher dimensions, in the physical world we have not yet caught up with that grand unified state of awareness. We must still respect each other's boundaries and diversity. To not scare other people, it's important to tune in to their needs for safety, to the rhythms and speed that feel natural for them. If you go too fast for someone or intrude into their reality with a new set of rules that requires them to make a quantum leap, don't be surprised if you get a cold or violent response. I have found that almost everyone wants to grow and share, and they will take the next steps that are appropriate for them if they can get a sense of how to do it and if it doesn't threaten their survival.

5. Don't give more or less than is required by the situation at hand. The Essenes believed that it is just as much a sin to have too little as to have too much. At either polarity, the optimal flow of creativity gets jammed up. But if you have just what you need, life flows perfectly. The same thing applies when healing and teaching others or in communicating your new knowledge to strangers, friends, and relatives. In healing or counseling, if you give more energy and information than the client's body and mind can absorb, you may actually make things worse. In teaching we are told not to "throw pearls before swine"—in other words, not to waste precious resources in inappropriate situations. *Balance* is the key word here. The universe doesn't waste energy. If you give less than a person needs, the resulting dissatisfaction can produce repercussions like pain, negative thought patterns, and the wasteful acting out of dramas. If you take two steps toward a relationship with someone when they take only one toward you, you will end up being rejected one step's worth so the energy can flow evenly. Give too much and you may feel insulted. Give too little and you'll never know your true self or anyone else. Use your truth and anxiety signals to know when to stop and go.

6. Practice right speech. Speech has the power to crystallize intangible

---

TROUBLESHOOTING TIP
When You Can't Tell
Who You Are
When you are in a close relationship or doing intuitive work for someone else and you become confused about whether something you're feeling is originating with you or with them, you are merged. Check to see if you've gone outside yourself for knowledge. Do you feel stretched, drained, or "over there"? Check whether they've come into you for knowledge. Do you feel crowded, smothered, or too warm?

Take a moment and get re-centered; draw all your energy back from the other person and inside the boundaries of your own skin, and send all their energy back to them. Breathe, feel your heartbeat, feel your nerves tingling. Your body holds a consistent, unique vibration. Feel it. Feel at home. Notice what feels natural to you right now. Feel the other person existing in their own reality, in their own space. Let it be OK.

Now reexamine the information you were dealing with. Does it match your feelings of deep comfort? Without leaving your center, let a new insight come to you. Let yourself know what to do without having the energetic support of the other person.

REMEMBER
▼
*What you focus on, you
become.*

realities, to bring visions to life. Be aware of the words you use. If your con- versations are peppered with disempowering language like "I don't know," "I can't," "I won't," "I never," "if," "but," or "maybe," it will be difficult for you to gain clarity about yourself. If you complain, gossip, and contin- ually describe what's wrong with situations, your life will be filled with depression, disappointment, and negativity. If you swear and use dull, ugly words that demean the sacred, your life will contain no miracles, no beauty. Try talking about what exists rather than what doesn't exist, what you *are* doing, what you *do* know, what you *like* and are interested in now. Tell the truth; say what you mean; keep your word. This way your reality can become the manifestation of your soul's real agenda.

Watching Your Words

1. Make a list of your swear words. How many of them are related to religion? How many to body functions? How many to the opposite sex/same sex? Write about how swearing affects your world view. What happens in your body when you swear?

2. List your "helplessness language"—words and phrases that keep you from knowing, deciding, and acting. What happens in your body when you talk this way?

3. List the people you gossiped or complained about this week. What were the key issues under the surface that made you say what you did out loud? What were you hoping to get from the people you told?

4. List the put-downs you've uttered this week. How would it feel if other people were saying these things about you?

7. Ask for help when you need it; offer help when you feel moved to. Another person's point of view can sometimes help loosen your perception and shift you into an insight you need. We need to make our own decisions, but we can't go it totally alone. Other people bring energizing new per- spectives and introduce us to new aspects of ourselves. You may even find that an occasional visit to a therapist, healer, or intuitive counselor can help speed your growth process. When someone helps you, either in the physi- cal or nonphysical world, "test the spirits." Check everything that comes into you against your own value system, common sense, and truth signals.

How can you tell if someone is enlightened? My sense is that the more evolved someone is, the more you'll naturally like yourself and feel free to express the full range of your personality in their presence; an evolved person does not foster dependency. Around trustworthy people, you'll feel safe and acknowledged yet open to self-improvement. Your heart will be activated, and you'll feel appropriate.

When other people offer help, consider accepting it. We all need to give and receive, and receiving allows others the chance to give; it's a gift in itself. If you feel impelled to share an insight with George or to give Judy a shoulder massage or to help carry an old man's packages, trust yourself and make the offer. They can always refuse you. Don't volunteer when you don't really feel like it or when you feel guilty. Don't help from a place of fear or superiority. Give to please yourself. Serve others to serve yourself.

Eye to eye, we are nearer but we truly enter each other's metaphysical immortal beings only through thought and forever only through utterly unselfish love.
Self is infinitely lonely; Love is infinitely inclusive.

R. Buckminster Fuller

Ways to Help
List specific ways you would like to help people, animals, plants, or the planet this week. List only things that you really intend to do and that you intend to have fun doing. Do them.

The poet Kabir says, "Suppose you scrub your ethical skin until it shines, but inside there is no music, then what? Mohammed's son pores over words, and points out this and that, but if his chest is not soaked dark with love, then what?"[1] Ethics only serve to remind us of the simple fact that it saves time and energy and produces joy to live according to the universal principles and to move down the river in the direction it's flowing. Wouldn't it be marvelous if we could just live by the harmonious order that governs the movements of nature rather than needing external regulations to keep ourselves in line? Then the ethics would be inside us, as us, and our chests would be soaked with love.

Entering the Flow and Staying There

My intuition tells me that intuition is going to be *the* skill of the future and that moving into the intuitive way of life and the intuitive age in history will bring profound transformations in our personal and societal world views, in the ways we relate to each other and manifest reality. To create the future and enter it gracefully, we must be able to know directly, *now*, without distortion. We must become transparent and fluid in our consciousness so we can dive in and swim with the universe's quantum particles and energy waves like dolphins leaping alongside the prow of a fast-moving ship.

As we look to the future, most of us see through the eyes of our old belief systems, through the density of a reality based on limitation, victimization, and suffering. We have not yet been able to grasp the fullness of what might be coming because our lens is still so filmy and refracted. But when we aren't motivated by fear of what might go wrong, we won't need to back through life avoiding experience after experience that reminds us of old pain. Our lives won't be about choosing the "least objectionable" options. We won't have to monitor our environment so paranoically, and our energy will be freed for direct involvement with life. As we experience more unity, life won't seem to bring random, senseless events. Instead it will feel like one huge creative act spontaneously bringing us what we need next.

In an intuitive world we'll live with much less resistance than we are currently accustomed to. It won't be as difficult to know things; all knowledge will be increasingly available and free and not tied to machines. Knowing so much, so fast, will speed up the process of creating; ignorance will no longer be an excuse or an obstacle. Ideas will seem to slide into manifestation rather than going through a grueling labor process to be born. Think of it and *presto!* it's real. Time will seem incredibly fast or perhaps even nonexistent. Without so much attachment and ego, we will be fluid and malleable in our perception, going wherever we need to go, thinking whatever we need to think, changing whenever we need to change—for our own good and the good of the whole. We may even feel that we are physically free from the pull of gravity, that we are made more of light force than solid matter. It's going to be so much fun!

You may realize already that when you trust your intuition, a door opens and the life that pours through the opening changes you forever. How can you maintain beliefs in limitation and difficulty in the face of such freely given provision, in the face of synchronous miracles and natural beneficence? After intuition gets hold of you, it takes an act of personal will

We shall not cease from exploration
And the end of all our exploring
Will be to arrive where we started
And know the place for the first time.

T. S. Eliot

to maintain a negative mind-set. So go ahead. Let go of your foursquare reality and your predictable way of knowing the world. You are the soul! Deep within you, you know how to move *with* life. Jump in! Dive, wave, swoop, swim, rise up and fall through, have passion, have peace, move in, move out, be yourself, be the all. Take a chance on the intuitive way.

⚡

I am new in the now.

BE INTUITIVE TODAY!
Be your soul all day.

1. First thing this morning, get quiet and centered. Ask for a higher vision of what the rest of your life is all about. What is your soul doing now toward that end at the highest levels? And how does that activity translate into today's experience? What are your soul's intentions and goals for this day? What does "it" want "you" to experience? Write on the back of your hand, "I = SOUL," and all day remember to be the soul as you say the word *I* and interact with others.

2. Accomplish your soul's goals for today. When you need something today, let your soul wisdom show it to you and bring it to you. Stay out of limited mental beliefs and habits.

Direct Writing Questions

Sit down with your journal and get quiet. Empty your mind. Pick one of the following questions and be with it for a few moments. Ask that you be able to receive creative insights from your deepest level of truth. Let the question serve as a magnet. Allow the first word to pop into your mind. Write it down. Let another word pop in. Write it down. Let words proceed forth, without judging them, without second-guessing where the answer is going. Don't jump ahead. Don't stop and read back over what you've written until the writing stops of its own accord. Helpful techniques: write as your own soul, innocent child, or future self; address your personality in the second person, by name; don't try to be too significant! Let your handwriting change shape. Change your speed and your rhythm, or write with your opposite hand.

- Write a dialogue between your accusing critic, your wise elder, and the wounded part of yourself that seeks approval. Write about your blind spots.
- Write from the viewpoint of your internalized parental authority figure: "I expect _____ of myself but not of others. I expect _____ of others but not of myself. Why?"
- "What are my biases, the ways I make subtle or not-so-subtle bids for attention, and the ways I maintain control?"
- "How have I changed and grown since beginning *The Intuitive Way?*"
- Write as your emotional self and as your physical self: "What kinds of situations drain me? Why?"
- Write a script for how you'd explain your intuitive experiences to a skeptical stranger.
- Write from the viewpoint of your soul: "What are my truest motives concerning other people and the planet?"

Delving Deeper

If you'd like to explore your intuition further,
try the exercises below in any order that appeals to you.

Soul Activities

Spend time thinking about your "soul activities." Write about what fascinates you to the point of total involvement. In what activities do you allow yourself to learn as you go, to be self-taught? Do you recall the effortless quality of your work at times like these? How work seems like play? How you magically proceed from one step to the next and everything seems just right? Describe in detail how it feels emotionally and physically to be involved in a soul activity.

Relaxing Your Masculine Mind

Pretend your brain-mind is a muscle. Tense it and contract it right now as if it were a fist. Tighten both fists as well and squinch your eyes closed. Make your brain-mind feel hard and tight. Hold it until you feel like shaking. Then suddenly let it go slack and loose, let your wrists go limp, and let your eyes drop open. Don't focus on anything in particular. Shake out your hands. Go blank, go blah. In fact, open your mouth and hang your jaw down, all the while moaning something like "Duhhhh." Just hang for a minute without commenting to yourself. Let your attention be soft.

Your Parents' Organizing Belief Systems

Write about the world views of your father and mother. For each parent, list the adages that epitomize his and her world view. You may have heard them repeat certain phrases, get upset by particular behaviors in other people, and say what they wished for.

By looking at what your parents did and didn't let themselves have and what brought them satisfaction versus upset, determine the "shoulds" your parents lived by and what they were unconsciously afraid might happen if the shoulds failed to be maintained. Now compose a statement that accurately describes each parent's basic assumptions about the nature of life. How have their beliefs affected yours?

Transforming Your Opinions

1. List five people you have negative opinions about. Bring each person into your awareness. Put your attention on that individual fully without making the person right or wrong. If your soul were explaining why the person is acting the way he or she is, what would the explanation be?

2. Do the same thing with five situations you have negative opinions about. What's your soul's explanation of why things are as they are?

Superconscious Insights

Write about a mystical experience that changed your view of yourself or of life. Perhaps it was a dream, perhaps a fleeting realization taking only a few seconds of "real time" but having a timeless feeling. These experiences often give you a feeling of profound love, a sense that there is a divine order to things, but they may simply be an ordinary experience of seeing to the heart of something.

Mining Your Subconscious

1. Save several pages in your journal to make an ongoing list pertaining to your subconscious blocks. Start by listing, as rapidly as you can, things you have a morbid curiosity about or can't stand seeing or thinking about. Then list things that make you blindly enraged or severely irritated.

2. Cut out images from magazines that trigger odd feelings of attraction and repulsion and paste them in this section of your journal. Let the words and images trigger associations from your past and present experiences. Write about the connections.

Who and What You're Not

Think about your life and focus on areas where you are wasting your energy and time. List three answers for each of the following statements, and be sure you mean what you say: (a) "I don't want to be _____ anymore. Instead I intend to be _____." (b) "I don't want to feel _____ anymore. Instead I intend to feel _____." (c) "I don't want to do _____ anymore. Instead I intend to do _____." (d) "I don't want to create _____ anymore. Instead I intend to create _____."

Your Primal Emotions

Describe three times in your life when you touched the primal emotions at the bottom of the subconscious mind. Did you feel terror? Rage? Hatred? Grief? Write in detail about the experiences in your journal. What was the trigger experience? What conclusions did you draw? Describe the deepest beliefs you hold about the nature of life, the physical plane, good and evil, and suffering: "I believe _____." Where might you be hung up in illusion concerning all this?

Cleaning the Energy in a Room

Have you ever had to spend time in a space that felt alien, dirty, unconscious, abused, or in some way negative? Have you ever walked into your own living room the morning after a party and still felt all the people's energy residue there? Or moved into a house where the previous tenant had been sick or died? Here's what you can do:

1. Open a window or door, if possible, and burn some aromatic, purifying herb like sage, cedar, or frankincense. Or spray or vaporize aromatic essential oils, like rosemary, eucalyptus, lemon, or pine. As you do this, hold the intention in your mind that energies incompatible with your own highest good will disperse.

2. Sit down in the room. Close your eyes and get centered. Visualize a column of diamond light coming up from the center of the earth, directly below the room, and see it rise slowly through the floor. As it inches its way up through the room, let

all the shadows and murky energy be absorbed and turned into sparkling light.

3. Wash the room with diamond light—every corner, every molecule. Let the air become purified by imagining fresh breezes blowing through from the ocean or the mountains. Imagine the sound of a hundred wind chimes tinkling. The space is now conducive to your own highest good and highest creativity.

A Hymn of Thanksgiving

In your journal, write a gratitude list, a poem, or a letter to the Earth, the Universe, or the Creator expressing your gratitude for your life. Include details from your observations of your body, your environment, what amuses you, what you find beautiful and amazing. Write from your feminine mind.

Mindfulness

Pick a small, mundane task: scrubbing your teeth, washing a pot, sweeping the sidewalk, booting up your computer, writing a check. Before you begin the task, pause and talk to your body and soul: "We are going to get this pot clean now." Then begin: "We are picking up the pot now; we are turning on the hot water now; we are getting the pot scrubber soapy now; we are holding the pot with our left hand and making scrubbing motions with our right hand now; Ah, look! Now the pot is shiny right here. Now we are getting this last dark spot off the pot; now the pot is perfectly clean; now we are rinsing it; now we are putting it on the dishrack to dry; now we are finished cleaning the pot." Feel every step, noticing how much your body, in its childlike simplicity, enjoys each part of the process. Thich Nhat Hanh says, "Washing the dishes is like bathing a baby Buddha."

Impeccability

Write about the people and areas of your life you tend to ignore, to gloss over, to go unconscious about. How could you improve your impeccability in these areas or with these people?

Making a Holy Sound

Close your eyes. Bring your attention into the geometric center of your head. Become aware of your breath. Take a slow, long inhale and gather your energy inside your skin. As you exhale, drop your jaw and slowly, evenly, loudly, from your chest and belly, make the sound *Aahhhhhh.* Hold it the entire length of your exhale. Let it fade gradually. Close your mouth and inhale. Exhale again through your mouth, this time creating the perfectly rounded sound *Oohhhhhh.* Make it full and loud with the inside of your mouth shaped to perfect roundness and the opening of your lips shaped in a perfect O. Draw in another breath. Exhale and create the long, smooth U sound *Ooooooo.* Narrow your lips to a tiny, perfect, puckered opening. Make the sound last as long as you can. Draw in one more breath. On the exhale, this time close your mouth, let your teeth come together, and make your tongue get fat and fill up your whole mouth cavity. Make the rich, earthy sound *Mmmmmmm,* letting it vibrate evenly through your bones, teeth, nose, tongue, and lips.

Do the whole sequence slowly several times. Then inhale and collect yourself. Exhale and blend all four sounds together, letting them flow into each other: *Aahhhhhh—Oohhhhhh—Ooooooo—Mmmmmmm.* Start with your mouth wide open, then let it close a bit and become round, then narrow to a tiny roundness, then close altogether and take the sound down into your body. Repeat slowly again and again, noticing where each sound resonates in your body. Let the mantra dissolve gradually into silence as it's ready.

Watching an Outer Image

Sit comfortably in front of a well-lit mirror with your eyes open. Relax the muscles around your eyes and in your face. Focus your attention in the center of your head. Watch your eyes in the mirror. Keep your attention focused on the energy coming out of the eyes. Hold the intention to understand (not verbally define): "Who am I?" Let the energy of the eyes in the mirror come into you. Keep opening and receiving. Keep your attention on the eyes. Watch for five minutes, then try ten minutes.

Balancing Your Three Brains

Get quiet, close your eyes, and bring your attention inside your skin. As you breathe in, imagine energy flowing up your spine, through the back of your neck, into your brainstem, and filling the reptile brain with warm (perhaps red or pink) light. Relax the area where your head and neck join. Let the warm light build and swell gently like a fruit becoming ripe. Let the light educate and heal that part of your brain, relaxing and opening it. As the light expands, let it gently lift off like a balloon, moving upward and outward, filling the midbrain.

Concentrate your attention on the clear, bright center point of your midbrain. Out of that center pours golden light. Visualize the pink light from the reptile brain gradually turning shiny gold as it merges into and circulates around the midbrain. Let the light educate, heal, and relax the second brain, opening it. See the golden light expand outward and upward, rising into the upper brain, the neocortex.

Concentrate your attention now at the top of your head. Watch the golden light from the midbrain rise and turn into a clear electric blue light. Feel your uppermost brain vibrating with energy and knowledge, and let the blue light educate and heal the tissues, circuitry, and neurotransmitters there.

Allow the blue light to cascade downward and gradually merge through your entire brain, dissolving into a transparent, glossy diamond light and radiating outward, beyond the head, like a halo. Sit for a while like this. Imagine that the data from the two lower brains is uploading to the neocortex and the understanding of the upper brain is downloading to the two brains below. Let the exchanges take place easily and naturally.

Developing Your Attention Span

1. Think about what you did yesterday. List the activities you concentrated on for the longest time to the shortest time, in descending order. How long did you hold your attention on activity number 1? Activity number 2? Activity number 3?
2. Think about what breaks your attention span. Is it a stimulus from the outside, like the telephone or your children, wanting

attention? Make a list of the most common external stimuli you blame for interrupting you. Or is it a force inside you, like an unnamed restlessness that makes you get up and go to the refrigerator looking for a snack? Make a list of your favorite ways to distract and interrupt yourself.

3. Visualize a situation in which you were concentrating and then distracted yourself. Just before you interrupted yourself, what did your body feel like? Is there a realization or an experience just under the surface that you're avoiding? Can you remember what triggered your desire to distract yourself? What would you discover if you continued to pay attention?

Clearing Your Energy Pathways

Imagine that your skin is porous and your tissues are transparent. Let every cell, molecule, and atom in your body feel cooperative with the rest. Visualize millions of tiny wavelike threads of light coming from every direction and entering your body, each running on a particular pathway and then going out the other side and back into space again. Relax and let yourself feel suspended in this wondrous, safe, loving web of light.

In your mind's eye, watch some of the light filaments, and see the waves of energy moving toward you from the highest, farthest reaches of the universe. Let the tiny waves of information enter your body and continue waving on through, imparting their vibration to the surrounding particles. Let the energy/information waves continue out the other side of you, perhaps changed slightly by your own truth. Release the energy once it's left your personal field. The departing energy waves are your loving gifts to the universe.

Sit for a while, simply tracing waves of energy, or light, through different parts of your body. Notice any tendency you might have to stop a wave and hold it. What happens when you do? Are there any places in your body where you've stopped waves in the past and jammed up your circuits? Let those waves pass through now and clear any spots that may seem flooded, chaotic, or "dead." Simply clear away the logjam and direct the flow along its natural pathway. (Hint: You won't know what wisdom the wave has for you until you let it pass all the way through.)

Dialoguing with Your Organs

Get quiet and pay attention to the inside of your body. Which of your organs seems to draw your attention? Perhaps you feel a throbbing in the area of your kidneys or sense that your lungs are giving off a greenish light. Whichever organ catches your attention, drop your roving eye down into the organ's territory and surround it with an aura of your full and loving attention.

Notice the energy state of the organ. Is it tense, hyper, sleepy? What emotional tones can you feel? Does it seem pressured, scared, wistful, lonely?

Ask the organ, "What do you need to tell me that I haven't been hearing? What are you the most worried about? What do you know about the current situation I'm dealing with?" Let the organ talk to you. When it seems complete, thank this part of you and ask it how you will know when it needs to talk to you again.

Affirmations

1. From your quiet, centered place, say: "I, (name), am infinite kindness." As you say it, pronounce each word and feel what it means. Let it be true. Continue: "I, (name), am infinite wisdom. I am infinite courage. I am infinite energy. I am infinite beauty. I am infinite strength. I am infinite patience. I am infinite creativity." Keep on going, thinking of divine qualities to associate with and become. Reown it all as truth.

2. Write an affirmation of your true nature and your deepest intent in life, as though you were applying for a job with God. As you write each description, each specific statement, make sure you know it to be true. If you don't believe it, don't write it down. Now, wouldn't you love to hire you?

A Prayer

Write a prayer to your own favorite spiritual figure or divine source. Make it personal and meaningful. Ask for what you want the most, and say what you want to give. Tell what you're grateful for and what your intentions are.

What's the Message?

1. Imagine that you have one of those days where every errand has to be done twice, everything you buy has to be returned, and most people either don't notice you or misunderstand what you're saying. Stop. Feel and describe what's happening in your body. What emotions are lurking below the surface? What's the message?

2. Imagine that your lottery ticket wins you a fair-sized amount of money. Stop. Feel and describe what's happening in your body. What emotions are lurking below the surface? What's the message in the day's event?

3. Imagine that you trip and sprain your right ankle, then later in the week come down with a head cold. Your eyes are watering badly, and everything feels swollen and sore. Stop. Feel and describe what's happening in your body. What emotions are lurking below the surface? What's the message in the week's events?

4. Imagine that you leave your wallet at a pay phone and go back to your restaurant table, and when you rush back to find it, your money, ID, and credit cards have been stolen. Stop. Feel and describe what's happening in your body. What emotions are lurking below the surface? What's the message?

Cultivating Surprises

1. Write about something or someone who surprised you this week. What was revealed to you about life or about some hidden aspect of yourself? Then write about how you surprised yourself or someone else this week.

2. This week, emphasize the words *oh, wow, ho-ho-ho, open, now,* and *so.* Notice how your mind responds to the exclamatory *O* sound.

Personal Symbols

1. Make a list of your positive character traits, the things you like about yourself. These traits should describe both the way you do

things and the way you are inside. Next to the words and phrases, list images that represent those characteristics. For example, for "free" you might list "horse, eagle, wind"; for "industrious" you might list "ant, bee, beaver, hammer."

2. Pick the traits you want to use to represent yourself to the business world. How do you want to feel when you're "out there"? What do you want others to notice about you? Design a logo for yourself.

3. Pick the traits you want to use to represent yourself to your mate or a potential soulmate. Design a logo for yourself.

4. Design a meditation symbol or mandala to help you focus on your essence.

Dream Recall Ceremonies

Your body loves ritual. Dreams are often easier to remember when you trigger the subconscious recall with a physical stimulus. Write a note to your dream self, fold it, put it under your pillow, and say to your subconscious, "In the morning, I'm going to reread this note, and it will trigger my memory."

You can set a glass of water, which you have held and charged with positive intentions to remember your dreams, by your bed. Say to your subconscious mind, "In the morning, when I take a drink of this water, it will trigger me to remember my dreams."

Work with these little rituals consistently so your body knows you mean it. Don't give up after the first or second try.

Interpreting an Omen

Think back and list three odd, perhaps surrealistic experiences you've had in the past few months. Or did you see something recently that you'd consider an omen? Did a huge flock of geese fly over you in a V from right to left? Did you get bitten by a black widow spider, or sprain an ankle, or find a $20 bill? Was there a synchronicity that seems to be pointing out a theme? Did three old friends from the distant past show up unexpectedly in town this month?

What question is each omen an answer to? What is the Source telling you via these symbols?

Meeting a Being from the Superconscious Realms

Imagine that you are camping in the desert under a bright full moon. Feel your desire to get help with a pressing problem. Or maybe you're hungry for higher teachings. Ask the Source to send you an appropriate teacher or guide from the superconscious realms.

Let the entity appear in front of you. Before any words are exchanged, let your body receive the full experience of their energy. Do you feel comfortable? You may set the parameters of how the other being can interact with you. Make sure you feel safe and receptive.

Let a dialogue occur, beginning perhaps with introductions. Receive the message, guidance, or teachings that the being has for you today. When you feel complete, thank the entity and offer a gift—your imagination will know what to give. Come back and write it all down.

Picking Up Impressions

Make a list of five people you know well but haven't seen for a while. Then quickly list three things you feel about each one's body or state of mind.

For each of those five people, next pretend that you are looking out from inside them, seeing through their eyes. List three things you see.

Now pretend you are inside each person and thinking their thoughts. List three things they are preoccupied with, issues they'd like help with.

The Four Elements

Close your eyes and imagine your partner's energy filling the space in front of you. Out of that field of energy will come the images you need.

First, look at the way your partner relates to and uses the earth element in life. Imagine a tunnel or hole in the ground. It can be large or small. Allow a being to emerge from the opening—this is the guardian of the earth element, and it will take you safely back into its realm to educate you about what your partner needs to know about being physical, safe, grounded, and financially secure. As you get the information, describe it to your partner. Then clear away the earth imagery.

Second, look at how your partner relates to and uses the water element. Imagine a body of water—a lake, river, or ocean. Allow the guardian of the water element to come up to greet you, and then let it take you safely into its world to educate you about what your partner needs to know about dealing with emotions and being more fluid, intuitive, feminine, or receptive. Share what you get. Then clear away the water imagery.

Third, look at how your partner relates to and uses the fire element in life. Imagine a huge bonfire, and allow the guardian of the fire element to come out to greet you and take you safely into its realm to educate you about what your partner needs to know about creative passion, purification, elimination, transformation, and letting go. Share your insights. Then clear away the fire imagery.

Finally, look at how your partner relates to and uses the air element. Imagine floating high in the sky, being blown through clouds by the winds. As you move, allow the guardian of the air element to emerge and greet you and take you into a safe experience of its kingdom to educate you about what your partner needs to know about communication, inspiration, mental skills, adaptability, and lightheartedness. Share your insights. Then clear away the air imagery.

Come back to normal reality, open your eyes, and discuss the information with your partner. What does it mean? What are the key pieces of advice?

Your Hidden Communication Agendas

1. This week, hold the intention to notice your negative communication and the underlying reasons for it. Pay attention to the negative obsessing that goes on inside your mind, your negative external comments and the negative self-talk directed by your critical mind at some aspect of yourself. What could cause you to want to damage another person? Are you jealous? Hurt? Why'd you give your power away? What can't you accept? If the other person were sitting with you, hearing you speak, how

would he or she feel? And what might that person say to you when speaking from the heart? Why can't you accept the part of your own self you are criticizing? Could you praise it instead?

2. Do a ruthless examination of the motives behind everything you say this week. To what extent does insecurity prompt you? Do you need attention to feel accepted or right? If you succeed in each communication, what might you gain by it? Might you be talking to maintain control? Remember, "If you can't say something positive, from a clear motivation, don't say anything."

Being Entirely Transparent and Honest

1. Make a list of all the things about yourself that you're afraid to have "the public" find out about. Imagine that everyone already knows about each of the items on your list and accepts you anyway. Integrate the way that feels. Let yourself be the composite of everything you've ever done—for better or worse. In your own mind, simply let yourself show up for who you are.

2. Make a list of the things you feel you have natural authority about. When you talk about these subjects this week, relax your will; let the pictures in your aura help you communicate.

3. This week when you speak on a topic about which you're not an authority, make a point of prefacing your comments with a short statement of truth: "I'm interested in this and I don't know a lot about it yet, but here are my ideas."

Sending a Telepathic Message

Close your eyes and get centered. Imagine stepping out of your physical body in your energy body. As you step away from your resting physical body, you are in the etheric realm where energy and knowledge travel faster.

Think of a person you want to send a message to. You must feel convinced about communicating with that individual. Visualize the person in as much detail as you can and call their name: "Michael, I call upon you to become aware of me now." See them appear in their energy body in front of you. Make eye contact.

Form the thought clearly in your mind. Walk up to them and

speak the message into their left ear, calmly and directly. Then ask the person, "Did you hear and understand what I said?"

Thank the person and imagine both of you going back to your physical bodies and reconnecting with your normal reality. Make a note later on of any response you get in your waking reality or in the dream world.

Public Conversations Soup

This week keep your ears open for tidbits and snatches of conversation you overhear at restaurants, on subways, on the radio and television, from your children, at the market or gas station, or from passersby on the street. Immediately write down or tape these random phrases or even interesting single words. At the end of the week put it all together in a poem or piece of creative writing, allowing the phrases to act as triggers for your imagination. Remember, it doesn't have to make sense.

Stream of Consciousness

Let your mind feel relaxed, like a loose muscle, and clear any images or thoughts. Then wait for a new image to appear. Take the first one you get. Let that image turn into something else; take the next image that appears. Let that one turn into yet another. Maybe your first image is a ladder. That turns into a giraffe, which turns into a tree, which turns into a green balloon, which turns into a parrot flying in the sky, which turns into a paperclip, which turns into a tiny whirlwind scooting across your desk. Keep going, entertaining yourself, keeping the process fluid and animated, like a living cartoon, for five minutes.

Patience

1. Make a list of five things you were impatient about this week, areas of your life where you wanted instant results. How could you transform each frustrating experience so it offers you greater depth? What might you learn from each thing if you gave it more time and attention?

2. List five times this week when someone was impatient with you. If they had taken more time with you, what might they have learned? What benefit did they not receive from you?

I'd Be Better If . . .

1. For each statement list five answers that you got by comparing yourself to someone else: (a) "I'd be more attractive if _____." (b) "I'd have more friends if _____." (c) "I'd make more money if _____." (d) "I'd be happier if _____."
2. For each statement list one answer that originates from your soul.

Excuses and Double Standards

1. Where in your life do you hear yourself saying, "Yes, but"? Make a list of five excuses you made to yourself this week to avoid doing something. What were you avoiding? How did you rationalize it? If you hadn't made an excuse and had done each thing, what would you have had to face? What would you have learned?
2. List five areas where you have double standards about your behavior. Do you meditate but drink too much alcohol? Do you work out aggressively but avoid returning phone calls? Why do you hold these expectations? How could you even out these areas of your life and what might you learn?

Balanced Giving and Receiving

1. Write about a time when you gave too much to someone else; describe that person's reaction and yours. Why didn't it work? Now write about a time when someone else gave too much to you; describe your physical and emotional reactions. Why didn't it work?
2. Write about a time when someone else gave you too little or gave something that didn't meet your needs; describe your physical and emotional reactions. Why didn't it work? Now write about a time you gave someone else too little or gave something that didn't meet that person's needs; describe your reactions. Why didn't it work?

Notes

How to Proceed: Guidelines and Tools

1. Brenda Ueland, *If You Want to Write* (St. Paul, Minn.: Graywolf Press, 1987), 133.
2. Ibid, 139.

Chapter 1

1. Yogananda, *The Science of Religion* (Los Angeles: Self Realization Fellowship, 1982), 83.
2. Robert Ornstein, *The Evolution of Consciousness* (New York: Prentice Hall, 1991), 278.

Chapter 3

1. Natalie Goldberg, *Writing Down the Bones* (Boston: Shambhala, 1986), 9.

Chapter 4

1. Satprem, *The Mind of the Cells* (New York: Institute for Evolutionary Research, 1982), 131.

Chapter 5

1. Alan Watts, *The Joyous Cosmology* (New York: Random House, 1962), 29.
2. Thomas Cleary, *The Japanese Art of War* (Boston: Shambhala, 1991), 59.
3. Ibid., 62.
4. Carlos Castaneda, *A Separate Reality* (New York: Simon & Schuster, 1971), 218–19.
5. Frances Vaughan, *Awakening Intuition* (New York: Doubleday, 1979), 177.
6. Carlos Castaneda, *The Eagle's Gift* (New York: Simon & Schuster, 1981), 260–61.
7. David Whyte, *Images of Fire*, audiotape (Boulder, Colo.: Sounds True Recordings, 1992).
8. Chogyam Trungpa, *Shambhala* (New York: Bantam, 1984), 74.

Alan Watts, *The Joyous Cosmology* (New York: Random House, 1962), 69.
Nick Herbert, *Elemental Mind* (New York: Plume/Penguin, 1993), 246.

Chapter 7
1. Anne Cushman, "The Spirit of Creativity," *Yoga Journal*, September/October 1991, 53.

Chapter 9
1. Julia Cameron, *The Artist's Way* (New York: Tarcher Putnam, 1992), 13, 21.
2. Carlos Castaneda, *Journey to Ixtlan* (New York: Simon & Schuster, 1976), 183–84.

Chapter 10
1. Robert Bly, ed., *The Soul Is Here for Its Own Joy* (Hopewell, N.J.: Ecco Press, 1995), 89.